PRENTICE HALL

UNITED STATES HISTORY

Reading and Note Taking Study Guide

PEARSON

Upper Saddle River, New Jersey   Boston, Massachusetts   Chandler, Arizona   Glenview, Illinois

PEARSON

ISBN-13: 978-0-13-368815-3
ISBN-10:   0-13-368815-1

16   V031   15   14

Contents

How to Use This Book

The **Reading and Note Taking Study Guide** will help you better understand the content of *Prentice Hall United States History*. This book will also develop your reading, vocabulary, and note taking skills. Each study guide consists of two components. The first component focuses on developing the graphic organizers that appear in your textbook.

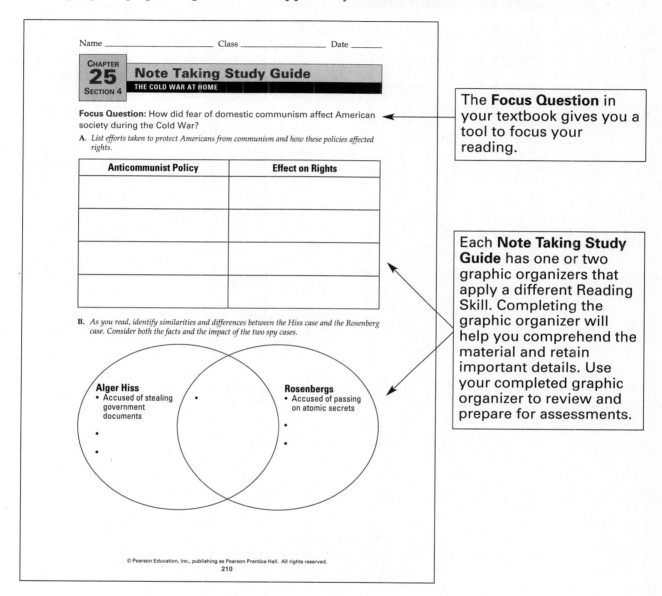

Name _____ Class _____ Date _____

Focus Question: How did fear of domestic communism affect American society during the Cold War?

A. *List efforts taken to protect Americans from communism and how these policies affected rights.*

Anticommunist Policy	Effect on Rights

B. *As you read, identify similarities and differences between the Hiss case and the Rosenberg case. Consider both the facts and the impact of the two spy cases.*

Alger Hiss
• Accused of stealing government documents
•
•

Rosenbergs
• Accused of passing on atomic secrets
•
•

The **Focus Question** in your textbook gives you a tool to focus your reading.

Each **Note Taking Study Guide** has one or two graphic organizers that apply a different Reading Skill. Completing the graphic organizer will help you comprehend the material and retain important details. Use your completed graphic organizer to review and prepare for assessments.

The second component highlights the central themes, issues, and concepts of each section.

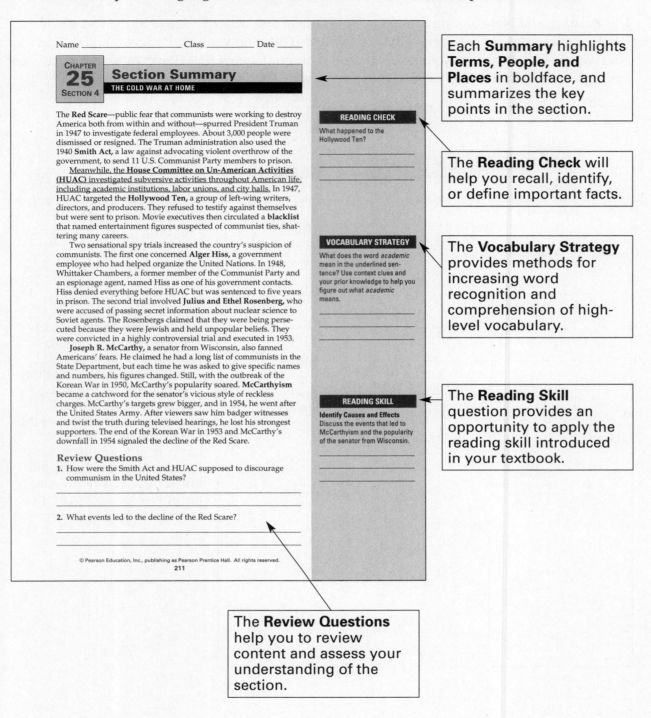

Name _____ Class _____ Date _____

CHAPTER
25
SECTION 4
Section Summary
THE COLD WAR AT HOME

The **Red Scare**—public fear that communists were working to destroy America both from within and without—spurred President Truman in 1947 to investigate federal employees. About 3,000 people were dismissed or resigned. The Truman administration also used the 1940 **Smith Act,** a law against advocating violent overthrow of the government, to send 11 U.S. Communist Party members to prison.

Meanwhile, the **House Committee on Un-American Activities (HUAC)** investigated subversive activities throughout American life, including academic institutions, labor unions, and city halls. In 1947, HUAC targeted the **Hollywood Ten,** a group of left-wing writers, directors, and producers. They refused to testify against themselves but were sent to prison. Movie executives then circulated a **blacklist** that named entertainment figures suspected of communist ties, shattering many careers.

Two sensational spy trials increased the country's suspicion of communists. The first one concerned **Alger Hiss,** a government employee who had helped organize the United Nations. In 1948, Whittaker Chambers, a former member of the Communist Party and an espionage agent, named Hiss as one of his government contacts. Hiss denied everything before HUAC but was sentenced to five years in prison. The second trial involved **Julius and Ethel Rosenberg,** who were accused of passing secret information about nuclear science to Soviet agents. The Rosenbergs claimed that they were being persecuted because they were Jewish and held unpopular beliefs. They were convicted in a highly controversial trial and executed in 1953.

Joseph R. McCarthy, a senator from Wisconsin, also fanned Americans' fears. He claimed he had a long list of communists in the State Department, but each time he was asked to give specific names and numbers, his figures changed. Still, with the outbreak of the Korean War in 1950, McCarthy's popularity soared. **McCarthyism** became a catchword for the senator's vicious style of reckless charges. McCarthy's targets grew bigger, and in 1954, he went after the United States Army. After viewers saw him badger witnesses and twist the truth during televised hearings, he lost his strongest supporters. The end of the Korean War in 1953 and McCarthy's downfall in 1954 signaled the decline of the Red Scare.

Review Questions
1. How were the Smith Act and HUAC supposed to discourage communism in the United States?

_____

_____

2. What events led to the decline of the Red Scare?

_____

_____

211

READING CHECK

What happened to the Hollywood Ten?

_____

_____

_____

VOCABULARY STRATEGY

What does the word *academic* mean in the underlined sentence? Use context clues and your prior knowledge to help you figure out what *academic* means.

_____

_____

_____

READING SKILL

Identify Causes and Effects
Discuss the events that led to McCarthyism and the popularity of the senator from Wisconsin.

_____

_____

_____

Each **Summary** highlights **Terms, People, and Places** in boldface, and summarizes the key points in the section.

The **Reading Check** will help you recall, identify, or define important facts.

The **Vocabulary Strategy** provides methods for increasing word recognition and comprehension of high-level vocabulary.

The **Reading Skill** question provides an opportunity to apply the reading skill introduced in your textbook.

The **Review Questions** help you to review content and assess your understanding of the section.

The **American Issues Journal** supports the **American Issues Connector** features found in your text. These worksheets will help you track key issues that Americans have debated throughout their history. Each worksheet covers one of the 21 recurring American issues over time.

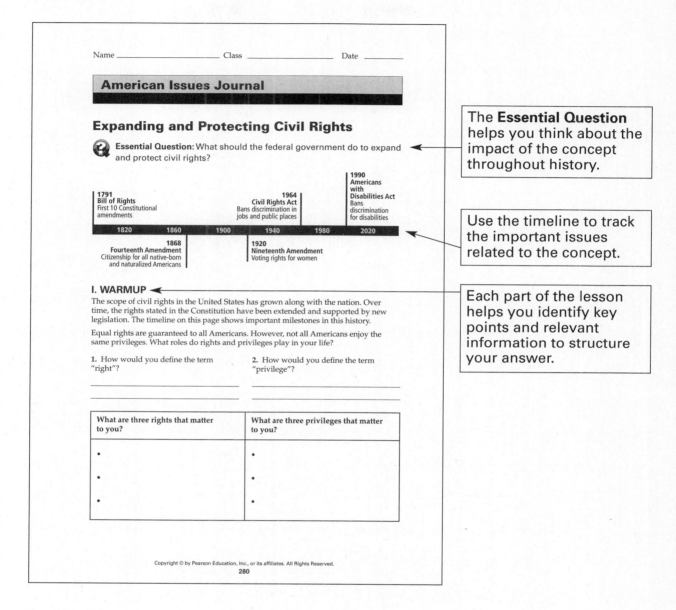

Name _____ Class _____ Date _____

American Issues Journal

Expanding and Protecting Civil Rights

Essential Question: What should the federal government do to expand and protect civil rights?

The **Essential Question** helps you think about the impact of the concept throughout history.

1791
Bill of Rights
First 10 Constitutional amendments

1964
Civil Rights Act
Bans discrimination in jobs and public places

1990
Americans with Disabilities Act
Bans discrimination for disabilities

| 1820 | 1860 | 1900 | 1940 | 1980 | 2020 |

1868
Fourteenth Amendment
Citizenship for all native-born and naturalized Americans

1920
Nineteenth Amendment
Voting rights for women

Use the timeline to track the important issues related to the concept.

I. WARMUP

The scope of civil rights in the United States has grown along with the nation. Over time, the rights stated in the Constitution have been extended and supported by new legislation. The timeline on this page shows important milestones in this history.

Equal rights are guaranteed to all Americans. However, not all Americans enjoy the same privileges. What roles do rights and privileges play in your life?

1. How would you define the term "right"?

_____

_____

2. How would you define the term "privilege"?

_____

_____

Each part of the lesson helps you identify key points and relevant information to structure your answer.

What are three rights that matter to you?	What are three privileges that matter to you?
•	•
•	•
•	•

CHAPTER 1 SECTION 1
Note Taking Study Guide
THE AMERICAN INDIANS

Focus Question: How did the spread of civilization begin in the Americas?

As you read this section, complete the outline below with the main ideas.

I. The First People of the Americas

    A. Paleoindians

        1. _____

        2. _____

    B. _____

    C. _____

        1. _____

        2. _____

II. _____

    A. _____

        1. _____

        2. _____

    B. _____

        1. _____

        2. _____

    C. _____

        1. _____

        2. _____

    D. _____

        1. _____

        2. _____

III. _____

    A. _____

    B. _____

CHAPTER 1 SECTION 1	Section Summary
	THE AMERICAN INDIANS

READING CHECK

What is adobe?

_____

_____

_____

Until recently, most scholars believed that Paleoindians, the first people in the Americas, arrived 15,000 years ago during an **ice age.** Since much of the planet's seawater was frozen and the sea level was lower, hunters crossed a land bridge between Siberia and Alaska. Now, some scholars theorize that the first Americans **migrated,** or traveled from Asia some 40,000 years ago.

About 12,000 to 10,000 years ago, the climate warmed, allowing the environment to become more diverse. Wild plants were domesticated and grown for food. The expanded food supply encouraged population growth, which led to larger, permanent villages. In Mexico, some villages grew into great cities ruled by powerful chiefs. Along the Gulf of Mexico and the Caribbean coast, the leading peoples were the Olmecs and later the **Mayas.** In the highlands of central Mexico, the **Aztecs** became the most powerful people. In the Southwest, the Hohokam and the Anasazi built villages and houses of **adobe,** a type of sun-dried brick.

The people who lived in the Mississippi River valley enjoyed a humid and temperate climate. These Mississippians built large towns, and developed trade. During the ninth century, some Mississippians moved westward onto the Great Plains, an immense, windy, and arid grassland. They built villages, planted crops, and hunted bison in mobile camps. These Great Plains villagers sometimes clashed with hunting nomads from the Rocky Mountains.

The Choctaws, Creeks, and other southeastern groups were primarily farmers, but they also depended on hunting and fishing. Northeastern people developed into two major language groups: the Algonquians and the Iroquoians. Five Iroquois people united to form the **Iroquois League,** a ritual forum for promoting peaceful cooperation among the members.

Despite their cultural diversity, most Native American groups shared several cultural features. American Indians believed that spirits could be found in every plant, animal, rock, cloud, and body of water. They possessed little private property and maintained a respectful equality among the various groups of Indians.

VOCABULARY STRATEGY

What does the word *diverse* mean in the underlined sentence? Circle the word below that is a synonym for *diverse.*
• varied
• similar

READING SKILL

Identify Main Ideas What cultural features did most Native American groups share?

_____

_____

_____

Review Questions

1. Describe the theories that scholars have about the arrival of Paleoindians in America.

_____

_____

2. What was life like for Great Plains villagers?

_____

_____

Note Taking Study Guide
THE EUROPEANS

Focus Question: How did Europeans begin to explore more of the world?

As you read this section, fill in the following chart to describe Europe before and after the 1400s.

Europe in the 1400s		
Economy	**Society**	**Politics**
• Agriculture	•	•
•		
	•	•
•		
	•	
•		•
	•	
•		
	•	
•		
	•	

CHAPTER 1

SECTION 2

Section Summary
THE EUROPEANS

READING CHECK

Which European country took the lead in maritime expansion?

_____

_____

_____

VOCABULARY STRATEGY

What does the word *adhered* mean in the underlined sentence? Look for context clues in the surrounding words, phrases, and sentences.

_____

_____

READING SKILL

Summarize Describe how life changed in Europe during the Renaissance.

_____

_____

_____

Europe was changing quickly in the 1400s. The **Middle Ages,** a period marked by limited trade, the absence of strong nations, and little interaction with the outside world, was ending. <u>During the Middle Ages, Church leaders sought to ensure that all thought adhered to their understanding of the world.</u> In the mid-1400s, the **Renaissance** brought renewed interest in learning and the arts. Trade with and awareness of the world beyond Europe also expanded, producing wealth and fueling exploration.

Western Europe was divided into warring kingdoms. Each kingdom was ruled by a monarch who let the elite govern. Nearly all land and wealth was held by the elite, who made up less than 5 percent of the population. Three out of five western Europeans were working poor and one tenth to one fifth were beggars.

Many Europeans felt hemmed in by the wealth, power, and technology of their neighbors, the Muslims, who were adherents of Islam rather than Christianity. The Muslims had won a series of religious wars launched by European Christians during the Middle Ages. The Muslim realm stretched across North Africa, around the southern and eastern Mediterranean Sea to parts of eastern Europe and the Middle East. They controlled most of the lucrative trade routes. Inspired by the travel accounts of explorers such as Marco Polo, Europeans dreamed of an alternative trade route around the Muslim world and longed for the fabled riches of India and China.

European expansionists found hope on the Iberian Peninsula. With the 1469 marriage of Prince Ferdinand and Queen Isabella, the kingdoms of Aragon and Castile joined to create the new nation of Spain. They completed the *reconquista* (reconquest) when Granada, the last Muslim stronghold in Iberia, was seized.

Close to Africa and facing the Atlantic, Spain and Portugal were well-placed to lead the maritime expansion of Europe. Portugal took the lead in 1419. Prince Henry, known as **Prince Henry the Navigator,** became a supporter of oceangoing exploration as a means to spread Christianity and outflank Muslim domination of trade. He helped finance a series of expeditions down the coast of West Africa and founded a school of navigation.

Review Questions

1. Explain why the Europeans felt hemmed in by the Muslims.

_____

_____

2. What developments on the Iberian Peninsula gave Europeans hope of finding a route around the Muslim world?

_____

_____

CHAPTER 1 SECTION 3

Note Taking Study Guide

THE WEST AFRICANS

Focus Question: What was life like in West Africa before the age of European exploration?

As you read, complete the following concept web with details about major West African kingdoms.

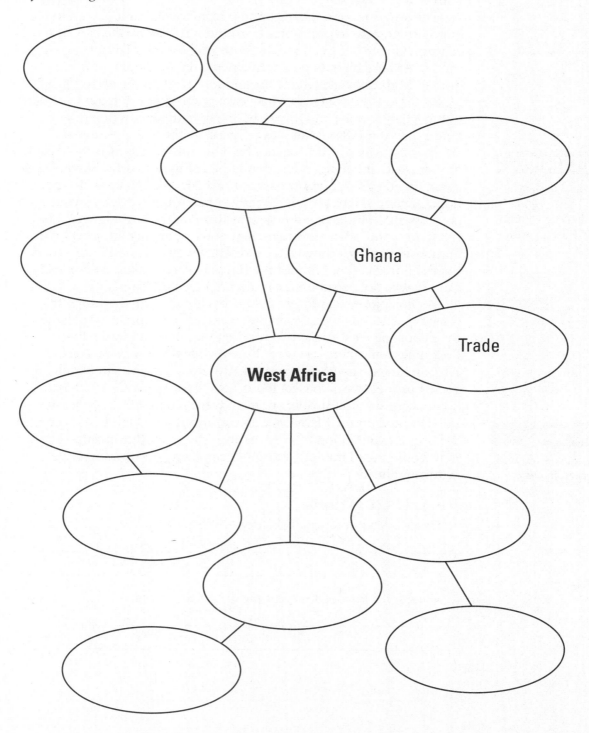

CHAPTER 1 / SECTION 3

Section Summary
THE WEST AFRICANS

Name two natural resources located in West Africa.

_____

_____

_____

VOCABULARY STRATEGY

What does the word *domain* mean in the underlined sentence? Look for context clues in the surrounding words, phrases, and sentences.

_____

_____

_____

READING SKILL

Identify Details How did Mansa Musa alter the Mali empire?

_____

_____

_____

West Africa is a diverse land with valuable natural resources such as salt and gold. Hundreds of years ago, these resources formed the basis of trade among the people in West Africa. Trade revolved around trading centers, which grew into great and powerful empires with rich and thriving cultures.

The kingdom of **Ghana**, running from the Atlantic Ocean to the Niger River, rose to prominence around A.D. 800. By the eleventh century, Ghana supplied much of the gold for the Mediterranean region. Attacks by outsiders weakened Ghana, and the new kingdom of **Mali** replaced Ghana around A.D. 1200. In the early 1300s, Mali's famous king **Mansa Musa** expanded Mali's domain westward to the Atlantic coast and increased the role of Islam within the empire. By the 1400s, Mali was eclipsed by the rise of **Songhai.**

In West Africa, land was not held by individuals as private property. Instead, it belonged to extended kinship networks. Slavery was common and an important part of West Africa's economic foundation. Owning slaves (or wives) rather than property determined one's wealth. Humans were used as items of trade along with gold, salt, ivory, and other resources. Slaves were usually adopted by the families into which they were sold. They were allowed to marry, and their children did not inherit the status of slaves. Most importantly, slavery was not based on the notion of racial inferiority.

As Portuguese explorers made voyage after voyage along the coast of Africa, they discovered a profitable enterprise: trade with the people of West Africa. To conduct their African trade, the Portuguese mariners received the assent of the powerful West African kings. The Portuguese greatly expanded the slave trade. By 1500, Europeans purchased about 1,800 African slaves each year. Some were sent to Europe, but most were sent to work on plantations located on the Madeira, Canary, and Azore islands. Thus began the brutal exploitation of West African slaves by Europeans—a fate that would befall millions more African men and women in the centuries ahead.

Review Questions

1. Describe the practice of slavery in West Africa.

_____

_____

2. Where did Europeans send most African slaves?

_____

_____

Name _____ Class _____ Date _____

Focus Question: How did European exploration affect the Americas?

As you read, complete the chart below with the effects of the arrival of the Europeans in the Americas.

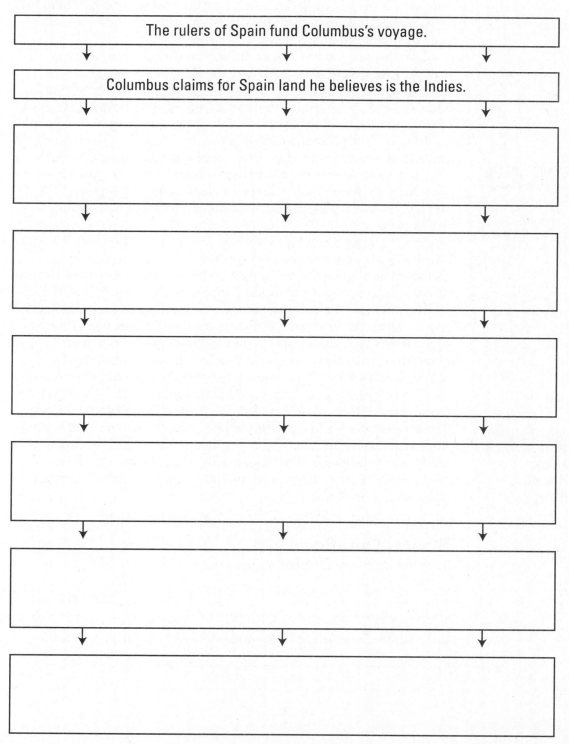

The rulers of Spain fund Columbus's voyage.

Columbus claims for Spain land he believes is the Indies.

CHAPTER 1

SECTION 4

Section Summary
FIRST ENCOUNTERS

READING CHECK

READING CHECK

Whose voyage circled the entire globe?

_____

_____

_____

VOCABULARY STRATEGY

What does the word *adjacent* mean in the underlined sentence? Look for context clues in the surrounding words, phrases, and sentences.

_____

_____

_____

READING SKILL

Understand Effects Describe the changes the Columbian Exchange brought about.

_____

_____

_____

Throughout the 1400s, the Portuguese sought a route around Africa's southern tip into the Indian Ocean. In 1487, the Portuguese mariner **Bartolomeu Dias** discovered how to use the counterclockwise winds of the South Atlantic to get around southern Africa. In 1498, **Vasco de Gama** used this discovery to reach India, opening a very profitable channel of trade.

Christopher Columbus, an Italian mariner, pursued Spain's dream of westward exploration in the Atlantic Ocean. <u>When Columbus reached the present-day Bahamas and adjacent islands, he mistakenly believed these islands were off the mainland of Asia.</u> He claimed the land for Spain despite the presence of native people.

In 1497, **John Cabot,** a Genoese mariner, sailed to Newfoundland, and a Portuguese fleet led by **Pedro Alvarez Cabral** discovered Brazil in 1500. A year later, another Genoese mariner, **Amerigo Vespucci,** deemed South America a new continent. Between 1519 and 1522, a voyage begun by **Ferdinand Magellan** circled the entire globe.

In 1519, **Hernán Cortés** marched to the inland home of the Aztec Empire in Mexico. The Spanish captured the capital city of Tenochtitlán and began building a Spanish capital, Mexico City, on its ruins. The Spanish expanded their empire deep into North and South America. The **conquistadors** were motivated by religious faith and loyalty to their monarch, as well as wealth. European diseases such as smallpox devastated native populations who had no natural defenses against them. With the death of so many Indians, the colonists turned to African slaves to work the new sugar plantations.

The colonizers also introduced plants and animals that were new to the Americas in what is referred to as the **Columbian Exchange.** These new plants and animals brought drastic changes to the environment. Europeans also began farming American plants such as maize and potatoes. Large harvests aided by these new American crops fueled European population growth while Native American populations declined.

Review Questions

1. What motivated the conquistadors?

_____

_____

2. Describe the effects of European diseases on native peoples.

_____

_____

CHAPTER 2 SECTION 1

Note Taking Study Guide

SPAIN'S EMPIRE IN THE AMERICAS

Focus Question: How did Spain strengthen its colonies in the Americas?

Complete the concept web below to summarize how each item strengthened the Spanish American Empire.

Missions
-
-

Presidios
-
-

Spanish America

Explorers
-
-

Native Americans
-
-

CHAPTER 2 SECTION 1

Section Summary
SPAIN'S EMPIRE IN THE AMERICAS

READING CHECK

What was the significance of the Pueblo Revolt?

_____

_____

_____

Enriched by conquests in the Americas, Spain financed an aggressive military policy in Europe. This aggression alarmed the Dutch, French, and English, who sought their own share of the riches in America. With the spread of the Protestant Reformation, religious divisions added to the conflict among nations in Europe.

The conquistadores were successful at conquering territory but not at running the colonies. Catholic **missionaries** aimed to convert Indians to Christianity and to persuade them to conform to Spanish culture. The missionaries relied on Spanish soldiers, who set up **presidios**, or forts, near the mission.

Spain's American empire was divided into two immense regions, New Spain and Peru. Each was ruled by a **viceroy** appointed by the king. Most of the colonists were men, and many took Indian wives. Their children became known as **mestizos.** The mestizos became the largest segment of Spain's colonial population by the eighteenth century. Next in proportion were enslaved Africans, especially in the Caribbean region. In both New Spain and Peru, the Spanish developed an urban and cosmopolitan culture.

VOCABULARY STRATEGY

What does the word *urban* mean in the underlined sentence? Use context clues from the surrounding words, phrases, and sentences to learn the meaning of *urban*.

_____

_____

_____

Hernando de Soto and Francisco Vásquez de Coronado led expeditions into the lands north of Mexico. De Soto's men explored present-day Florida and other areas, leaving behind deadly new diseases. Coronado searched for a golden kingdom named Quivara, but found only villages of grass-thatched lodges. After the failures of De Soto and Coronado, the Spanish Crown lost interest in the northern lands. Friars tried to transform Indians into Hispanics by building **missions** in native villages. In New Mexico, the Pueblo Indians would not give up all their traditional beliefs. The missionaries' harsh punishments for these infractions angered the Pueblos.

Conditions worsened during the 1660s and 1670s. A prolonged drought undercut the harvests, reducing many Pueblos to starvation. In 1680 the Pueblos revolted under the leadership of a shaman named Popé. The rebels destroyed and plundered missions, farms, and ranches. The Pueblo Revolt was the greatest setback that the Indians ever inflicted on colonial expansion. After Popé's death, the Spanish reclaimed New Mexico. The bloody revolt taught the Pueblos and the Spanish to compromise.

READING SKILL

Summarize What were three ways that the Spanish colonies negatively affected Native Americans?

_____

_____

_____

Review Questions

1. How did Spain run its American empire?

_____

_____

2. What role did missionaries play in the Spanish colonies?

_____

_____

CHAPTER 2 SECTION 2

Note Taking Study Guide

THE FRENCH EMPIRE

Focus Question: How did France's American colonies differ from Spain's American colonies?

Fill in the Venn diagram below comparing Spanish America and French America.

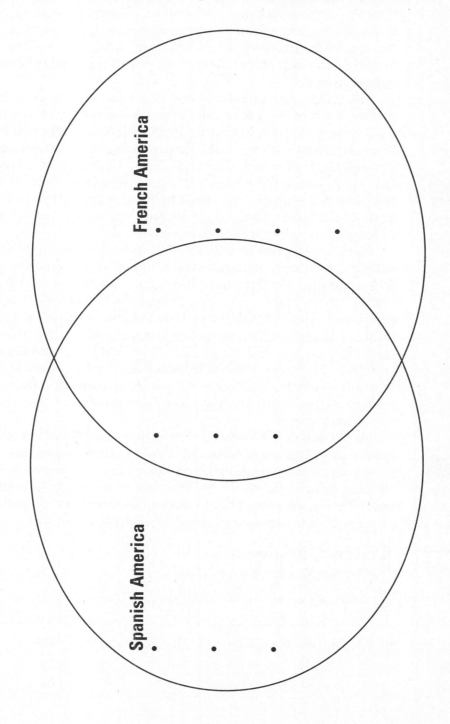

Section Summary
THE FRENCH EMPIRE

Who were the *metis?*

_____

_____

_____

What does the word *dominated* mean in the underlined sentence? Circle the phrase below that means the same thing as *dominated.*
- gave up power
- had control

Compare and Contrast Contrast the economies of Spanish America and French America.

_____

_____

_____

During the early 1500s, French explorers wanted to find a **Northwest Passage** to Asia. They probed the eastern coastline of North America, from present-day North Carolina to Newfoundland. The French king claimed the region around the St. Lawrence River as New France. French mariners fished for cod and hunted for whales and seals. They met Indian hunters who offered beaver fur in trade. The coastal Indians sought new stocks of beaver by invading the hunting territories of their neighbors, provoking wars between Indian groups.

The traders also plundered and killed one another in their competition for furs. To repel rivals, a French company built a fortified trading post on the St. Lawrence River in 1608. **Quebec** was the first permanent settlement in Canada. Its founder, **Samuel de Champlain,** traded with the Montagnais, Algonquin, and Huron Indians. In return, they expected Champlain to help them against their foes, the Iroquois, who lived to the south in what is now New York. The Iroquois acquired guns from Dutch traders on the Hudson River, becoming better armed than their enemies.

New France grew slowly. By 1700, the colony had only 15,000 colonists. Its government resembled that of New Spain. The French king appointed a military governor-general, a civil administrator, and a Catholic bishop. Like the Spanish, the French used Catholic priests as missionaries to convert the Indians. <u>To the west, Indians dominated the vast hinterland of forest and lakes, where the colonists were few and scattered.</u> In the Great Lakes and Illinois countries, the French established some small settlements. They lived by a mix of farming and trade. Known as *coureurs de bois,* many fur traders married Indian women. The children of these marriages were known as the *metis.*

At the end of the 1600s, the French also established a southern colony along the lower Mississippi Valley. They named this Louisiana, in honor of King Louis XIV. In 1718, they founded New Orleans, which became the colony's largest town and leading seaport. The French valued Louisiana as a military base to keep the English from taking control of the Mississippi watershed.

Review Questions
1. Why was Quebec founded?

_____

_____

2. Why did the French value Louisiana?

_____

_____

CHAPTER 2 SECTION 3

Note Taking Study Guide

ENGLAND'S SOUTHERN COLONIES

Focus Question: What were the characteristics of the government and the economy in the Southern Colonies?

As you read this section, use the flowchart below to list the important events in the founding of the Southern Colonies.

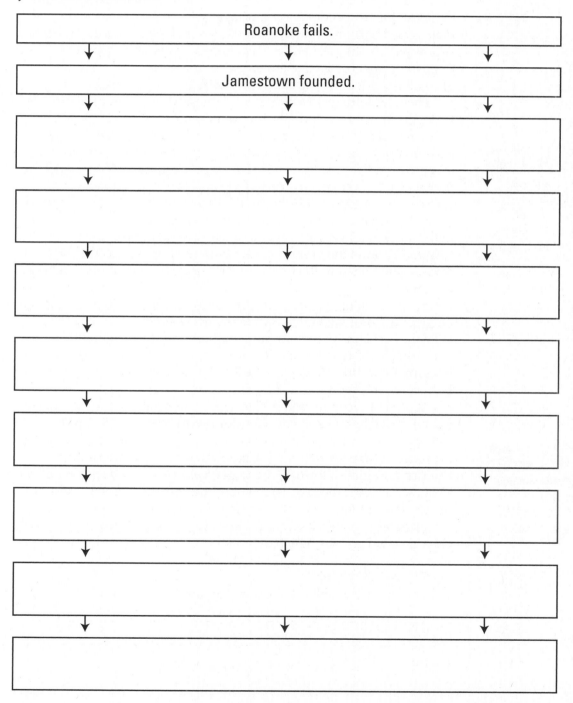

Roanoke fails.

↓ ↓ ↓

Jamestown founded.

↓ ↓ ↓

Section Summary
ENGLAND'S SOUTHERN COLONIES

READING CHECK

What was the headright system?

_____

_____

_____

VOCABULARY STRATEGY

What does the word *intense* mean in the underlined sentence? The words *fierce* and *deep* are synonyms of *intense*. Use these synonyms to learn the meaning of *intense*.

_____

_____

_____

READING SKILL

Sequence List in chronological order the colonies that formed between 1632 and 1732. Provide the date each colony was established.

_____

_____

_____

The first English colonies were promoted by wealthy gentlemen who obtained a **charter,** or certificate of permission, from the king. Then, the group formed a **joint-stock company** run by several investors. During the 1580s, Sir Walter Raleigh twice tried to colonize Roanoke, a small island on the North Carolina coast. In 1607, the Virginia Company established a colony on Chesapeake Bay, a region that offered many good harbors and navigable rivers, as well as more fertile land. A powerful Native American chief named **Powhatan** hoped to use the English against his own enemies and to trade for their metal weapons. The colonists, led by Captain **John Smith,** wanted Indian lands.

The new settlement was named Jamestown to honor the king. By taking food from the Indians, the colonists provoked conflicts. By 1616, the colony was an unprofitable town of 350 diseased, hungry, and unhappy colonists. Then the planters learned how to cultivate tobacco, and the profits attracted more immigrants to Virginia. Under the headright system, anyone paying passage to Virginia received 50 acres of land. In 1619, the Virginia Company allowed the planters to create the **House of Burgesses,** the first representative body in colonial America. It had the power to make laws and raise taxes. In 1624, Virginia became the first royal colony in the English empire. **Royal colonies** belonged to the Crown, while **proprietary colonies** belonged to powerful individuals or companies.

In 1675, intense fighting erupted between the Indians and the settlers in the Potomac Valley. When the royal governor of Virginia, William Berkeley, protested the slaughter of Indians, Nathanial Bacon marched his armed followers to Jamestown in a revolt called **Bacon's Rebellion.** Although the rebellion collapsed, it undermined Berkeley's credibility.

In 1632, a second colony, Maryland, was established at the northern head of Chesapeake Bay. Charles I gave Maryland to **Lord Baltimore,** who owned and governed it as a proprietary colony. He provided refuge for his fellow Catholics, who were discriminated against in England. In 1670, the English established Carolina south of Virginia. In 1691, they set aside the northern half of their territory as the distinct colony of North Carolina. Georgia was founded in 1732 as a proprietary colony. Its leader, **James Oglethorpe,** wanted to make Georgia a haven for English debtors.

Review Questions
1. What finally enabled the colony of Jamestown to thrive?

_____

_____

2. Why was the colony of Maryland established?

_____

_____

CHAPTER 2 SECTION 4

Note Taking Study Guide
THE NEW ENGLAND COLONIES

Focus Question: What were the goals of the Plymouth and Massachusetts Bay colonies?

Fill in the chart below to identify the reasons the Pilgrims left Europe.

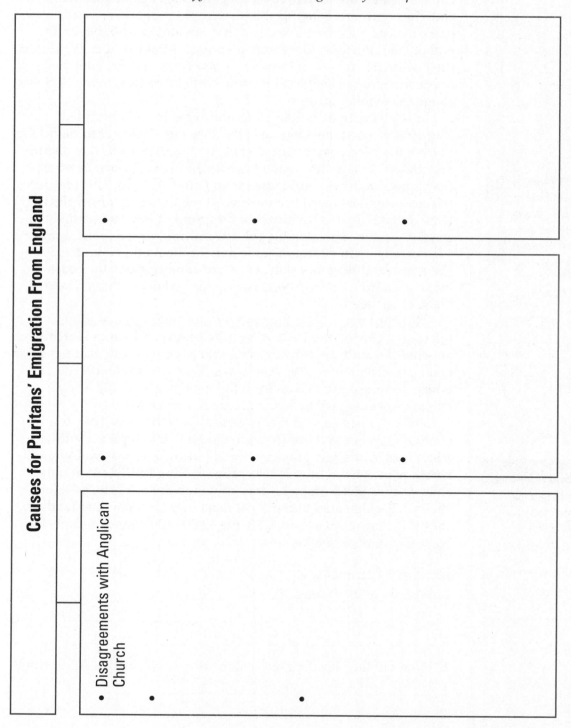

Causes for Puritans' Emigration From England

- Disagreements with Anglican Church

CHAPTER 2 SECTION 4

Section Summary
THE NEW ENGLAND COLONIES

Most of the New England colonists were religious dissidents. Known as **Puritans,** they wanted to purify the Church of England, which they believed retained too many ceremonies from the Catholic Church. Other dissidents, called **Separatists,** began their own churches. Puritans believed that they could prepare for God's saving grace by leading moral lives, and that salvation depended on the will of God. Puritans came from all ranks of English society. Most of them were farmers, shopkeepers, and skilled artisans. They were persecuted for challenging England's official church. Some Puritans sought a colonial refuge.

In 1620, the first Puritan emigrants, who were later called **Pilgrims,** crossed the Atlantic in the ship the *Mayflower* to found the Plymouth Colony on the south shore of Massachusetts Bay. Before they disembarked, they made the **Mayflower Compact,** in which they agreed to form a government and obey its laws. This idea of self-government would become one of the founding principles of the United States. In 1630, a much larger group of Puritans settled the town of Boston. Their leader, **John Winthrop,** urged them to make their colony an inspirational example for the mother country. From Plymouth and Boston, colonists spread rapidly along the coast and into the interior, settling New Hampshire, Maine, Rhode Island, and Connecticut.

The Puritans in New England did not champion religious toleration. During the 1630s, **Roger Williams** and **Anne Hutchinson** angered the authorities by arguing that Massachusetts had not done enough to break with Anglican ways. They fled to Rhode Island, which became a rare haven for religious toleration. The Rhode Islanders also agreed to separate church and state.

The colonists viewed the Indians as lazy savages. They tried to subdue, convert, and transform the Indians into replicas of English Christians in special "praying towns." In 1675, a massive Indian rebellion erupted. The colonists called it **King Philip's War,** after a chief named **Metacom,** who was known to the colonists as "King Philip." The defeated Indians lost most of their remaining lands in southern New England. In 1700, the 92,000 colonists outnumbered New England's 9,000 Indians.

Review Questions
1. Who were the Puritans?

_____

_____

2. How did the New England colonists treat the Native Americans?

_____

_____

Note Taking Study Guide
THE MIDDLE COLONIES

Focus Question: What were the characteristics of the Middle Colonies?

As you read this section, complete the outline below.

I. The Dutch Establish New Netherland

    A. Government in New Netherland

        1. No elected assembly

        2. Religious tolerance

        3. _____

    B. Push-Pull Factors

        1. _____

        2. _____

II. _____

    A. _____

    B. _____

III. _____

    A. _____

        1. _____

        2. _____

    B. _____

        1. _____

        2. _____

IV. _____

    A. _____

        1. _____

        2. _____

    B. _____

        1. _____

        2. _____

        3. _____

V. _____

    A. _____

    B. _____

CHAPTER 2 SECTION 5

Section Summary
THE MIDDLE COLONIES

Beginning in 1609, Dutch merchants sent ships across the Atlantic and up the Hudson River to trade for furs with the Indians. In 1614, they founded a permanent settlement at Fort Nassau on the upper river. To guard the mouth of the river, the Dutch built New Amsterdam at the tip of Manhattan Island in 1626. It became the colony's largest town, major seaport, and government headquarters. The Dutch West India Company appointed the governor and an advisory council of leading colonists. New Netherland tolerated various religious groups, including Jews. However, the colony attracted few immigrants. **Push factors** motivate people to leave their home countries, while **pull factors** attract people to a new location. There was less cause for the Dutch to leave home than the English.

In 1638, traders founded New Sweden on the lower Delaware River, within the present state of Delaware. Some of the colonists were Swedes, but most came from Finland. These colonists introduced many frontier techniques that eventually became classically American, such as log cabins. In September 1655, New Sweden was forced to surrender to its Dutch neighbors.

In 1664, the English forced the Dutch governor to surrender New Amsterdam, which the English renamed New York, after its proprietor, the Duke of York. The region between the Chesapeake and New England colonies became known as the Middle Colonies. The Duke of York granted lands between the Hudson and Delaware rivers as a new colony called New Jersey.

Pennsylvania began as a debt paid to **William Penn** by King Charles II of England. <u>Penn belonged to a radical form of Protestantism whose members were called **Quakers.**</u> They relied on mystical experience to know God and understand the Bible. They considered women spiritually equal to men, refused to bear arms, and tolerated other faiths. In 1680, the king granted to Penn the land west of the Delaware River as the colony of Pennsylvania, or "Penn's Woods." In 1682, Penn arrived and established a city named Philadelphia. Cultivating peace with the local Indians, the Pennsylvanians avoided the sort of native rebellions that devastated other colonies. In their ethnic and religious pluralism, the Middle Colonies anticipated the diversity of America's future population.

Review Questions

1. How did the Dutch colony of New Netherland become the English colony of New York?

_____

_____

2. Who were the Quakers? What did they believe?

_____

_____

Name _____ Class _____ Date _____

Focus Question: Which major groups of immigrants came to Britain's American colonies in the 1700s?

As you read the section, use the concept web below to list main ideas about population in the colonies.

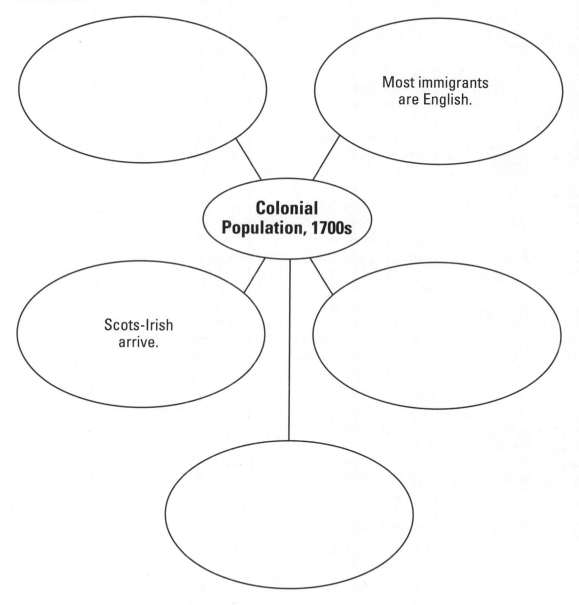

Most immigrants are English.

Colonial Population, 1700s

Scots-Irish arrive.

CHAPTER 3 SECTION 1

Section Summary
IMMIGRATION AND SLAVERY

READING CHECK

What is the name for the voyage of enslaved Africans from Africa to the colonies?

_____

_____

_____

VOCABULARY STRATEGY

What does the word *status* mean in the underlined sentence? Look for context clues in the surrounding words, phrases, and sentences to learn the meaning of *status*.

_____

_____

_____

READING SKILL

Identify Main Ideas Why did the practice of slavery develop in the colonies?

_____

_____

_____

As the English colonies developed, Europeans began to arrive in greater numbers. In the 1600s, about 90 percent of the migrants came from England. About half of the colonial immigrants were **indentured servants.** Too poor to afford the cost of passage, they paid by agreeing to work for a period of four to seven years. Instead of receiving a wage, they received food, clothing, and shelter.

After 1660, English emigration decreased, but Scottish emigration soared. Generally poorer than the English, the Scots had more reasons to seek their fortunes elsewhere. Germans were second only to the Scots-Irish as immigrants to British America. Most of the German immigrants were Protestant, seeking to escape war, taxes, and religious persecution.

Immigration made colonial society more diverse. Although the different groups often distrusted one another at first, they all gradually accepted that a diverse society was an economic boon and the best guarantee for their own faith.

As the number of indentured servants declined in the late 1600s, many colonists turned to another source of labor: enslaved Africans. By law, the position as slave was passed from parent to child. This change in legal status promoted the racist idea that people of African origin were inferior to whites. Once firmly established in the colonies, slavery expanded rapidly. Enslaved Africans came to the Americas as part of a three-part voyage called the **triangular trade.** In the **Middle Passage,** shippers carried the enslaved Africans across the Atlantic to the American colonies. The brutality of the Middle Passage was extreme, and at least 10 percent of those making the trip in the 1700s did not survive.

Slavery varied considerably by region. In 1750, slaves made up small minorities in New England and the Middle Colonies. Many more slaves lived in the Southern Colonies, where they raised labor-intensive crops of tobacco, rice, indigo, or sugar. A lifetime of enslavement was the fate of most African Americans, but some did obtain their freedom. A rare few, such as **Phillis Wheatley,** managed to overcome enormous obstacles to distinguish themselves.

Review Questions

1. How did European immigration to the colonies change in the late 1600s and 1700s?

_____

_____

2. How did slavery vary by region?

_____

_____

Name _____ Class _____ Date _____

Focus Question: How did English ideas about government and the economy influence life in the 13 colonies?

Use the format below to outline the section's main ideas and supporting details.

I. **Government in the Colonies**

  A. Traditions of English Government

    1. Magna Carta

    2. _____

  B. _____

  C. _____

  D. _____

    1. _____

    2. _____

II. _____

  A. _____

  B. _____

  C. _____

  D. _____

III. _____

  A. _____

  B. _____

  C. _____

    1. _____

    2. _____

Name _____ Class _____ Date _____

CHAPTER 3 SECTION 2

Section Summary
THE AMERICAN COLONIES AND ENGLAND

READING CHECK

Which document protected the right of habeas corpus?

_____

_____

_____

VOCABULARY STRATEGY

What does the word *asserted* mean in the underlined sentence? The words *ignored* and *overlooked* are antonyms of *asserted*. Use these antonyms to learn the meaning of *asserted*.

_____

_____

_____

READING SKILL

Identifying Supporting Details
Give an example of how England tried to control colonial commerce.

_____

_____

_____

Compared with the Spanish or French rulers, the English monarch exercised little direct control over the colonists. The English monarchs were bound to uphold the provisions of the **Magna Carta.** This document limited the king's ability to tax nobles; it also guaranteed due process, or the right to a trial. During the 1300s, the lawmaking body known as **Parliament** evolved.

Most settlers in the English colonies asserted that they were entitled to the same rights as any other English subject. In 1689, the colonists learned that James II had been overthrown in England. The new monarchs signed an **English Bill of Rights** guaranteeing a number of freedoms, including that of **habeas corpus**—the idea that no one can be held in prison without being charged with a specific crime. The Glorious Revolution encouraged England to adopt a policy of **salutary neglect,** which allowed its colonies virtual self-rule.

In the mid-1600s, Parliament passed a series of trade laws in order to control colonial commerce. The **Navigation Acts** stated that only English ships with English sailors can trade with English colonies. These acts expressed an economic philosophy known as **mercantilism,** which holds that a nation can build wealth and power by developing its industries and exporting manufactured goods in exchange for gold and silver. The Navigation Acts promoted the dramatic growth of English colonial commerce. The expanding transatlantic commerce produced a "consumer revolution" that brought more and cheaper goods to the colonies.

During the 1600s and 1700s, Europe experienced an intellectual movement known as the **Enlightenment.** It challenged old ways of thinking about science, religion, and government. Enlightenment ideas changed the way American colonists such as **Benjamin Franklin** viewed the world as well. As a result, a new movement of heightened religious fervor, known as the **Great Awakening,** arose. Preachers such as Jonathan Edwards and George Whitefield stressed an emotional and deeply personal religious experience. The Great Awakening inspired the American people with a sense of their own power as individuals. It also led many colonists to believe that if they could choose their method of worship, they could decide on their form of government.

Review Questions

1. How did most settlers in the English colonies view themselves in relation to England?

_____

_____

2. How did the Great Awakening affect Americans?

_____

_____

CHAPTER 3
SECTION 3
Note Taking Study Guide
COMPARING REGIONAL CULTURES

Focus Question: How did life differ in each of the three main regions of the British colonies?

Complete the chart below by comparing the three regions of the 13 colonies.

	New England	**Middle Colonies**	**Southern Colonies**
Economy	• Fishing • • • •	• • •	• • •
Society	• • • • • • • •	• Religious diversity • • •	• • • • •

Name _____ Class _____ Date _____

READING CHECK

Where were the most valuable and profitable colonial crops grown?

_____

_____

_____

VOCABULARY STRATEGY

What does the word *commodities* mean in the underlined sentence? Use context clues from the surrounding words, phrases, and sentences to learn the meaning of *commodities*.

_____

_____

_____

READING SKILL

Compare and Contrast How did climate affect the economies of New England and the Middle Colonies?

_____

_____

By the mid-1700s, the colonies had developed important regional distinctions based on geography and climate. New England has cold winters, a short growing season, and a rugged landscape. Most New Englanders worked small farms where they raised livestock and grew wheat, rye, corn, and potatoes for their own use. <u>Since none of these commodities could profitably be shipped to England, they exported lumber and fish and used their abundant wood to build ships.</u>

As in New England, family farms prevailed in the Middle Colonies. However, their farms were more prosperous than those to the north. A more temperate climate allowed farmers to produce and export wheat. The Middle Colonies boomed during the eighteenth century.

Because of a warm climate and long growing season, the Southern Colonies could raise the most valuable and profitable colonial crops. In Virginia and Maryland, planters raised **staple crops,** such as tobacco, which were in steady demand. These crops were also **cash crops,** crops grown for sale. North Carolina produced cattle and lumber, while South Carolina and Georgia harvested rice and indigo.

The three colonial regions also varied in the shape and form of the social life that developed there. European immigrants seemed to prefer the Middle Colonies, which became the most ethnically and culturally diverse region in the entire British Empire. In addition to religious tolerance, the Middle Colonies offered immigrants greater economic opportunities.

Though a less desirable destination for immigrants, New England provided a healthier environment. New England was free of the malaria and dysentery that killed so many colonists elsewhere, allowing the population to grow rapidly. New England leaders favored compact settlement in towns to support public schools and to sustain local churches. By law and custom, there were few opportunities for women outside the home. Some girls received an education in **dame schools,** private schools operated out of a woman's home. Outside of New England, education was less widely available.

In the Southern Colonies, the plantation economy based on slavery produced great profits at the expense of cultural development and economic opportunity. A few white people became rich planters, but most remained common farmers.

Review Questions

1. What did the Middle Colonies offer immigrants?

_____

_____

2. Why did New England leaders favor a town system?

_____

_____

Name _____ Class _____ Date _____

Focus Question: How did Great Britain's wars with France affect the American colonies?

As you read, keep track of the sequence of events that led to the French and Indian War.

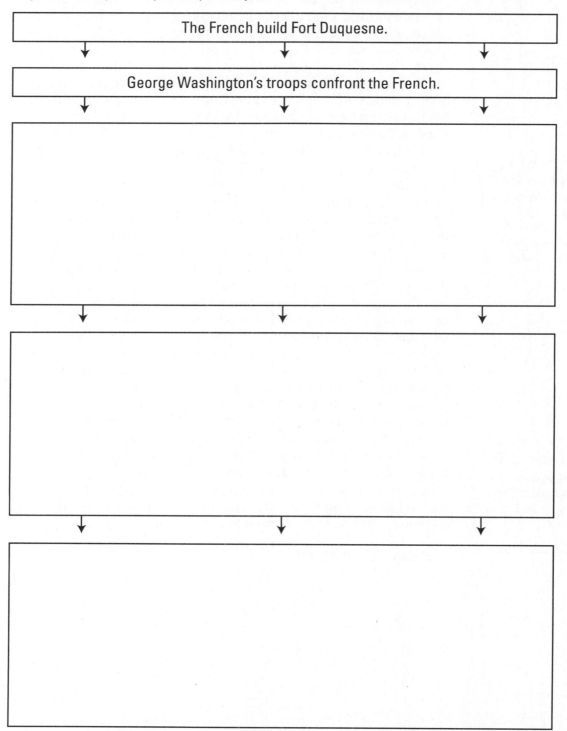

The French build Fort Duquesne.

⬇   ⬇   ⬇

George Washington's troops confront the French.

⬇   ⬇   ⬇

CHAPTER 3 SECTION 4

Section Summary
WARS OF EMPIRE

Between 1689 and 1748, the British and the French fought a series of wars. Each side gave generous gifts to woo the Indians. The Indians recognized the importance of preserving the balance of power between the French and the British. However, that balance began to tip as the British colonial population grew and the French were more restrained, treating most Native Americans with respect and generosity. The outnumbered French worked with their Indian allies to resist British colonial expansion.

To discourage British colonists from moving into the rich Ohio River valley, the French built Fort Duquesne. The new fort angered the British governor of Virginia. He sent troops led by **George Washington** to evict the French. They did not succeed, and the incident helped start the **French and Indian War.**

The British fared poorly in North America until 1758 and 1759, when they managed to cut off French shipping to the Americas. Many Indians deserted the French in order to receive better goods from the British. In 1760, the British captured Montreal and forced the surrender of the rest of Canada. In 1763, the Treaty of Paris ended the war triumphantly for the British, who kept Canada, the Great Lakes country, the Ohio River valley, and Florida. They had driven the French from North America.

The conquest of Canada was dreadful news to Indians of the interior. During the spring of 1763, members of several Indian groups surprised and captured most of the British forts in the Ohio River valley and along the Great Lakes. Their goal was to weaken the British and lure the French back into North America. **Pontiac's Rebellion** ended when the Indian nations made peace in return for British promises to restrain the settlers. The **Proclamation of 1763** ordered colonial settlers to remain east of the Appalachian Mountains.

With British encouragement, colonial delegates met in 1754 to review Benjamin Franklin's **Albany Plan of Union.** The plan called on the colonies to unite under British rule and cooperate with each other. At the time, none of the colonies would accept the plan for fear of losing some autonomy. The British also feared that the united colonies might be even more difficult to manage.

Review Questions
1. Why did the Indians work with the French?

_____

_____

2. How was Pontiac's Rebellion resolved?

_____

_____

CHAPTER 4 SECTION 1 — Note Taking Study Guide
CAUSES OF THE REVOLUTION

Focus Question: What caused the colonists to rebel against the British?

Record the events that increased tension between Britain and its colonies.

Colonial assemblies win the right to levy taxes.

↓   ↓   ↓

Parliament passes the Sugar Act, an indirect tax.

↓   ↓   ↓

↓   ↓   ↓

↓   ↓   ↓

↓   ↓   ↓

↓   ↓   ↓

↓   ↓   ↓

↓   ↓   ↓

CHAPTER	**Section Summary**
4	
SECTION 1	**CAUSES OF THE REVOLUTION**

Who were the Sons of Liberty?

_____

_____

_____

What does the word *virtual* mean in the underlined sentence? Look for context clues in the surrounding words, phrases, and sentences.

_____

_____

_____

Recognize Sequence What event led to the first eruption of violence by the colonists?

_____

_____

Colonial governments were supposed to be miniature versions of the British government. However, the British constitution was not a formal document but a collection of laws and traditions. In contrast, the colonists' rights were spelled out in written contracts such as the Mayflower Compact or royal charters. Still, members of Parliament saw themselves as "virtual representatives" of all British citizens, including the colonists.

After the Seven Years' War, Parliament decided that the colonists should pay more to help the British Empire. The **Stamp Act,** passed in March 1765, required colonists to pay a tax on almost all printed materials. This was the first time that Parliament had imposed a direct tax on the colonies. The colonists protested angrily. **Patrick Henry** of Virginia argued that only the colonial assemblies had the right to tax the colonists. Those who opposed the British taxes began to call themselves "Patriots." To lead the protests, some men joined together as the **Sons of Liberty.**

In 1767, Parliament passed the Townshend Acts, which levied new import duties on items such as glass and tea. When riots broke out in Boston, the Crown sent in 4,000 troops. In March 1770, soldiers fired into a crowd, killing five colonists. Patriots called the killings the **Boston Massacre.** They formed **committees of correspondence** to provide leadership and promote cooperation. The British withdrew their troops from Boston, but kept the tax on tea. On December 16, 1773, the Boston Sons of Liberty dressed as Indians and boarded three British ships laden with tea, which they dumped into the harbor. The event became known as the **Boston Tea Party.**

To punish Boston, Parliament passed the Coercive Acts, which became known as the **Intolerable Acts.** These acts closed the port of Boston and forced colonists to house British troops. Leaders from other colonies watched the situation in Boston closely. In the fall of 1774, delegates from every colony except Georgia met in Philadelphia, Pennsylvania, for the **First Continental Congress.** They announced a boycott of all British imports and established new governments that bypassed the Parliament and the Crown.

Review Questions

1. How did the colonists respond to the Stamp Act?

_____

_____

2. What was the significance of the First Continental Congress?

_____

_____

Name _____ Class _____ Date _____

Focus Question: What events led the colonists to declare their independence from Britain?

Use the timeline below to keep track of events in this section.

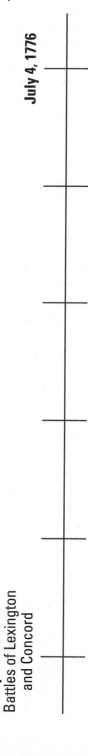

July 4, 1776

April 18, 1775
Battles of Lexington and Concord

CHAPTER 4 SECTION 2

Section Summary
DECLARING INDEPENDENCE

READING CHECK

What course of action did Thomas Paine propose in *Common Sense*?

_____

_____

_____

VOCABULARY STRATEGY

What does the word *stereotype* mean in the underlined sentence? Use context clues from the surrounding words, phrases, and sentences to help you figure out what *stereotype* means.

_____

_____

_____

READING SKILL

Recognize Sequence What role did the publication of *Common Sense* play in leading the colonies to declare their independence?

_____

_____

_____

On April 19, 1775, war erupted with battles at Lexington and Concord, small towns west of Boston. British troops that had been sent to seize Patriot weapons stockpiled in Concord encountered the Patriot **militia,** full-time farmers who were part-time soldiers. The British were pushed back to Boston, and provincial assemblies of Patriots seized control of the New England colonies. **Loyalists,** or colonists who remained loyal to Britain, fled to take refuge with the British troops in Boston. In May 1775, delegates from all the colonies assembled in Philadelphia for the **Second Continental Congress.** The Congress assumed responsibility for the war and gave the command of the new **Continental Army** to **George Washington.**

Most colonists supported the actions of the Continental Congress, but a large minority preferred British rule. The Loyalists feared that the resistance would lead to a deadly and destructive war that Britain would certainly win. According to stereotype, Loyalists were wealthy elitists. In reality, many were ordinary farmers and artisans.

In January 1776, **Thomas Paine** published a pamphlet called *Common Sense,* in which he made a radical proposal: independence from Britain, a republican government, and a union of the colonies. Paine argued that ordinary people should elect their entire government. Although the colonies had enormous social and economic differences, Paine insisted that Americans could create a model that would inspire common people everywhere.

By the spring of 1776, Paine's ideas had built momentum for American independence. Congress selected a committee to draft a document declaring American independence. On July 4, Congress approved the **Declaration of Independence.** Drafted by **Thomas Jefferson,** it drew on Paine's ideas to denounce the king. Congress embraced the Enlightenment ideas that all men are born with **natural rights** that cannot be taken away by a government. Jefferson called them "inalienable rights." However, to achieve independence, the poorly organized colonists would have to fight against one of the strongest military powers on Earth.

Review Questions

1. How did the Second Continental Congress respond to the eruption of fighting?

_____

_____

2. Trace the origins of the "inalienable rights" referred to by the Declaration of Independence.

_____

_____

CHAPTER 4 SECTION 3

Note Taking Study Guide

TURNING POINTS OF THE WAR

Focus Question: What factors helped the Patriots win the war?

A. *Record the British and Patriot strengths and weaknesses on the chart below.*

British	
Strengths	**Weaknesses**
•	•
•	•
•	
•	
•	

Patriot	
Strengths	**Weaknesses**
•	•
•	•
•	•
•	•
•	•
	•

CHAPTER 4 SECTION 3

Note Taking Study Guide
TURNING POINTS OF THE WAR

Focus Question: What factors helped the Patriots win the war?

B. *Use the timeline below to record the sequence of important events and battles during the war.*

September 15, 1776
British capture
New York City

CHAPTER 4 SECTION 3

Section Summary

TURNING POINTS OF THE WAR

Britain seemed to have great advantages at the beginning of the war, which led the British to underestimate the Patriots as an enemy. In 1775, British soldiers under Lord **William Howe** tried to take the hills overlooking Boston. Although they succeeded, they suffered more than twice the Patriot casualties. Six months later, Patriot reinforcements arrived with cannons they had captured, and the British were forced to abandon the city in March 1776.

The British never fully understood that they were fighting a revolutionary war. They further angered colonists by hiring German **mercenaries.** Patriot persistence owed much to the leadership of George Washington and his use of guerrilla warfare and unorthodox tactics to hold off the British. Continental troops worked with local militias and relied on the aid and support of the civilian population.

After leaving Boston, the British attacked New York City to cut off New England from the rest of the colonies. Howe captured the city on September 15. After a modest victory at the **Battle of Trenton,** Washington began 1777 with another victory when he inflicted heavy casualties on General **Charles Cornwallis**'s troops at the **Battle of Princeton.** After a Patriot victory at **Saratoga, Benjamin Franklin** secured help in February 1778. <u>France agreed to become an ally of the Patriots.</u> Some French volunteers, including the **Marquis de Lafayette,** were already providing military expertise.

Washington's army spent a harsh winter at **Valley Forge** outside of Philadelphia. Despite their hardships, the soldiers benefited from drilling exercises supervised by a German officer. The Continental soldiers demonstrated their improved discipline at **Monmouth,** New Jersey, in June 1778.

The outbreak of war between the colonists and the British escalated the frequent skirmishes between settlers and Indians. Most Indians sided with the British, who had promised to keep the colonists in the east. Native Americans and white settlers increasingly attacked each other, beginning a cycle of revenge that continued for years.

Review Questions

1. In what ways did the British underestimate the Patriots?

_____

_____

2. Why did most Indians side with the British?

_____

_____

READING CHECK

Who negotiated an alliance with the French?

_____

_____

_____

VOCABULARY STRATEGY

What does the word *ally* mean in the underlined sentence? Look for context clues in the surrounding words, phrases, and sentences.

_____

_____

_____

READING SKILL

Summarize What advantages did the Patriots have against the British?

_____

_____

_____

CHAPTER 4
SECTION 4

Note Taking Study Guide
WAR'S END AND LASTING EFFECTS

Focus Question: What did the Revolution accomplish, and what ideas did it set in motion?

A. *Use the flowchart below to record the events leading up to the Treaty of Paris.*

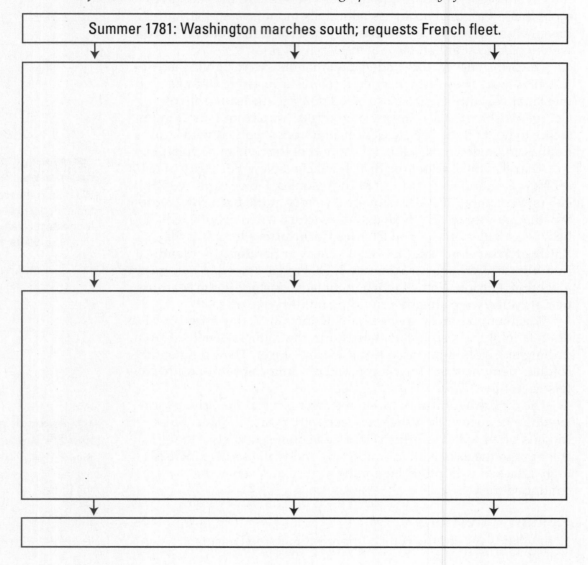

Summer 1781: Washington marches south; requests French fleet.

Name _____ Class _____ Date _____

Focus Question: What did the Revolution accomplish, and what ideas did it set in motion?

B. *Use the concept web below to summarize how the Revolution affected different groups.*

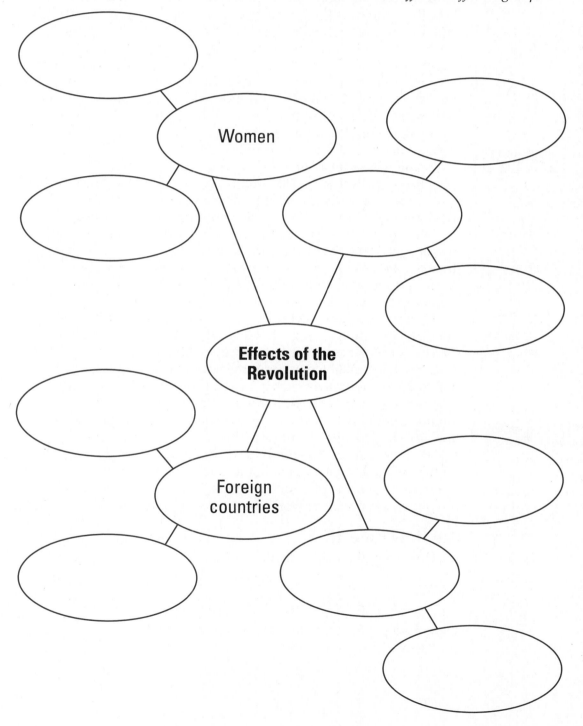

CHAPTER 4 SECTION 4

Section Summary
WAR'S END AND LASTING EFFECTS

What were the terms of the Treaty of Paris?

_____

_____

_____

VOCABULARY STRATEGY

What does the word *frustrated* mean in the underlined sentence? Look for context clues in the surrounding words, phrases, and sentences to help you learn the meaning of *frustrated*.

_____

_____

_____

READING SKILL

Recognize Sequence What effect did the American Revolution have on other nations in the world?

_____

_____

_____

The British knew they would find more Loyalist support in the South. They won most of the battles and captured the leading seaports, yet failed to control the southern countryside. In October 1780 at **Kings Mountain** in North Carolina, the Patriots crushed a Loyalist militia. As the Loyalists lost men and territory, neutral civilians swung over to the Patriot side, which frustrated the British.

During the summer of 1781, Washington marched most of his troops south. He planned to trap Cornwallis's army at **Yorktown,** Virginia. The French fleet arrived at just the right moment, trapping the British navy. Cornwallis surrendered his army on October 19. The British negotiated a peace treaty with an American delegation led by Benjamin Franklin. The **Treaty of Paris** recognized American independence and granted generous boundaries to the United States.

Some Americans won far more rights than others. About 90,000 Loyalists—including 20,000 former slaves—became refugees. About half of them resettled in Britain's northern colonies. During the Revolutionary War, the Americans fought on their western frontier to defeat the Native Americans. When the British abandoned the Indians in 1783, the Patriots forced the Indians to give up massive tracts of land as the price of peace. Women gained few political or legal rights as a result of the Revolution, but they won greater respect based on the new conception of women as "republican mothers."

African Americans were excluded from the rights demanded by the Patriots. After the war, the Revolution led to emancipation in the North, where slavery was not critical to the economy. Emancipation was much less likely to occur in the South, where slaves were essential to the plantation economy. In Maryland and Virginia, many planters voluntarily freed their slaves, a practice known as **manumission.** After 1810, however, southern states passed laws to discourage further manumissions.

Perhaps the greatest effect of the Revolution was the spreading of the idea of liberty, both at home and abroad. Over the next three centuries, the principles for which the Patriots fought would inspire revolutions around the world, beginning with the French Revolution.

Review Questions

1. How were the British finally defeated?

_____

_____

2. Why did African Americans not benefit from the American Revolution?

_____

_____

CHAPTER 5 SECTION 1

Note Taking Study Guide

A CONFEDERATION OF STATES

Focus Question: What form of national government did the Patriots create initially, and what events revealed that a new government was necessary?

Use the table below to list characteristics of early state governments and characteristics of the national government under the Articles.

Early State Governments	Early National Government
• All states established republics, in which voters chose representatives.	• Each state had one vote, regardless of size.
•	•
•	•
•	•
	•

CHAPTER 5 SECTION 1

Section Summary
A CONFEDERATION OF STATES

READING CHECK

What was the name of the plan the Congress created to provide a government for the Northwest Territory?

_____

_____

_____

Upon declaring independence in 1776, the Congress invited each new state to create a constitution. The constitutions all called for **republics,** or governments in which officials are representatives elected by the people. The more liberal Patriots preferred a **unicameral legislature,** or a single house elected by the people. Most states chose to create state governments made up of a **bicameral legislature,** a lawmaking body with two houses—a Senate and a House of Representatives. In most states, conservatives preserved colonial property requirements for voting. Most state constitutions guaranteed freedom of religion.

In 1777, the Continental Congress drafted the **Articles of Confederation,** the new constitution for the union of the states. Under the leadership of **John Dickinson,** Congress designed a loose confederation of states rather than a centralized nation. The new **federal,** or national, government included no executive branch. However, the powers to make, implement, and enforce the laws were placed with the Congress.

The national Congress created plans for settling and governing the **Northwest Territory,** the territory north of the Ohio River and west of Pennsylvania to the Mississippi River. In the **Land Ordinance of 1785,** the Congress designed a system for distributing the public lands. The **Northwest Ordinance of 1787** provided a government for the western territory, as well as a process for statehood. Slavery was barred from the territory.

Spain and Britain did not take the new United States seriously. Spain forbade American trade with Spanish-held New Orleans. Britain imposed restrictions that hurt American shipping interests. Britain also kept its forts on American territory.

The weaknesses of the Articles of Confederation contributed to the troubles of the fledgling government. Under the Articles, the federal Congress could not establish a common currency, regulate interstate commerce, or levy taxes. Meanwhile, most Americans were farmers, and most farmers were in debt. They faced the loss of their crops, livestock, and even their farms to foreclosure. In 1786, the Massachussetts army suppressed an uprising by farmers that became known as **Shays' Rebellion.** Most Americans hoped to save the Republic by establishing a stronger national government.

VOCABULARY BUILDER

What does the word *implement* mean in the underlined sentence? Look for context clues in the surrounding words, phrases, and sentences to learn the meaning of *implement.*

_____

_____

_____

READING SKILL

Identify Main Ideas Identify three provisions of the Articles of Confederation that weakened the new U.S. government.

_____

_____

_____

Review Questions

1. What was one cause of tension between the United States and Britain?

_____

_____

2. What was one characteristic of early state governments?

_____

_____

CHAPTER 5 SECTION 2

Note Taking Study Guide

DRAFTING THE CONSTITUTION

Focus Question: What new system of national government did the delegates agree upon at the Constitutional Convention of 1787?

In the concept web below, write details about each plan or compromise that led to the creation of the United States Constitution.

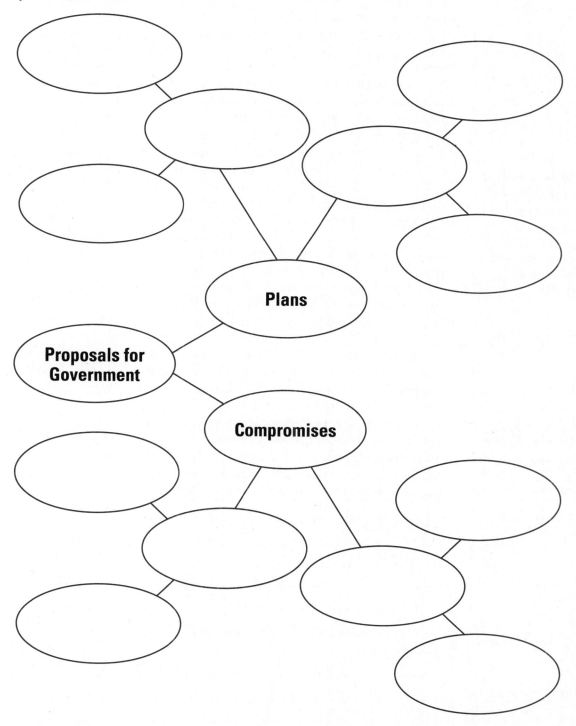

Section Summary
DRAFTING THE CONSTITUTION

What was the name of the compromise that helped resolve the conflict between the northern and southern states over the issue of slavery?

_____

_____

_____

What does the word *subsequent* mean in the underlined sentence? Look for context clues in the surrounding words, phrases, and sentences. Circle the word below that is a synonym for *subsequent*.

• following

• preceding

Identify Supporting Details List details of both the Virginia Plan and the New Jersey Plan.

_____

_____

_____

By 1787, it was clear that the Articles of Confederation needed major changes. Most agreed that Congress should have the power to regulate interstate and international commerce and to tax the people. To draft amendments to the Articles, 12 of the 13 states sent delegates to a convention in Philadelphia. Two of the convention's leading thinkers were **Alexander Hamilton** and **James Madison.**

During the subsequent weeks and months, delegates debated a number of proposals for the new constitution. Most of the delegates favored a scheme proposed by Madison called the **Virginia Plan.** The plan proposed creating a government that divided power among the legislative, executive, and judicial branches. The plan would establish a bicameral legislature with a House of Representatives and a Senate. In both houses, representation would be based on population. The Virginia Plan also called for a strong President and gave the Congress the power to veto any state law.

The **New Jersey Plan** proposed only modest changes and was favored by the small states. This plan gave the Congress the powers to regulate commerce and to tax, but it kept the three chief principles of the Articles: a unicameral legislature representing the states as equals, an executive committee rather than a President, and sovereignty for the states in most areas.

Led by Roger Sherman, the delegates worked out a compromise between the Virginia and the New Jersey plans, known as the **Great Compromise.** The Senate would equally represent every state by allowing two senators per state. The House of Representatives would represent states based on population, granting more power to the more populous states. The delegates supported a system known as **federalism,** which divided government power between the national and state governments.

During the debates, the delegates discovered that slavery was their greatest division. A compromise known as the **Three-Fifths Compromise** counted each slave as three fifths of a person to be added to a state's free population in allocating representatives to the House of Representatives and electoral college votes.

Review Questions

1. In 1787, what two powers did most Americans believe Congress should have?

_____

_____

2. What was the name of James Madison's plan for a new constitution?

_____

_____

Note Taking Study Guide
RATIFYING THE CONSTITUTION

Focus Question: How did Americans ratify the Constitution, and what are its basic principles?

Use the table below to record the arguments for and against ratification of the Constitution.

Ratification of the Constitution	
Arguments For	**Arguments Against**
• A strong central government would be able to handle the problems that faced the nation. • •	• A strong central government would undermine basic liberties. • •

CHAPTER 5 SECTION 3

Section Summary
RATIFYING THE CONSTITUTION

Who wrote the essays in
The Federalist?

_____

_____

_____

What does the word *convened*
mean in the underlined sentence? Look for context clues in
the surrounding words, phrases,
and sentences.

_____

_____

_____

Identify Main Ideas How did the
ratified Constitution reflect the
views of both Federalists and
Antifederalists?

_____

_____

_____

The delegates to the Constitutional Convention drafted a new constitution. After being signed, the proposed Constitution was printed,
circulated, and hotly debated. The delegates ruled that nine states
had to **ratify** the new Constitution in specially elected conventions.
Two groups emerged in the debate: the Federalists, who supported
ratification, and the Antifederalists, who opposed it.

The **Federalists** argued that a strong central government could
overcome the difficulties facing the new nation. The checks and balances in the proposed Constitution would prevent any of the three
branches from gaining too much power. The **Antifederalists** disliked the lack of a bill of rights. They believed that liberty could not
survive unless the federal government was weak.

The proposed Constitution lacked majority support in 1787. However, the Constitution had the support of George Washington and
Benjamin Franklin, two of the most trusted men in America. The case
for ratification of the Constitution was set forth in *The Federalist,* a
series of 85 essays written by Madison, Hamilton, and **John Jay.** These
essays were published in New York newspapers in 1787 and 1788.

The Federalists pushed for ratifying conventions in five states
and won ratification in all of them. The promise of a bill of rights
helped the Federalists to win most of the remaining states. The resistance of the Antifederalists obliged the Federalists to make the
concession to add the **Bill of Rights,** the first ten amendments to the
Constitution that provide basic rights. <u>In 1789, the new Congress
convened in New York City.</u>

The writers of the Constitution created an indirect democracy in
which voters elect representatives to govern. Similarly, an **electoral
college,** or group of persons chosen from each state, indirectly elects
the President. The Constitution established a representative government based on these basic principles: **popular sovereignty, limited
government, separation of powers,** federalism, and **checks and
balances.** The Constitution has survived, in part, because it provides a
process for its own amendment.

Review Questions

1. Why did the Federalists want the new Constitution to be ratified?

_____

_____

2. Why were the Antifederalists opposed to the ratification of the
   new Constitution?

_____

_____

Focus Question: How did debate over the role of government lead to the formation of political parties?

Summarize information about the early American government in the outline below.

I. **Building the Federal Government**

    A. Electing Washington as President

    B. Forming the Cabinet

    C. Setting up the Judiciary

II. _____

    A. _____

    B. _____

    C. _____

        1. _____

        2. _____

    D. _____

III. _____

    A. _____

    B. _____

CHAPTER 6 SECTION 1

Section Summary
GOVERNMENT AND PARTY POLITICS

Name two political parties that formed in the aftermath of the Whiskey Rebellion.

_____

_____

_____

What does the word *suppress* mean in the underlined sentence? Circle any words or phrases in the paragraph that help you figure out what *suppress* means.

_____

_____

_____

Summarize Summarize how the two-party system emerged in the new nation.

_____

_____

_____

In 1789, the new electoral college unanimously elected George Washington as President of the United States. John Adams became Vice President. The **administration** began with only Washington, Adams, and some clerks. Besides the newly elected Congress, there were no other federal officers. After taking office, Washington began setting important **precedents,** or acts that become traditions to be followed. One precedent was the formation of a **Cabinet,** or the group of federal leaders who headed the major departments of the executive branch and served as advisers to the President. Congress passed the Judiciary Act, which set up the judicial branch.

As Secretary of the Treasury, Alexander Hamilton was given the task of paying off the nation's immense debts. Hamilton meant to pay the national debt by selling government bonds. He also called for high **tariffs** to raise revenue for the federal government. Hamilton thought his system would promote the accumulation of wealth needed for commercial and industrial growth.

Thomas Jefferson and James Madison led the opposition to Hamilton's plan, framing it in terms of how the Constitution should be interpreted. Hamilton's broad interpretation, or **loose construction,** relied on the Constitution's "implied powers" and its clauses empowering Congress to enact laws for the "general welfare." Jefferson and Madison favored a **strict construction,** or limiting the federal government to powers explicitly granted by the Constitution.

In 1794, the excise tax on whiskey led to rebellion. Farmers resisted the whiskey tax by attacking tax collectors. <u>Washington and Hamilton demonstrated the new power of the nation by sending militia to suppress the **Whiskey Rebellion.**</u>

In the aftermath of the Whiskey Rebellion, the growing division in American politics became more apparent. The federal government, headed by Washington and Hamilton, sought to secure its power and authority. Meanwhile the opposition, led by Madison and Jefferson, grew stronger. The authors of the Constitution wanted to avoid organized **political parties.** However, practical politics resulted in the formation of two parties: the Federalists, led by Hamilton and John Adams, and the **Democratic Republicans,** led by Jefferson.

Review Questions

1. What was the purpose of the Cabinet?

_____

_____

2. What was Hamilton's plan to pay off the national debt?

_____

_____

Name _____ Class _____ Date _____

Focus Question: How did foreign policy challenges affect political debate and shape American government?

Record details about early U.S. foreign policies in the chart below.

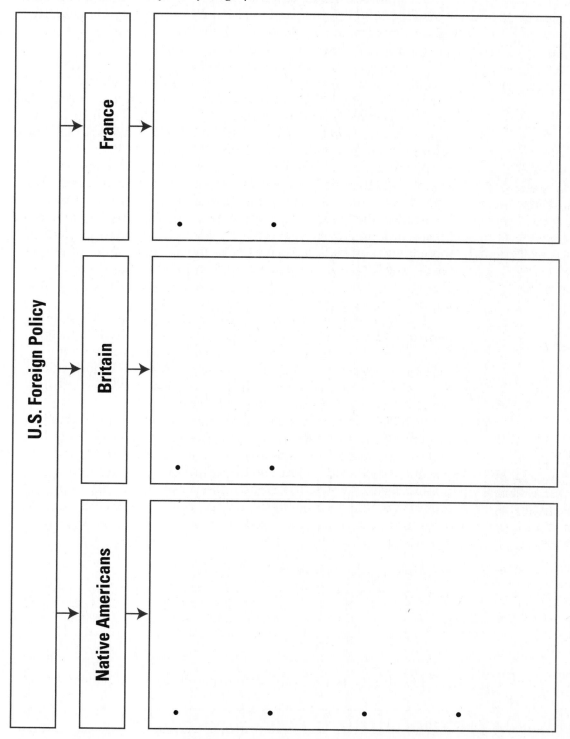

CHAPTER 6 SECTION 2

Section Summary
THE STRUGGLE OVER FOREIGN POLICY

READING CHECK

Which event roused public sentiment against France?

_____

_____

_____

As President, Washington helped unify the country during the difficult times of the early 1790s. In 1791 in the Ohio Valley, British guns helped Native Americans, led by war chief **Little Turtle,** crush an American force. Britain hoped to limit American settlement. But in 1794, federal troops defeated the Miami Confederacy at the **Battle of Fallen Timbers.** In the Treaty of Greenville, twelve tribes ceded most of present-day Ohio to the U.S. government.

In 1793, leaders of the **French Revolution** declared war on European monarchies. As a result, Britain and France were at war. Too weak to get tangled in the war, President Washington issued a proclamation of American neutrality. The British navy tested that neutrality by seizing American ships in the West Indies. Chief Justice **John Jay** went to London to negotiate a treaty with Britain.

At the same time, the United States signed a treaty with Spain. Spain controlled the Mississippi River and New Orleans. The treaty guaranteed Americans shipping rights and access to New Orleans.

In 1796, the French began seizing American ships. Newly-elected President John Adams sent envoys to Paris to negotiate peace. But three French officials, known as X, Y, and Z, demanded humiliating terms. The **XYZ Affair** roused public sentiment against France. Though not officially at war, Congress expanded the military and imposed unpopular taxes to pay for the increase.

The Federalists exploited the war fever to pass the **Alien and Sedition Acts.** Arguing that criticism undermined trust in the government, the Federalists used the act to silence Democratic Republican opposition. Virginia and Kentucky, two Democratic Republican states, passed the **Virginia and Kentucky resolutions,** which declared the Sedition Act unconstitutional.

In 1800, Adams lost the presidential election. Jefferson and his running mate, **Aaron Burr,** tied with 73 electoral college votes. The voters had meant for Jefferson to become President and Burr to become Vice President, but the Constitution did not allow a distinction in electoral votes. The House of Representatives decided that Jefferson would become President. To avoid another electoral crisis, a constitutional amendment required electors to vote separately for President and Vice President.

VOCABULARY STRATEGY

What does the word *unify* mean in the underlined sentence? What do you think Washington's goal was during this time? Circle any words or phrases in the paragraph that help you figure out what *unify* means.

_____

_____

_____

READING SKILL

Identify Supporting Details How did the election of 1800 lead to a constitutional amendment?

_____

_____

_____

Review Questions

1. Why did the British supply guns to Native Americans in the Ohio Valley in 1791?

_____

_____

2. How did the treaty with Spain benefit the United States?

_____

_____

Note Taking Study Guide

THE AGE OF JEFFERSON

Focus Question: What were the successes and failures of the Jefferson administration?

A. *Record main ideas about Jefferson's presidency in the concept web below.*

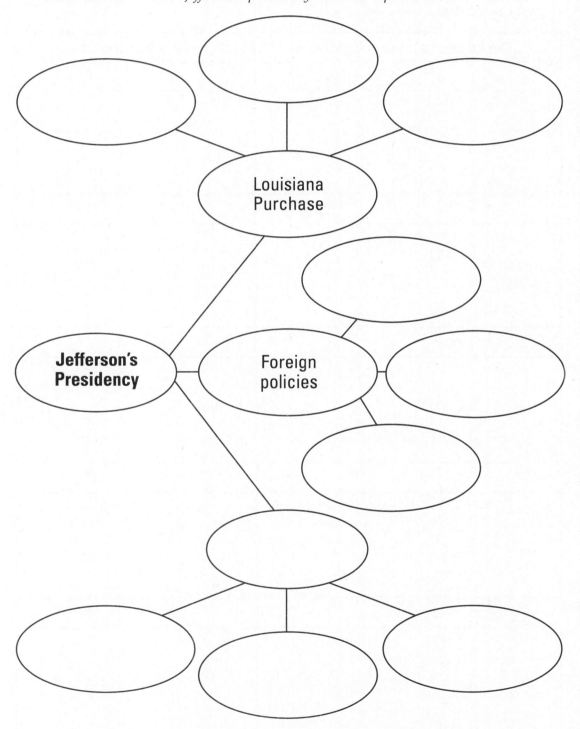

CHAPTER
6
SECTION 3

Note Taking Study Guide
THE AGE OF JEFFERSON

Focus Question: What were the successes and failures of the Jefferson administration?

B. *As you read, trace events that led to the recognition that the Supreme Court would have the power to review federal laws.*

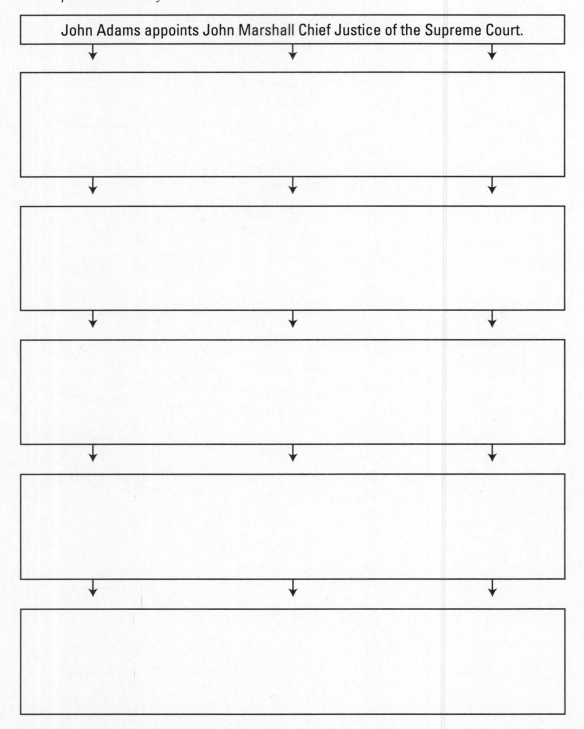

John Adams appoints John Marshall Chief Justice of the Supreme Court.

CHAPTER 6 SECTION 3

Section Summary
THE AGE OF JEFFERSON

The Jefferson administration set out to do things differently. Jefferson recognized the popularity of a common style. Many saw his election as a "revolution." Jefferson encouraged Congress to abandon the Alien and Sedition Acts, as well as the hated federal taxes. He cut the national debt. He made major cuts in the military and streamlined the government's **bureaucracy,** or the departments and workers that make up the government.

When Jefferson became President in 1801, **John Marshall** became the Chief Justice. Marshall's appointment had a major impact. His Supreme Court claimed the power to review the acts of Congress and the President to determine whether they were constitutional. This power is known as **judicial review.** The case of *Marbury* v. *Madison* established the power of judicial review.

In 1803, the **Louisiana Purchase** from France nearly doubled the size of the United States. Beginning in 1804, Jefferson sent Meriwether Lewis and William Clark to explore the new territory, in what became known as the **Lewis and Clark Expedition.**

While Jefferson succeeded in his plans to expand to the west, he also needed to solidify the position of the United States as an international power. The Barbary States of North Africa were seizing American ships and sailors in the Mediterranean Sea. Jefferson had paid protection money to the Barbary States, but when the price increased, Jefferson blockaded the port of Tripoli, winning a favorable peace in the **Barbary War** in 1805.

The government dealt with surplus produce by selling it to overseas markets. From 1793 to 1807, war in Europe aided this goal.

Engaged in a tough war and desperately needing sailors, Britain relied on **impressment,** or taking American sailors from their ships and forcing them to be British sailors. As an alternative to war in 1807, Jefferson persuaded Congress to declare an **embargo,** or suspending trade by ordering American ships to stay in port. The British found other markets, while the embargo hurt American merchants, sailors, and farmers. Exploiting voter anger, the Federalists staged a political comeback in the northern states.

Review Questions

1. In what ways was Jefferson's election a "revolution"?

_____

_____

2. What was the importance of the Louisiana Purchase?

_____

_____

READING CHECK

What Supreme Court case established the power of judicial review?

_____

_____

_____

VOCABULARY STRATEGY

What does the word *surplus* mean in the underlined sentence? This word comes from two French words: *sur,* which means "over," and *plus,* which means "more." Using this information, circle the phrase below that means the same as *surplus.*

• more than is needed

• an inadequate amount

READING SKILL

Identify Main Ideas Identify three accomplishments of Jefferson's presidency.

_____

_____

_____

CHAPTER

6

SECTION 4

Note Taking Study Guide

THE WAR OF 1812

Focus Question: Why did the United States go to war with Britain, and what was the outcome of that war?

Record the causes of the War of 1812 in the following chart.

Conflict with Native Americans	Foreign Conflict
•	• The embargo fails.
	•
•	

On the western frontier, Native American resistance was increasing. The warrior **Tecumseh** wanted to unite the Indian nations in armed resistance against American expansion. William Henry Harrison led troops in the **Battle of Tippecanoe.** This battle ended in stalemate, but as a result of it, the Native American movement lost momentum.

In 1811, some young aggressive politicians known as the **War Hawks** pushed for war against Britain. Angry about the continued impressments of American sailors and British support for Native Americans, the War Hawks insisted that invading British-held Canada would drive the British out of North America. In the **War of 1812,** the United States went to war with Britain.

The United States' attempts to invade Canada were unsuccessful. The small British and Indian forces repeatedly defeated the poorly trained U.S. army and state militias. To the surprise of many Americans, the small American navy performed well, capturing four British ships during 1812.

In 1814, British forces invaded the United States in Maine, New York, Maryland, Washington, D.C., and New Orleans. Except for the occupation of Maine, the British attacks ended in defeat. The British did capture the national capital and burned the White House and the Capitol. **Francis Scott Key** celebrated the American victory at Fort McHenry in a poem called **"The Star-Spangled Banner."** The Americans won their greatest victory at the **Battle of New Orleans** under **Andrew Jackson.**

The Americans had failed to conquer Canada, while the British had failed in their American invasions. In the **Treaty of Ghent,** both sides agreed to prewar boundaries.

The outcome of the war discredited the Federalists, who looked weak for opposing a war that became popular once it was over. By 1820, the Federalist Party was dead.

Events during the War of 1812 ended most Indian resistance to American expansion for the time being. The Treaty of Ghent forced the British to give up their forts in America, opening the way to American expansion.

Review Questions

1. Why did the War Hawks push for war against Britain?

_____

_____

2. Name two results of the War of 1812 that benefited the United States.

_____

_____

READING CHECK

What was the Americans' greatest victory in the War of 1812?

_____

_____

_____

VOCABULARY STRATEGY

What does the word *momentum* mean in the underlined sentence? A bicycle loses *momentum* as it goes uphill. What do you think *momentum* means in the underlined sentence?

_____

_____

_____

READING SKILL

Recognize Sequence Identify the causes of the War of 1812.

_____

_____

Note Taking Study Guide

Focus Question: How did transportation developments and industrialization affect the nation's economy?

Fill in the table below with the causes and effects of the transportation revolution and industrialization.

Transportation and Industry	
Causes	**Effects**
• Invention of commercial steamboat •	• Drastically increased speed of traveling upstream •
•	•
•	•
•	•
•	•
•	•
•	

CHAPTER 7 SECTION 1 — Section Summary
INDUSTRY AND TRANSPORTATION

In the early 1800s, the transportation revolution changed the economy of the United States. As new methods of transportation developed, the cost of moving goods dropped and businesses grew.

Some states chartered companies to operate **turnpikes**—roads for which users had to pay a toll. However, most of these roads did not succeed in increasing the speed of travel. The country's first major road was the **National Road,** which was funded by the federal government.

Steamboats provided the first major advance in transportation. This invention allowed goods and people to be carried upstream much faster. The construction of canals also made water transportation more efficient. Most canals were built by the government. The **Erie Canal** connected Lake Erie to New York City. Later, the growth of railroads allowed vast new areas to gain access to new markets.

New technology was also changing manufacturing in a transformation that came to be known as the **Industrial Revolution.** Entrepreneurs began this revolution by developing machines to perform the work that had once been done by hand. These machines were powered by steam or moving water.

Samuel Slater, a skilled English worker, moved to America and built the nation's first water-powered textile mill in 1793. A flowing river provided power for the mill's machinery to make cotton thread. In 1813, Boston merchant **Francis Cabot Lowell** built a fully operational mill that could make all parts of cloth, instead of just thread. The growth of factories like these changed the working lives of thousands of people. Machines increased the pace of work and divided labor into many small tasks that required less skill. The invention of **interchangeable parts,** identical components that could be used in place of one another, also improved manufacturing efficiency. **Eli Whitney** is credited with this innovation.

Other areas of American life were also changed by technology. **Samuel F.B. Morse** invented the electric telegraph in 1837, which made communication much faster. Food production also greatly increased when new farming methods were developed.

Review Questions
1. How did improved transportation help businesses?

_____

_____

2. How was the production of goods affected by the Industrial Revolution?

_____

_____

READING CHECK
Who built the first textile mill in the United States?

_____

_____

_____

VOCABULARY STRATEGY
What does the word *components* mean in the underlined sentence? Circle the words in the surrounding phrases or sentences that could help you learn what *components* means.

_____

_____

_____

READING SKILL
Identify Causes and Effects Provide at least two effects of the transportation revolution and industrialization.

_____

_____

_____

CHAPTER 7 SECTION 2

Note Taking Study Guide

SECTIONAL DIFFERENCES

Focus Question: How did the North and South differ during the first half of the 1800s?

Use the Venn diagram below to compare and contrast the North and the South.

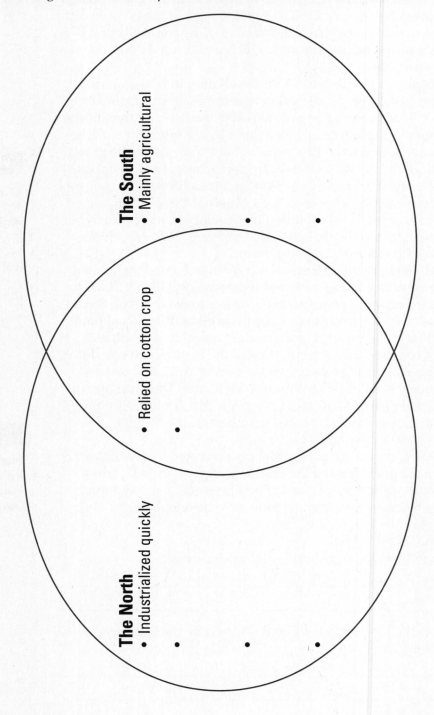

The South
- Mainly agricultural
- •   •   •

Relied on cotton crop
- •   •

The North
- Industrialized quickly
- •   •   •

CHAPTER 7 SECTION 2

Section Summary

SECTIONAL DIFFERENCES

In the early 1800s, the North became more industrialized while the South became mostly agricultural. Industrialization spread across the North for several reasons. The **Tariff of 1816** was a protective tariff that helped American manufacturers by increasing the cost of imported goods, which encouraged Americans to buy products made in the United States. Factories also appeared in the North because there was greater access to **capital,** or the money needed to buy equipment and factories. In the South, capital was tied up in land and slaves.

Another reason for industrialization was the abundance of labor. Millions of immigrants came to the United States during this period. Most of them were poor and went to work in northeastern cities. Often these immigrants were treated poorly. Many Protestant workers resented the competition from poor, Catholic immigrants. Some politicians, called **nativists,** campaigned for laws to discourage immigration or to deny political rights to newcomers.

Industrialization changed how people worked. New jobs required less skill, and skilled workers saw their wages go down. Some workers formed **labor unions**—groups of workers who unite to seek mutual goals. One tactic of labor unions was to go on strike, hoping to force employers to pay higher wages.

Many Americans benefited from new office jobs that were created during industrialization. These well-paid workers made up a new social and economic class—a middle class.

In the South, a boom in agriculture was caused by the cotton gin, western expansion, and industrialization in the North. The **cotton gin** was an invention that made cotton cultivation easier and more profitable. More and more farmers began to grow cotton, including those who lived in new territories to the west. Demand for cotton continued to increase from factories in the North and in Europe.

The culture of the South was affected by its agriculture. The cotton boom was an incentive for farmers to acquire more slaves. Southerners claimed that slavery was good for society, and they had a sense of racial superiority. Education was not a high priority, so illiteracy was higher in the South than it was in the North.

Review Questions

1. How did the presence of capital affect industrialization in the North?

_____

_____

2. What factors caused a boom in southern agriculture?

_____

_____

READING CHECK

What caused an abundance of labor in the North?

_____

_____

_____

VOCABULARY STRATEGY

What does the word *access* mean in the underlined sentence? Circle the words in the surrounding phrases or sentences that could help you learn what *access* means.

_____

_____

_____

READING SKILL

Compare and Contrast Describe the similarities and differences between the new American immigrants and Protestant workers.

_____

_____

_____

Name _____ Class _____ Date _____

Focus Question: How did domestic and foreign policies reflect the nationalism of the times?

Fill in the concept web below to identify the effects of nationalism on the nation's domestic and foreign policies.

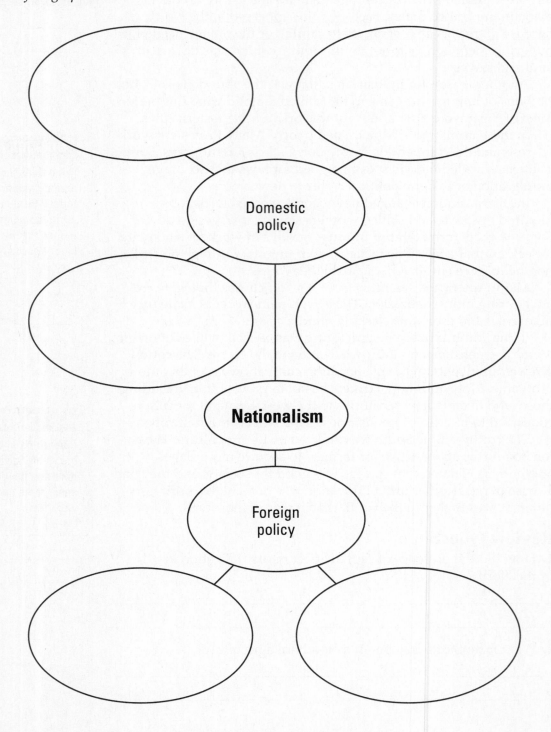

CHAPTER 7 SECTION 3

Section Summary

AN ERA OF NATIONALISM

After the War of 1812, **nationalism** swept the country. This was a feeling of glorification and promotion of the nation.

When Congress passed tariffs, it was expressing nationalism by using federal power to help industrialists and their workers. <u>**Henry Clay** was one of the leading advocates of this new economic nationalism.</u> He supported a large federal program called the **American System** for building new roads and canals to connect regions and help business.

The Supreme Court also took measures to strengthen the federal government. In several rulings, it interpreted the Constitution in a way that gave wide powers, such as the principle that federal law was superior to state law, to the government.

Nationalism also affected art and literature. Artists celebrated the nation's beautiful landscape, and novelists expressed pride in the nation's immense potential.

During this period of time, the economy experienced periodic shocks called panics, the results of "busts" in a "boom-and-bust" cycle that is common in capitalism.

The effects of nationalism also appeared in the government's foreign policy. **John Quincy Adams,** the Secretary of State under James Monroe, used the First Seminole War to expand the nation. In this war, American soldiers fought the Seminoles in Florida, which was a part of Spain. General Andrew Jackson led troops into Florida and captured some Spanish forts, making it clear that Spanish control over Florida was very weak. Adams pressured Spain to sell Florida to the United States as part of the **Adams-Onís Treaty.** The treaty also ended Spanish claims to the territory of Oregon.

Adams also formulated the **Monroe Doctrine.** This statement of policy, named for President Monroe, declared that European powers should stay out of the Western Hemisphere. The doctrine showed the nation's growing sense of its own importance.

Despite strong feelings of nationalism, there were still differences between regions in the United States. In 1820, the **Missouri Compromise** addressed the heated debate over slavery. The act maintained the balance of slave and free states. The compromise was only a temporary solution, however.

Review Questions

1. How did the American System express nationalism?

_____

_____

2. How did artists and writers express nationalism?

_____

_____

READING CHECK

What was the Monroe Doctrine?

_____

_____

_____

VOCABULARY STRATEGY

What does the word *advocates* mean in the underlined sentence? Circle the words in the surrounding sentences that could help you learn what *advocates* means.

_____

_____

_____

READING SKILL

Understand Effects The capture of some Spanish forts by General Andrew Jackson led to what effect?

_____

_____

_____

CHAPTER 7 SECTION 4

Note Taking Study Guide

DEMOCRACY AND THE AGE OF JACKSON

Focus Question: What changes did Andrew Jackson represent in American political life?

Use the flowchart below to record the effects of Jackson's presidency.

Andrew Jackson's Presidency

[flowchart with four empty boxes]

CHAPTER 7 SECTION 4

Section Summary

DEMOCRACY AND THE AGE OF JACKSON

In the election of 1824, the four candidates who ran for President were from the Democratic Republican Party, the only major political party at the time. War hero **Andrew Jackson** enjoyed wide public support. However, the election was so close that the House of Representatives had to declare the winner. Jackson was upset over losing and spent the next four years campaigning to win the presidency in 1828.

Jackson traveled the country, hoping to exploit the increasingly democratic character of national politics. In the 1824 presidential election, some states chose electors based on popular votes, a shift from earlier elections in which state legislatures chose the electors. A key Jackson aide was New York's **Martin Van Buren.** Van Buren worked behind the scenes to build support for Jackson.

Andrew Jackson became the symbol of this expanded democracy. Historians refer to the movement as **Jacksonian Democracy.** In public, Jackson celebrated majority rule and the dignity of common people. He also had an appealing personal story. He was born in a log cabin and orphaned as a boy. Jackson won the election of 1828 easily. His party was now called the Democratic Party, and it promised a return to strong states and a weak federal government.

The party created a new, more disciplined and professional organizational structure. It rewarded loyal supporters with government jobs, a practice called the **spoils system** by critics.

One of Jackson's highest priorities was removing the 60,000 American Indians living in the South. Southern whites wanted the land for themselves, and they got their wish with the **Indian Removal Act** of 1830. This act sought to exchange Indian lands for new lands in Indian Territory.

Although most Indians agreed to leave their homelands, some did not. U.S. soldiers forced 16,000 Cherokees to walk to their new home in modern-day Oklahoma. This forced march came to be called the **Trail of Tears** because at least 4,000 Cherokees died of disease, exposure, and hunger. Some Seminoles violently resisted the government's demands by fighting the Second Seminole War.

Review Questions

1. Why was Jacksonian Democracy popular with the public?

_____

_____

2. What was the goal of the Indian Removal Act?

_____

_____

READING CHECK

What was the spoils system?

_____

_____

_____

VOCABULARY STRATEGY

What does the word *exploit* mean in the underlined sentence? Use context clues in the surrounding words and phrases to help you learn the meaning of *exploit.*

_____

_____

_____

READING SKILL

Understand Effects Describe the effects resulting from Jackson's desire to remove the 60,000 American Indians living in the South.

_____

_____

Name _____ Class _____ Date _____

Focus Question: What major political issues emerged during the 1830s?

Fill in the table below to compare the viewpoints of Jackson and Calhoun on the issue of nullification.

Nullification	
Andrew Jackson	**John C. Calhoun**
•	•
•	•
•	•

CHAPTER 7 SECTION 5 — Section Summary

CONSTITUTIONAL DISPUTES AND CRISES

The presidency of Andrew Jackson featured a number of conflicts. In 1828, Congress adopted a high tariff that became known as the **Tariff of Abominations.** In general, tariffs were favored by the North and disliked by the South. The fact that President Adams signed this tariff helped to bring about his defeat in 1828. Although Jackson was against tariffs, he did not remove them as President.

When the tariff was not abolished, Vice President **John C. Calhoun** got upset. Calhoun was from South Carolina and strongly against tariffs. He argued for **nullification,** the idea that states could nullify, or void, any federal law they deemed unconstitutional.

Even though Jackson did not support tariffs, he signed a new one into law. In 1833, South Carolina took action by nullifying the protective tariff and prohibiting the collection of tariff duties. The state also threatened to secede from the Union.

Jackson supported states' rights and low tariffs, but he rejected nullification and secession. <u>He felt the Union must be perpetual and states must honor federal law.</u> Congress gave Jackson the authority to use troops to enforce federal law in South Carolina. At the same time, Congress also reduced the tariff. This reduced South Carolina's anger, and the state ended its policy of nullification.

Jackson faced another conflict over the national bank. The second Bank of the United States had been created by Congress in 1816. Jackson and his supporters opposed the Bank and argued that it mostly benefited the rich. However, the Bank had many supporters in Congress, and in 1832, they voted to renew the Bank's charter. Jackson vetoed the bill, stating that the bank was unconstitutional and did not benefit the public.

Anger over Jackson's veto led to the creation of the political party known as the **Whigs.** The Whigs wanted a strong federal government to manage the economy. When the economy soured after Jackson's replacement Martin Van Buren served as President, the Whigs managed to get their candidate, William Henry Harrison, elected President. However, he died shortly after taking office, and his replacement rejected Whig policies.

Review Questions

1. How did South Carolina react to the high tariff?

_____

_____

2. Why did Jackson and his supporters oppose the Bank?

_____

_____

READING CHECK

Who was Vice President under Andrew Jackson?

_____

_____

_____

VOCABULARY STRATEGY

What does the word *perpetual* mean in the underlined sentence? Look for context clues in the surrounding words, phrases, and sentences to help you learn the meaning of *perpetual*.

_____

_____

_____

READING SKILL

Compare Compare the viewpoints of President Jackson and the Whigs.

_____

_____

_____

Name _____ Class _____ Date _____

Focus Question: How did the Second Great Awakening affect life in the United States?

Note the main ideas under each blue heading in the chart below.

Religion in the Early 1800s

Second Great Awakening	Discrimination	Other Religious Movements
• Camp meetings	•	•
•		
	•	•
•		
	•	•
	•	
	•	

CHAPTER 8 SECTION 1

Section Summary
A RELIGIOUS AWAKENING

In the early 1700s, Americans experienced a burst of religious energy known as the Great Awakening. Another revival of religious feeling, the **Second Great Awakening,** swept the country in the early 1800s. Protestant preachers known as **revivalists** taught that religion was vital to the nation.

This excitement about religion started in Kentucky and spread across the nation. Revivalists such as **Charles Grandison Finney** taught listeners in large outdoor gatherings called "revivals." Finney gave passionate sermons that were emotionally moving. This **evangelical** style of preaching proved very successful in winning converts. African Americans were also part of this movement. They attended revivals and sometimes started their own churches.

Excitement about religion also led to the formation of two new religious groups. In 1830, **Joseph Smith** established the Church of Jesus Christ of Latter-day Saints. His followers were commonly called the **Mormons.** In New England, some members of Puritan churches broke away into a new group called the **Unitarians.** They believed that God was a single divine being instead of a "Trinity."

As Protestant believers grew in their enthusiasm and political power, some non-Protestants faced persecution. Mormons faced violence when their neighbors opposed their beliefs. <u>Catholics and Jews faced discrimination in the early 1800s, too.</u> In some places, Protestants rioted against Catholic worshippers. State constitutions, from New England to the South, barred Jews from holding public office. Americans often ostracized Jews.

Some groups took advantage of abundant land and established **utopian communities.** They hoped these settlements would be perfect worlds where all residents worked together.

In New England, a group known as the **Transcendentalists** developed a new way to look at humanity, nature, and God. Writers like **Ralph Waldo Emerson** and **Henry David Thoreau** thought that people could transcend, or go beyond, their senses to learn about the world and to learn the truth about the universe.

Review Questions

1. How did revivalists win so many converts?

_____

_____

2. What was Transcendentalism?

_____

_____

READING CHECK

Which religious group believed that God was a single divine being?

_____

_____

_____

VOCABULARY STRATEGY

What does the word *discrimination* mean in the underlined sentence? Circle any words or phrases in the paragraph that help you figure out what *discrimination* means.

_____

_____

_____

READING SKILL

Identify Main Ideas How were African Americans involved in the Second Great Awakening?

_____

_____

Note Taking Study Guide
A REFORMING SOCIETY

Focus Question: What were the main features of the public school, penitentiary, and temperance reform movements?

As you read, note the different problems facing society in the early 1800s, what reformers did to address each problem, and the effects of their efforts.

Causes	Efforts to Reform	Results
Educating all Americans	•	• • •
	•	•
	•	•
	•	• •

CHAPTER 8 SECTION 2

Section Summary
A REFORMING SOCIETY

In the early and middle 1800s, many Americans worked to reform American life and to help disadvantaged people. Reformers tackled problems in several areas of public life.

Many reformers thought that education in America was inadequate. Because there were no tax-supported schools that children were required to attend, most children did not receive a formal education. The **public school movement** tried to establish state-supported schools. <u>Reformers thought that education would give Americans the intellectual tools needed to keep the nation strong.</u> School reformers, such as **Horace Mann,** also tried to ensure that schools were funded and had good teachers. Over the next few decades, public schools became common nationwide. Many women, such as Catharine Beecher, played key roles in the school reform movement. Beecher helped establish schools for women.

Some reformers tried to help the mentally ill. **Dorothea Dix** discovered that many mentally ill patients were placed in prisons along with criminals. By encouraging her state and many others to build humane hospitals for the mentally ill, she promoted the creation of the first modern mental hospitals.

Dorothea Dix also collaborated with others to reform the prison system. The **penitentiary movement** sought to change prisons and make them less cruel. Due to the efforts of these reformers, prisoners were less isolated and received better treatment.

Some reformers blamed societal ills on the abuse of alcohol, believing it was the root cause of most crime, poverty, and family neglect. Reformers launched the **temperance movement** to end alcohol abuse. Temperance means drinking alcoholic beverages in moderation. Reformers warned the public that drinking alcohol led to many social problems.

The temperance movement only had real success when reformers, such as **Neal Dow,** won changes in the law. Dow became the mayor of Portland, Maine. He passed a law restricting the sale of alcohol, setting a precedent that many other states chose to follow.

Review Questions

1. What was the goal of the public school movement?

_____

_____

2. Why did temperance reformers oppose the use of alcohol?

_____

_____

READING CHECK

Who led the reform movement to help the mentally ill?

_____

_____

_____

VOCABULARY STRATEGY

What does the word *intellectual* mean in the underlined sentence? Circle any words or phrases in the paragraph that help you figure out what *intellectual* means. Ask yourself how education would keep the nation strong.

_____

_____

_____

READING SKILL

Understand Effects Provide an example of a reform that resulted from a reform movement.

_____

_____

_____

Name _____ Class _____ Date _____

Focus Question: How did reformers try to help enslaved people?

A. *Summarize what life was like for African Americans in the 1800s in the chart below.*

Life Under Slavery		
Daily Life	**Ways of Surviving**	**Lives of Free Blacks**
• Heavy labor • • • • • •	• • •	• • • •

Name ______________________ Class __________________ Date ________

CHAPTER 8 SECTION 3

Note Taking Study Guide

THE ANTISLAVERY MOVEMENT

Focus Question: How did reformers try to help enslaved people?

B. *Use the chart below to contrast the opinions held by abolitionists and people who opposed abolition.*

Debate Over Slavery	
Against	**For**
• Abolitionists believed that slavery was immoral. •	• Slaveholders argued that slavery was justified because it formed the basis of the South's economy. • • • •

Name _____ Class _____ Date _____

CHAPTER
8
SECTION 3

Section Summary
THE ANTISLAVERY MOVEMENT

READING CHECK

What was Nat Turner's greatest achievement?

_____

_____

_____

VOCABULARY STRATEGY

What does the word *inevitable* mean in the underlined sentence? Circle any words or phrases in the paragraph that help you figure out what *inevitable* means.

_____

_____

_____

READING SKILL

Summarize How did abolitionists and slaveholders differ in their views about slavery?

_____

_____

_____

In the early 1800s, around two million Africans and African Americans were held as slaves in the United States. Most of these men, women, and children labored all day at difficult tasks. They faced physical punishment if they did not do their work, and were provided with barely enough food, clothing, and shelter.

Slaves tried to maintain some hope and dignity by relying on networks of family and friends and taking comfort in their religion, a mix of African and Christian beliefs. Other slaves resisted their masters by escaping or revolting. Denmark Vesey, a **freedman,** or former slave, planned a large slave revolt in 1822. His plan failed, but **Nat Turner's** revolt was more successful. Turner was a slave who led followers on a violent revolt that alarmed slaveholders.

Many northerners had objected to slavery for decades on moral grounds. Many of these Americans were part of the **abolition movement,** and they wanted slavery abolished, or ended. One leading abolitionist, **William Lloyd Garrison,** published an antislavery newspaper called *The Liberator.* Garrison tried to convince the public that slavery was morally wrong. He also created the American Anti-Slavery Society, whose 150,000 members worked across the nation to abolish slavery.

Another famous abolitionist was **Frederick Douglass.** This former slave was an effective lecturer against slavery and even served as an adviser to President Lincoln during the Civil War.

Most Americans still opposed abolishing slavery. Slaveholders argued that the southern economy would collapse without slavery. Some southerners claimed that Christianity supported slavery or that slaves could not survive without their masters. They felt that Africans were inferior and that their enslavement was historically inevitable. Many northerners opposed abolition, too. Some feared that African Americans would take their jobs.

Most white northerners did not like the controversy about slavery and did not want to discuss abolition. In 1836, southern politicians helped pass a **Gag Rule** in Congress. This law prohibited Congress from discussing abolition for many years.

Review Questions

1. List two ways that some slaves resisted their masters.

_____

_____

2. What was Frederick Douglass' role in the abolition movement?

_____

_____

Note Taking Study Guide

CHAPTER 8
SECTION 4

THE WOMEN'S MOVEMENT

Focus Question: What steps did American women take to advance their rights in the mid-1800s?

Use the chart below to record the causes and effects of the women's rights movement in the 1800s.

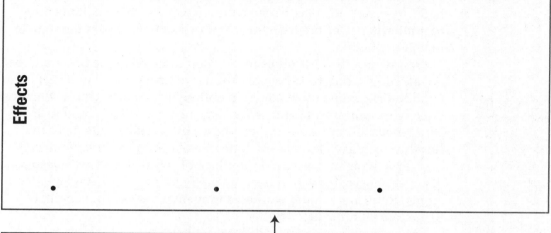

Effects

-
-
-

Events

- Birth of women's rights movement
-
-

Causes

- Limited rights
-
-

CHAPTER
8
SECTION 4

Section Summary

THE WOMEN'S MOVEMENT

In the 1800s, American women's freedom and rights were sharply limited. Women were not allowed to have a visible role in public life, and they lacked many basic legal and economic rights. They could not own property, hold office, or vote, and very few received a formal education.

Some groups living in America, such as certain Native Americans, had different traditions. Some cultures were **matrilineal,** meaning that inheritance of family names and property followed the female line in the family.

Many new opportunities for women came from the Second Great Awakening. Churches sponsored some reform groups, and many abolitionist groups were made up entirely of women. One of the most effective abolitionist lecturers was **Sojourner Truth,** a former slave. Women also found some opportunities by working outside of the home, which gave them a small degree of economic independence.

Many women compared their lack of rights to slavery. Despite some advances, there had been virtually no progress in women's rights. Reformers in the **women's movement** across the country began to call for greater rights.

Most women reformers did not seek full equality. However, **Lucretia Mott** and **Elizabeth Cady Stanton** did. These two abolitionists organized the nation's first Women's Rights Convention. Often called the **Seneca Falls Convention,** the meeting attracted hundreds of men and women. The meeting inspired many women, including **Amelia Bloomer,** who went on to publish a newspaper that advocated equality for women.

By the middle of the 1800s, American women had laid the foundation for a future in which equality seemed like a real possibility. For example, in 1848, New York passed the **Married Women's Property Act.** This law guaranteed many property rights for women. Over time, the women's movement narrowed its focus to one goal: **suffrage,** or the right to vote.

Review Questions

1. What were some of the limits American women faced in the 1800s?

_____

_____

2. Why was the Seneca Falls Convention significant?

_____

_____

Note Taking Study Guide

CHAPTER 9 SECTION 1

MIGRATING TO THE WEST

Focus Question: What were the causes of westward migration?

Outline the main ideas relating to westward migration.

I. Settling the Spanish Borderlands

    A. Spain Settles New Mexico

        1. Colony is sparsely populated.

        2. _____

    B. _____

        1. _____

        2. _____

    C. _____

    D. _____

        1. _____

        2. _____

II. _____

    A. _____

        1. _____

        2. _____

    B. _____

        1. _____

        2. _____

    C. _____

    D. _____

III. _____

    A. _____

        1. _____

        2. _____

    B. _____

        1. _____

        2. _____

    C. _____

CHAPTER 9 SECTION 1

Section Summary
MIGRATING TO THE WEST

In the 1600s and 1700s, Spanish settlers spread into New Mexico, Texas, and California, where they set up ranches, missions, and *presidios*. However, these areas remained sparsely populated. Lacking colonists, the Spanish leaders in California sought to convert Indians to Christianity. Franciscan priests led by Father **Junípero Serra** set up a string of missions that became more successful than those in Texas or New Mexico. However, conflicts between the Spanish and Native American groups remained a problem.

In 1821, a revolution ended Spanish rule in Mexico. The U.S. government recognized Mexico's independence. However, **expansionists** quickly began to covet the territories of northern Mexico. These Americans thought that the Mexican government and economy were weak and that the territory should belong to the United States. This idea, known as **Manifest Destiny,** claimed that it was God's plan for the United States to own most or all of North America.

Mexican independence spurred U.S. trade with Mexico, allowing merchants to establish an active trading route along the **Santa Fe Trail.** This trade benefited Mexico, but the U.S. traders and settlers would come to threaten the security of Mexico's border.

Adventurous men known as **Mountain Men** also traveled west. They worked as fur trappers, explored the Rocky Mountains, and established new trails, which settlers used to travel westward. By the 1840s, large wagon trains were taking settlers west in great numbers. Commencing in springtime in Missouri, the demanding journey covered nearly 2,000 miles and took about five months to complete. One popular trail became known as the **Oregon Trail.**

The religious group called the Mormons had a different reason than most for moving west. They were fleeing religious persecution. Their leader, **Brigham Young,** led migrants west to establish a colony on the eastern shore of the Great Salt Lake.

Most settlers were left alone by Native Americans during their move west. However, the federal government still sought to ensure their safety. The 1851 **Treaty of Fort Laramie** bound the Indians to territories away from the major trails.

Review Questions

1. What did expansionists want to acquire?

_____

_____

2. What role did Mountain Men play in the settlement of the West?

_____

_____

Name _____ Class _____ Date _____

Focus Question: How did the revolution in Texas lead to war with Mexico?

Look for the steps that led to war with Mexico.

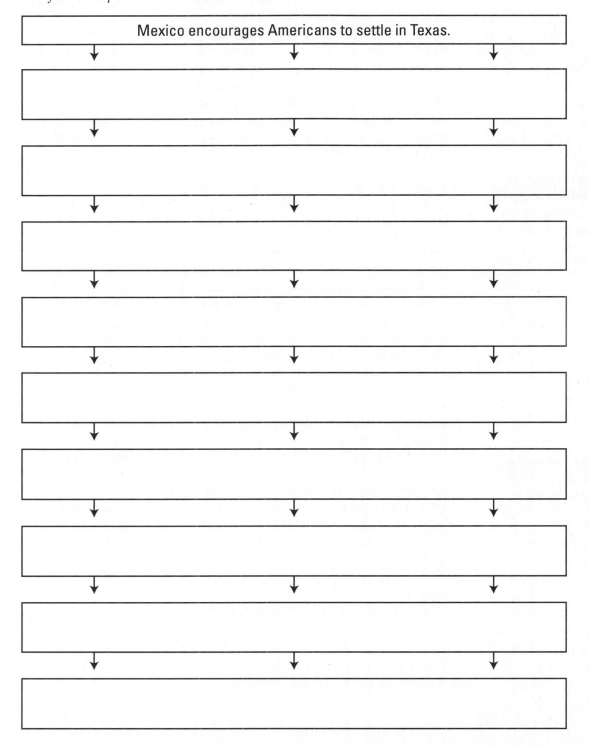

Mexico encourages Americans to settle in Texas.

CHAPTER 9 SECTION 2

Section Summary
TEXAS AND THE MEXICAN-AMERICAN WAR

In 1821, only a few thousand Hispanics, known as *Tejanos,* lived in Texas. To develop the territory, Mexico invited Americans to settle there. In return for cheap land grants, Americans had to agree to become Mexican citizens, to become Roman Catholics, and to accept the Mexican constitution banning slavery.

Led by **Stephen F. Austin,** these settlers came in large numbers. By 1835, American settlers outnumbered Tejanos by six to one. However, tension was growing between the settlers and the Mexican government. The settlers were reluctant to honor the agreement they had made with Mexico when they accepted the land grants. They were also unhappy with Mexico's ruthless leader, **Antonio López de Santa Anna.** The settlers wanted greater **autonomy,** or more control over their own affairs. In 1835, the Texans rebelled against the Mexican government. The rebels declared independence and called their new nation the **Lone Star Republic.**

Santa Anna led his army north to attack the Texans. At the **Alamo,** a former mission in San Antonio, Mexican troops slaughtered the Texans. The bloody defeat motivated the Texans to fight even harder. **Sam Houston** led the Texan army in a surprise attack on Santa Anna's army. Houston's men won, and Santa Anna was forced to sign a treaty recognizing Texan independence.

The Mexican government refused to honor the treaty. A border war persisted for the next decade. When the U.S. Congress voted to annex Texas as a state in 1845, Mexico was outraged. President **James K. Polk** supported the annexation.

Polk won the election by supporting the annexation of Texas and Oregon. Americans who opposed Polk feared that he planned to annex the Mexican provinces adjacent to Texas, including New Mexico and California. Polk pushed the nation closer to war by ordering U.S. troops into the contested borderlands in Texas. General **Zachary Taylor** led these troops. In May 1846, a border clash between U.S. and Mexican troops in which Americans were killed led Polk to declare war on Mexico.

The United States had many advantages, including its size, wealth, and larger population. In 1847, General **Winfield Scott** captured Mexico City. America had won a sweeping victory over Mexico.

Review Questions

1. How did Texas come to be dominated by American settlers?

_____

_____

2. What was the Lone Star Republic?

_____

_____

Name _____ Class _____ Date _____

Focus Question: What were the effects of the Mexican-American War and the California Gold Rush?

Trace the effects of the Mexican-American War.

Effects

• Treaty of Guadalupe Hidalgo; United States gains territory

•

•

•

•

•

•

•

Event

Mexican-American War →

Section Summary
EFFECTS OF TERRITORIAL EXPANSION

READING CHECK

What was the name for people who moved west during the California Gold Rush?

_____

_____

_____

In February 1848, the defeated Mexicans made peace with the United States in the **Treaty of Guadalupe Hidalgo.** Mexico was forced to give up the northern third of their country. In 1853, the United States gained territory in southern Arizona and New Mexico from Mexico in the **Gadsden Purchase.** The new lands comprised present-day New Mexico, California, Nevada, Utah, Arizona, and half of Colorado.

The Mexican-American War had many far-reaching effects. The new territories made the fight over slavery even more heated. Whigs proposed the **Wilmot Proviso,** a law that would have prohibited slavery in the new territories. Congress broke into northern and southern groups, and major political parties were divided. The Wilmot Proviso never passed, but it brought the slavery issue to the forefront and weakened the two major parties.

In 1848, workers at a sawmill on the West Coast discovered gold. The discovery set off the **California Gold Rush.** This mass migration brought tens of thousands of people west. About half of these **forty-niners** traveled by land, and another half went by sea. Forty-niners also came from South America and China. In just five years, California's population jumped by more than 200,000 people. Most of these miners had a difficult, violent life. They worked hard, earned little, and suffered from disease and terrible living conditions.

At first, most miners used **placer mining,** in which each miner tried to find gold in rivers and streams and along the banks with little equipment. Over time, however, better equipment was used. **Hydraulic mining,** which employed jets of water to erode gravel hills, and "hard rock mining" were both more effective, but they also damaged the environment more.

The rapid settlement of California had unforeseen consequences. Native Americans were killed and terrorized by the thousands. Many Mexican Americans lost their land and their rights.

California also caused a problem when it applied for statehood. At that time, the number of slave and free states was equal. However, if California became a free state, it would tip the balance. Northern and southern congressmen debated slavery yet again.

VOCABULARY STRATEGY

What does the word *comprised* mean in the underlined sentence? Circle the words in the surrounding phrases or sentences that could help you learn what *comprised* means.

_____

_____

_____

READING SKILL

Understand Effects What unforeseen consequences occurred during the settlement of California?

_____

_____

Review Questions
1. Why was the Wilmot Proviso controversial?

_____

_____

2. How did California contribute to the slavery debate?

_____

_____

Name _____ Class _____ Date _____

Focus Question: How did Congress try to resolve the dispute between North and South over slavery?

Organize people, groups, and ideas by their position on slavery.

Position on Slavery		
For	**Against**	**Compromise**
•	• Wilmot Proviso	•
•	•	
•	•	•
•	•	
•	•	•
•	•	•

Name _____ Class _____ Date _____

Section Summary
SLAVERY, STATES' RIGHTS, AND WESTERN EXPANSION

READING CHECK

What was popular sovereignty?

_____

_____

_____

VOCABULARY STRATEGY

What does the word *component* mean in the underlined sentence? Use context clues to help you figure out the meaning of *component*.

_____

_____

_____

READING SKILL

Categorize Which two political parties supported the policy of popular sovereignty?

_____

_____

_____

After the American Revolution, the North and the South developed different ways of life. The North developed busy cities, embraced technology and industry, and built factories. The South remained an agrarian, or agricultural, society. By the mid-nineteenth century, cotton cultivation and slavery had spread across the Deep South.

Americans faced this question: Should slavery be allowed in the new territories west of the Mississippi River? The balance of power between the North and the South—free and slave—depended on this decision. During the early days of the Mexican-American War, Pennsylvania congressman David Wilmot had proposed a law banning slavery from the lands won from Mexico. The northern-dominated House of Representatives approved the **Wilmot Proviso,** but the Senate voted it down.

Democrats and Whigs hoped to attract voters from all sides of the slavery debate. Members of the new **Free-Soil Party** wanted to limit slavery in the territories. Democrats and Whigs embraced the idea of **popular sovereignty,** a policy stating that the voters in a territory—not Congress—should decide whether to allow slavery. The election was won by the Whig candidate, Zachary Taylor, a general and a hero of the Mexican-American War. He was also a slaveholder.

In 1848, gold was discovered in California, attracting people from all over the world. In 1849, the people of California drafted a constitution and asked that California be admitted to the Union as a free state. Because admitting California would tip the balance in favor of the free states, the southern states threatened to **secede,** or break away, from the Union. Senator Henry Clay put forth a number of compromise resolutions. <u>Illinois Senator Stephen A. Douglas steered each component of Clay's plan through Congress separately.</u> The Senate adopted legislation based on Clay's proposals, known as the **Compromise of 1850.** California was admitted as a free state, and the policy of popular sovereignty was applied to the territory acquired from Mexico. In addition, a new **Fugitive Slave Act** required that private citizens help apprehend runaway slaves. Though the Compromise of 1850 restored calm for the moment, it carried the seeds of new crises to come.

Review Questions

1. Contrast the economies and ways of life that developed in the North and the South.

_____

_____

2. How did Congress try to settle the slavery issue in 1850?

_____

_____

Focus Question: How did the Fugitive Slave Act and the Kansas-Nebraska Act increase tensions between the North and the South?

A. *Use the concept web below to record the effects of the Fugitive Slave Act on different groups of people.*

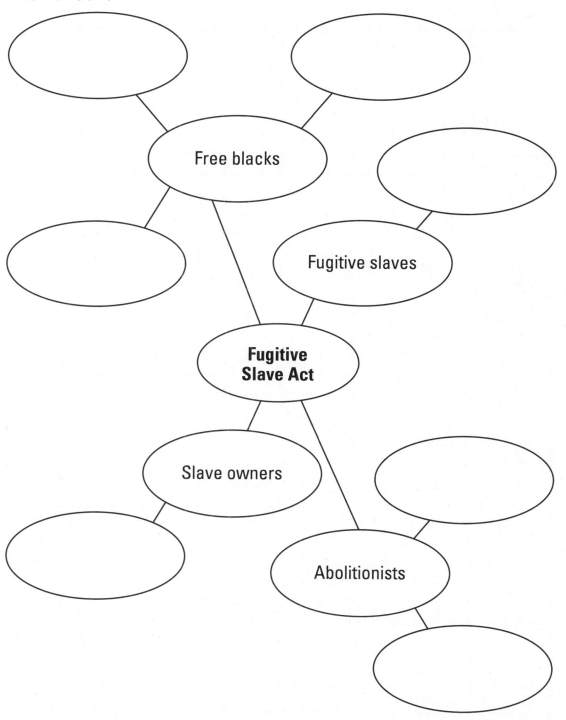

CHAPTER 10 SECTION 2

Note Taking Study Guide

A RISING TIDE OF PROTEST AND VIOLENCE

Focus Question: How did the Fugitive Slave Act and the Kansas-Nebraska Act increase tensions between the North and the South?

B. *Use the chart below to trace the series of events that led up to and followed the passage of the Kansas-Nebraska Act.*

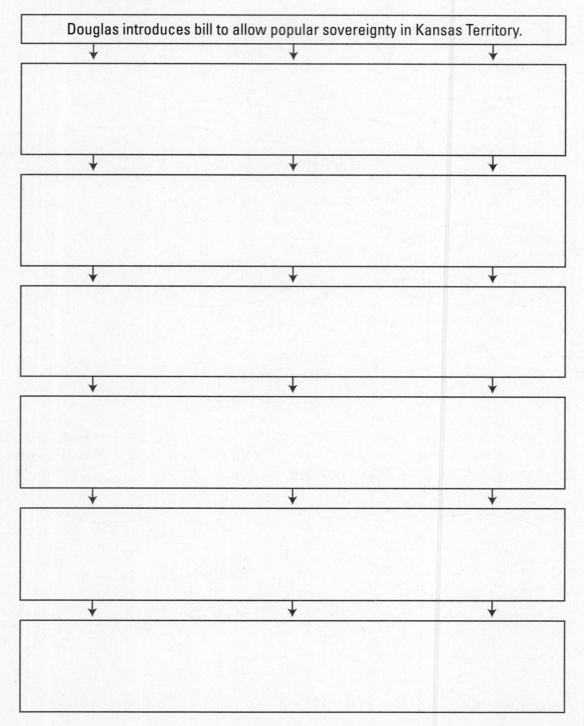

Douglas introduces bill to allow popular sovereignty in Kansas Territory.

The new Fugitive Slave Act, which required citizens to catch and return runaway slaves, enraged many northerners. Some northern states passed **personal liberty laws,** which nullified the Fugitive Slave Act. They also allowed the state to arrest slave catchers for kidnapping. <u>Northern white bystanders refused to intervene to help slave hunters.</u> A network known as the **Underground Railroad** helped runaway slaves escape to the North or to Canada. One of its most courageous conductors was former slave **Harriet Tubman.** She was known as "Black Moses" for leading her people out of bondage. In 1852, **Harriet Beecher Stowe** published the novel *Uncle Tom's Cabin,* a powerful condemnation of slavery.

The repeated attempts of Congress to resolve the question of slavery resulted in a jumble of contradictory policies. In 1854, Senator Douglas introduced a bill to set up a government in the Nebraska Territory. Under pressure from the South, Douglas amended the bill to divide the region into two territories, Kansas and Nebraska. Each territory would be organized according to popular sovereignty. The **Kansas-Nebraska Act** nullified the Missouri Compromise, allowing slavery to spread to areas that had been free for more than 30 years.

Most of the people who came to the new Kansas Territory were farmers looking for land. However, Kansas also attracted settlers with political motives. By 1855, a proslavery government near the Missouri border developed a proslavery constitution. Free-state advocates set up an antislavery government in Topeka. In 1856, the Topeka government petitioned Congress for statehood. On May 21, 1856, a proslavery group raided the antislavery town of Lawrence, Kansas. The abolitionist **John Brown** quickly retaliated. With his sons and a few friends, Brown executed five proslavery settlers. Throughout the fall of 1856, violent outbreaks occurred in various locales around Lawrence, leading reporters to characterize the situation as **"Bleeding Kansas."** It became clear that popular sovereignty was not the solution to the slavery question. Kansas was finally admitted as a free state in 1861.

Review Questions

1. How did northerners show their disapproval of the Fugitive Slave Act?

_____

_____

2. What was the outcome of the Kansas-Nebraska Act?

_____

_____

READING CHECK

What was the Underground Railroad?

_____

_____

_____

VOCABULARY STRATEGY

What does the word *intervene* mean in the underlined sentence? The prefix *inter-* means "between." The root *-vene* means "to come." Use these clues to help you figure out what *intervene* means.

_____

_____

_____

READING SKILL

Understand Effects What effects did the Fugitive Slave Act have on African Americans?

_____

_____

_____

Name _____ Class _____ Date _____

CHAPTER
10
SECTION 3

Note Taking Study Guide
POLITICAL REALIGNMENT DEEPENS THE CRISIS

Focus Question: What developments deepened the divisions between North and South?

Use the timeline below to record significant political events.

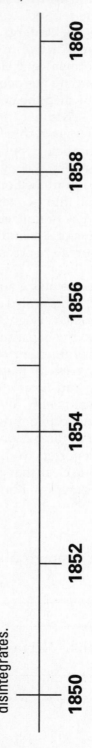

1860

1858

1856

1854

1852

Early 1850s—
Whig Party
disintegrates.

1850

CHAPTER 10 SECTION 3

Section Summary
POLITICAL REALIGNMENT DEEPENS THE CRISIS

Millard Fillmore was the last Whig President. He angered the South by supporting California's entry as a free state. Northerners left the party in large numbers because of his support for the Fugitive Slave Act and popular sovereignty. By the mid-1800s, increasing immigration was changing the country. An anti-immigrant movement developed. Dubbed the **"Know-Nothings"** because its members pretended to know nothing when questioned about their organization, the group grew rapidly. By 1855, they had formed the American Party. However, the new party soon divided over the issue of slavery in the western territories. Antislavery zeal gave rise to the new **Republican Party** in 1854, which grew rapidly in the North.

In the 1856 presidential election, the Republican candidate made a strong showing. However, Democrat James Buchanan won the election, supported by the large majority of southerners. Then, in 1857, the Supreme Court ruled in the case of a Missouri slave, **Dred Scott,** who had sued for his freedom. The court, under Chief Justice **Roger B. Taney,** ruled that slaves and their descendants were property, not citizens, and not entitled to sue in the courts. It also ruled that the Missouri Compromise was unconstitutional because it was illegal for Congress to deprive an owner of property—in this case, a slave—without due process of law.

In 1850, a series of debates between two candidates for an Illinois Senate seat attracted attention. Republican **Abraham Lincoln** opposed the Kansas-Nebraska Act and its implicit support for the expansion of slavery. His rival was **Stephen A. Douglas,** who promoted popular sovereignty as a solution to regional tensions. Douglas won the election by a slim margin.

Both men believed that the slavery issue had to be resolved within the law. Abolitionist John Brown felt no such constraints. He believed he was God's angel avenging the evil of slavery. He mounted an armed assault on slavery. In the fall of 1859, Brown and his followers set out to seize the federal arsenal in **Harpers Ferry,** Virginia. Brown hoped local slaves would join a revolution to destroy slavery. The effort failed. Some of the rebels were killed, and some escaped. Brown's attack deepened the division between the North and the South.

Review Questions
1. Explain how John Brown's raid affected the slavery debate.

_____

_____

2. Compare the positions of Abraham Lincoln and Stephen Douglas on the issue of slavery.

_____

_____

READING CHECK
What was the significance of the *Dred Scott* decision?

VOCABULARY STRATEGY
What does the word *implicit* mean in the underlined sentence? Ask yourself what kind of support the Kansas-Nebraska Act gave to the expansion of slavery. Use this strategy to figure out what *implicit* means.

READING SKILL
Sequence Look at your timeline. What do the dates and events tell you about the relationship between the North and the South?

Name _____ Class _____ Date _____

Focus Question: How did the Union finally collapse into a civil war?

Fill in the cause-and-effect chart below to show the events that led to secession.

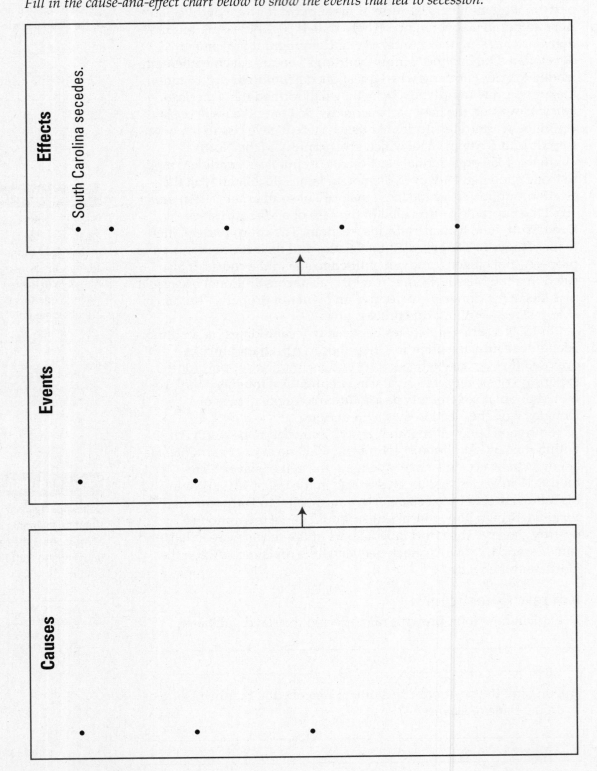

Effects

- South Carolina secedes.
- •
- •
- •
- •

Events

- •
- •
- •

Causes

- •
- •
- •

CHAPTER 10 SECTION 4

Section Summary

LINCOLN, SECESSION, AND WAR

In 1860, anxiety ran high in both the North and the South as the presidential election approached. Mississippi Senator **Jefferson Davis** convinced Congress to restrict federal control over slavery in the territories and assert that the Constitution prohibited Congress or any state from interfering with slavery in states where it already existed. During the election of 1860, the Democrats split into two parties. Northern Democrats backed Stephen A. Douglas, who supported popular sovereignty, while southern Democrats nominated Vice President **John C. Breckinridge,** who wanted to expand slavery into the territories. The Republicans nominated Abraham Lincoln. Their platform called for an end to slavery in the territories. They stipulated that there should be no interference with slavery in the states. The split in the Democratic Party kept those candidates from getting enough votes to win the election. Instead, Lincoln won with 40 percent of the popular vote—but not a single southern electoral vote.

When Lincoln's election was confirmed, South Carolina seceded from the Union. In the next few weeks, six other states of the Deep South seceded. In February 1861, they established the **Confederate States of America.** The Confederate constitution stressed each state's independence and protected slavery. However, to win the support of Britain and France, it prohibited importing new slaves. The Confederacy chose Jefferson Davis as its President. In an attempt to compromise with the South, Kentucky Senator John Crittenden proposed a new constitutional amendment. If it had passed, the **Crittenden Compromise** would have allowed slavery in western territories south of the Missouri Compromise line. In his last weeks in office, President Buchanan told Congress that he had no authority to prevent secession.

In his inaugural address, Lincoln said that he did not intend to interfere with slavery in states where it existed. He intended to preserve the Union, but he would not start a war. When South Carolinians fired on **Fort Sumter,** a Union fort guarding the harbor at Charleston, President Lincoln called for 75,000 volunteers to fight against the Confederacy.

Review Questions

1. What was Lincoln's position on slavery during the presidential campaign of 1860?

_____

_____

2. What events led to the outbreak of war?

_____

_____

READING CHECK

What was the Crittenden Compromise?

_____

_____

_____

VOCABULARY STRATEGY

What does the word *stipulated* mean in the underlined sentence? Circle the word below that is a synonym for *stipulated*.

- denied
- specified

READING SKILL

Identify Causes and Effects
How did the split in the Democratic Party lead to Lincoln's victory in the 1860 election?

_____

_____

_____

CHAPTER 11 SECTION 1

Note Taking Study Guide
RESOURCES, STRATEGIES, AND EARLY BATTLES

Focus Question: How did each side's resources and strategies affect the early battles of the war?

A. *As you read, use the table below to note the advantages of the North and the South at the beginning of the war.*

Wartime Advantages	
Union	**Confederacy**
• Population	• Strong military tradition
•	•
•	•
•	•
•	•
•	•
•	•
•	

CHAPTER 11 SECTION 1

Note Taking Study Guide

RESOURCES, STRATEGIES, AND EARLY BATTLES

Focus Question: How did each side's resources and strategies affect the early battles of the war?

B. *Use the timeline below to note how the fighting developed during the early years of the Civil War.*

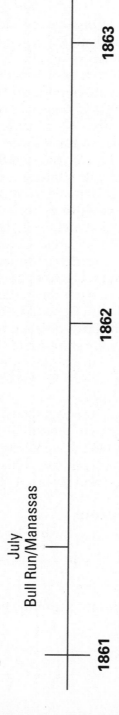

CHAPTER 11 SECTION 1

Section Summary
RESOURCES, STRATEGIES, AND EARLY BATTLES

READING CHECK

What was the Anaconda Plan?

_____

_____

_____

VOCABULARY STRATEGY

What does the word *thereby* mean in the underlined sentence? Circle any words or phrases in the paragraph that help you figure out what *thereby* means.

_____

_____

_____

READING SKILL

Categorize Explain the types of advantages each side had at the beginning of the war.

_____

_____

_____

The Union initially appeared to have the most advantages in the Civil War, due to its greater population and preparedness for war. In addition, the Union possessed most of the nation's mines, a large railroad network for moving troops and material and a well-organized navy. The South had no navy at all, leaving it vulnerable to a naval **blockade** in which Union ships prevented merchant vessels from entering or leaving the South's few good ports, thereby crippling southern trade. The Confederacy had the psychological advantage: it was fighting for survival. The South also had a strong military tradition, strategic advantages, and fine leaders like **Robert E. Lee.**

The initial Union strategy was the **Anaconda Plan.** Union forces would blockade southern ports and take control of the Mississippi River, splitting the Confederacy in two. They faced the tricky question of keeping Missouri, Kentucky, Delaware, and Maryland in the Union. These **border states** allowed slavery but had not seceded. To reduce this threat, Lincoln insisted that his only goal was to save the Union. The Confederate strategy was to preserve its small armies while doing enough damage to erode the Union's will to fight. It also hoped for formal recognition from Britain and France.

In July 1861, Union and Confederate troops met at Bull Run, a creek near Manassas, Virginia. Confederate General Thomas J. Jackson earned the nickname **Stonewall Jackson** for his refusal to yield to Union armies. His troops sent the Union army scrambling back to Washington. After the Battle of Bull Run, Lincoln replaced the Union general with General **George B. McClellan.** Meanwhile, General **Ulysses S. Grant** pursued the Mississippi Valley wing of the Anaconda Plan. Union ships under David Farragut seized the port of New Orleans, Louisiana, at the mouth of the Mississippi. Both Farragut and Grant aimed for the Confederate stronghold of Vicksburg, Mississippi.

Major fighting in the East focused on Virginia. One notable naval battle was between two ironclad warships, the *Virginia* and the *Monitor*, in March 1862. It signaled the beginning of the end of wooden warships. Meanwhile, Lincoln had become impatient with McClellan's caution and replaced him.

Review Questions

1. Identify and describe the border states.

_____

_____

2. What was significant about the naval battle between the *Virginia* and the *Monitor?*

_____

_____

CHAPTER
11
SECTION 2

Note Taking Study Guide
AFRICAN AMERICANS AND THE WAR

Focus Question: How did the Emancipation Proclamation and the efforts of African American soldiers affect the course of the war?

As you read, use the outline below to record details about African Americans during the war.

I. **The Push Toward Emancipation**
   A. Enslaved African Americans Seek Refuge
      1. Enslaved people come under Union control.
      2. _____

   B. _____
      1. _____
      2. _____

   C. _____
      1. _____
      2. _____

II. **Emancipation at Last**
   A. _____
      1. _____
      2. _____

   B. _____
      1. _____
      2. _____
      3. _____

III. _____
   A. _____
      1. _____
      2. _____

   B. _____
      1. _____
      2. _____

   C. _____
      1. _____
      2. _____

CHAPTER 11 SECTION 2

Section Summary
AFRICAN AMERICANS AND THE WAR

With the slavery debate ongoing, Union officers had to decide what to do with enslaved African Americans who came under their control. One general declared them to be **contraband,** or captured war supplies. Another declared the slaves free, but Lincoln reversed that order, fearing retaliation from the border states. Lincoln secretly began working on a plan for the emancipation of enslaved African Americans living in Confederate states.

Confederate General Lee attempted to lead a pro-Confederate uprising in Maryland. <u>On September 8, Lee issued the "Proclamation to the People of Maryland," which invited them to ally themselves with the South.</u> Marylanders responded to the invitation with little enthusiasm, and Lee's proclamation failed.

Union and Confederate troops met at Sharpsburg, Maryland on September 17 to fight the Battle of **Antietam.** It became the bloodiest day of the war with more than 23,000 soldiers dead or wounded.

On September 22, 1862, following the Battle of Antietam, Lincoln formally issued the **Emancipation Proclamation.** It stated that, as of January 1, 1863, all slaves in states in rebellion against the United States would be forever free. His decree did not apply to loyal border states. Although the Emancipation Proclamation did not actually free a single slave, it was an important turning point in the war. For northerners, it redefined the war as being "about slavery." For southerners, the call to free the slaves prevented any chance for a negotiated end to the war.

At the start of the war, many African Americans in the North were eager to fight but had been turned down. In the summer of 1862, Congress passed the **Militia Act,** mandating that black soldiers be accepted into the military. After the Emancipation Proclamation, the Union began to actively recruit black troops. The governor of Massachusetts supported the formation of the all-black **54th Massachusetts Regiment.** Although African American troops distinguished themselves on the battlefield, they still faced prejudice. If captured, they would be killed. Enslaved African Americans in the South also played an important role in the war, often finding ways to help Union forces.

Review Questions

1. What were the terms of the Emancipation Proclamation?

_____

_____

2. How did African Americans contribute to the war effort?

_____

_____

CHAPTER
11
SECTION 3

Note Taking Study Guide
LIFE DURING THE WAR

Focus Question: How did the Civil War bring temporary and lasting changes to American society?

Note the similarities and differences between the northern and southern home fronts during the war.

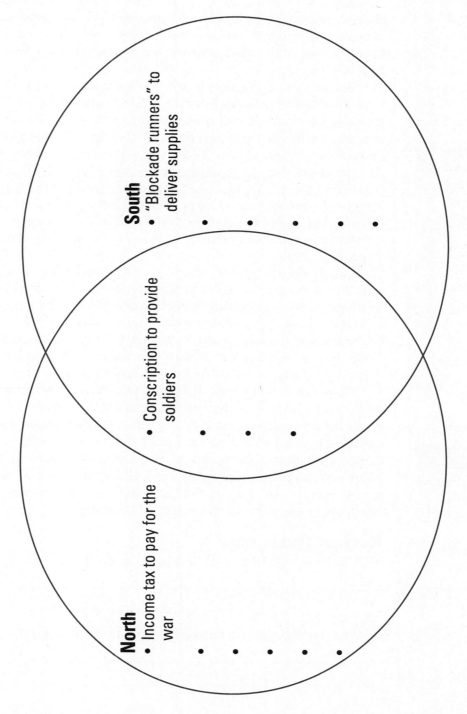

South
- "Blockade runners" to deliver supplies
- •
- •
- •
- •

Conscription to provide soldiers
- •
- •
- •

North
- Income tax to pay for the war
- •
- •
- •
- •

READING CHECK

What was the Homestead Act?

_____

_____

_____

VOCABULARY STRATEGY

What does the word *faction* mean in the underlined sentence? Circle any words or phrases in the paragraph that help you figure out what *faction* means.

_____

_____

_____

READING SKILL

Compare and Contrast What did the North and the South do to raise money for the war effort?

_____

_____

_____

The war had a huge impact on northern industry. As demand for clothing, arms, and other supplies spiked, industry became more mechanized. To raise funds for the war, the government introduced an **income tax** of 3 percent on all income over $800 a year. This tax increased as the war continued. The Union also raised tariffs. The biggest source of wartime funds came from the sale of **bonds.** To increase the amount of cash in circulation, Congress passed the Legal Tender Act in 1862, creating the nation's first single, common currency.

Also in 1862, Congress passed the **Homestead Act,** making western land available at very low cost to those who would farm it. In 1863, the Union instituted **conscription,** or the draft. Under this system, any white man between the ages of 20 and 45 might be called for required military service. Many groups of northerners opposed the war effort. <u>A faction calling themselves "Peace Democrats" criticized Lincoln's conduct and called for an end to the war.</u> Their opponents dubbed them **Copperheads,** after a poisonous snake. Lincoln suspended the constitutional right of **habeas corpus,** which protects a person from being held in jail without being charged with a specific crime.

As the war dragged on, the South's economic and social underpinnings seemed in danger of collapse, due to the Union blockade of southern ports. Agriculture was often complicated by nearby military operations, and getting food to market was difficult because rivers and rail lines were often blocked. Like the Union, the Confederacy issued paper money, enacted conscription laws, seized private property, and suspended habeas corpus.

Many families suffered divided loyalties, with members fighting on different sides. New technology resulted in killing on a scale never before seen in America. Camp life was dangerous due to poor drinking water and lack of sanitation. Even worse were the prison camps. In both the North and the South, the most notable military role for women was nursing. In 1861, **Clara Barton** obtained permission to travel with army ambulances and assist in "distributing comforts to the sick and wounded" of both sides.

Review Questions

1. What effect did the Civil War have on northern industry?

_____

_____

2. What challenges and hardships were faced by Civil War soldiers?

_____

_____

CHAPTER
11
SECTION 4

Note Taking Study Guide

TURNING POINTS OF THE WAR

Focus Question: How did the Battles of Vicksburg and Gettysburg change the course of the Civil War?

As you read, use the timeline to trace how the tide of the war turned toward Union victory.

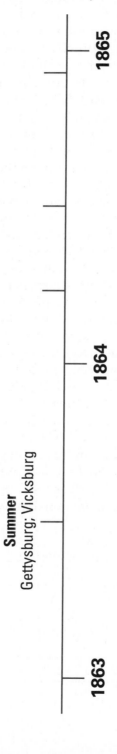

CHAPTER 11 SECTION 4

Section Summary

TURNING POINTS OF THE WAR

Who replaced General McClellan?

_____

_____

_____

What does the word *successor* mean in the underlined sentence? Circle any words or phrases in the paragraph that help you figure out what *successor* means.

_____

_____

_____

_____

Summarize What events marked the major turning points in the Civil War? Explain.

_____

_____

_____

The major focus of the Union's western campaign remained the Mississippi River. In the spring of 1863, Grant decided on a new approach in trying to capture **Vicksburg,** Mississippi. He cut Vicksburg off from its source of supply and then, after two failed attempts to storm the stronghold, he placed it under **siege.** Constant gunfire and lack of supplies weakened Vicksburg's defenders, and on July 4, 1863, the Confederate commander surrendered. This victory completed the Anacanda Plan of cutting the South in half.

The situation was different in the East, where Lincoln replaced General McClellan. McClellan's successor, General Ambrose Burnside, headed south, hoping to win a decisive victory over the Army of Northern Virginia. Lincoln quickly replaced Burnside with General Joseph Hooker, and in the spring, Hooker and Lee met at Chancellorsville, Virginia. Again the Confederates completely overwhelmed the Union army, but Lee lost Stonewall Jackson.

Lee sensed an opportunity to win international support, demoralize the Union, and perhaps even force an end to the war. He decided to invade the North, and in June 1863, his army crossed into Union territory in Pennsylvania. Under General George Meade, the Army of the Potomac set out to find the Confederates. On July 1, the two armies faced off in **Gettysburg,** Pennsylvania, in a battle that lasted for three days. On July 3, Confederate forces charged up Cemetery Ridge, only to be mowed down, thus ending the battle with over 50,000 dead and wounded. About half of these were Confederate—nearly a third of Lee's force. The South had suffered a devastating defeat. In November 1863, Lincoln came to the battlefield to dedicate a cemetery for the fallen soldiers. His **Gettysburg Address** described the United States as a single, unified nation.

In early 1864, Lincoln recalled Grant from the Mississippi Valley to take charge of the entire Union military effort. Grant used a strategy of **total war.** Part of that strategy was illustrated by the campaign of **William Tecumseh Sherman.** He cut a swath of destruction in his march across Georgia to the Atlantic. Sherman called the capture of Savannah his Christmas present for Lincoln.

Review Questions

1. Why was the Battle of Gettysburg important?

_____

_____

2. What was significant about the Gettysburg Address?

_____

_____

Name _____ Class _____ Date _____

CHAPTER
11
SECTION 5

Note Taking Study Guide
THE WAR'S END AND IMPACT

Focus Question: What was the final outcome and impact of the Civil War?

A. *As you read, use the flowchart below to note what happened during the final days of the Civil War.*

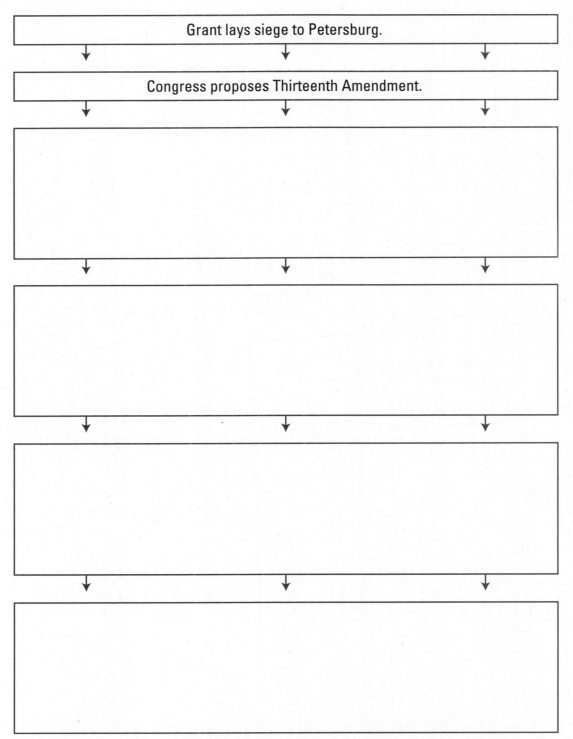

Grant lays siege to Petersburg.

↓ ↓ ↓

Congress proposes Thirteenth Amendment.

↓ ↓ ↓

↓ ↓ ↓

↓ ↓ ↓

↓ ↓ ↓

Note Taking Study Guide
THE WAR'S END AND IMPACT

Focus Question: What was the final outcome and impact of the Civil War?

B. *Use the concept web below to identify the effects of the Civil War.*

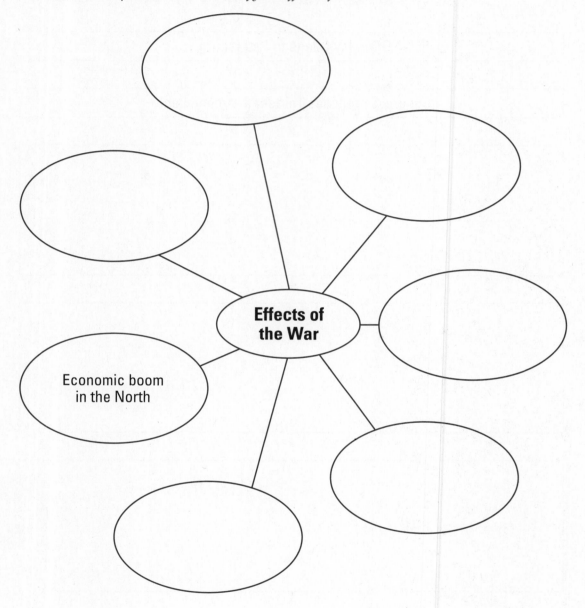

CHAPTER 11 SECTION 5

Section Summary
THE WAR'S END AND IMPACT

If the Union captured Petersburg, Virginia, a vital railroad center, it would control all supply lines into the Confederate capital at Richmond. As at Vicksburg, Grant used siege tactics. Lee's forces struck effective blows against the Union troops, which suffered over 40,000 casualties. The Confederates lost 28,000 men, but Lee had no replacement troops in reserve. Southerners began to talk of peace.

In February, a party led by Confederate Vice President Alexander Stephens met with Lincoln to discuss a feasible end to the war, but these discussions produced no results. Congress had recently proposed the **Thirteenth Amendment,** which would outlaw slavery in the United States. The South was unwilling to accept a future without slavery. On April 2, Lee ordered a retreat from Petersburg. On April 9, 1865, Lee formally surrendered to Grant at Appomattox Court House, Virginia. On April 14, Lincoln was assassinated by **John Wilkes Booth** while attending a play at Ford's Theater. His death had a deep political impact, uniting his northern supporters and critics, who saw him as a hero and symbol of freedom.

When the Civil War began, it was unclear who would be victorious. However, the North was able to marshal its greater technological prowess, larger population, and more abundant resources. Meanwhile, the South used up its resources, unable to call upon fresh troops and supplies. In the long run, the North's Anaconda Plan succeeded. When opinion in the North was bitterly divided, Lincoln's steady leadership helped keep the nation together.

When the war was over, more than 600,000 Americans were dead. The Civil War ushered in the harsh reality of modern warfare, as ordinary citizens viewed the carnage of the battlefield through the photographs of **Mathew Brady.** The southern landscape was in shambles, with many people left homeless and in shock. African Americans were disoriented, but they also had a new sense of hope. In the North, the industrial boom that was fueled by the war continued. In the decades following the war, factories, banks, and cities underwent sweeping industrialization. Debates over states' rights did not end with the Civil War, although the war helped cement federal authority.

Review Questions

1. What factors enabled the North to win the Civil War?

_____

_____

2. How did the Civil War affect ordinary citizens in both the North and the South?

_____

_____

READING CHECK

What was the Thirteenth Amendment?

_____

_____

_____

VOCABULARY STRATEGY

What does the word *feasible* mean in the underlined sentence? Circle any words or phrases in the paragraph that help you figure out what *feasible* means.

_____

_____

_____

READING SKILL

Recognize Sequence What effect did the proposal of the Thirteenth Amendment have on discussions to end the war?

_____

_____

_____

Note Taking Study Guide

CHAPTER 12 SECTION 1

RIVAL PLANS FOR RECONSTRUCTION

Focus Question: How did the Radical Republicans' plans for Reconstruction differ from Lincoln's and Johnson's?

Use the chart below to record main ideas about Reconstruction.

Plans for Reconstruction		
Lincoln	**Johnson**	**Congress**
•	•	•
•	•	•
•	•	•
•		
•		

CHAPTER 12 SECTION 1

Section Summary

RIVAL PLANS FOR RECONSTRUCTION

During the era of **Reconstruction** (1865–1877), the federal government struggled with how to return the southern states to the Union, rebuild the South's ruined economy, and promote the rights of former slaves. Some argued that states should be allowed to rejoin the Union quickly with few conditions. But many claimed that the defeated states should first satisfy certain stipulations, such as swearing loyalty to the federal government and adopting state constitutions that guaranteed freedmen's rights.

President Lincoln wanted to readmit southern states as soon as ten percent of a state's voters took a loyalty oath to the Union. **"Radical Republicans"** in Congress opposed this plan, insisting that the Confederates had committed crimes. Congress passed the **Wade-Davis Bill** in 1864. It required a majority of a state's prewar voters to swear loyalty before the state could be readmitted, and it demanded full equality for African Americans. Lincoln killed the bill with a "pocket veto." However, he supported the **Freedmen's Bureau.** Its goal was to provide food, clothing, healthcare, and education for both black and white refugees in the South.

Lincoln's assassination in April 1865 thrust his Vice President, **Andrew Johnson,** into the presidency. Johnson wanted to restore the political status of the southern states as quickly as possible. He did not want African Americans to have the vote and had little sympathy for their plight. All the southern states instituted **black codes,** laws that limited the rights of African Americans. When Congress sought to overturn them by passing the **Civil Rights Act of 1866,** Johnson vetoed it.

Violence against African Americans in the South increased. To protect freedmen's rights, Congress passed the **Fourteenth Amendment,** which guaranteed equality under the law for all citizens. The Military Reconstruction Act of 1867 divided the South into five military districts and set requirements for states to reenter the Union. A power struggle between Congress and the President continued. The House of Representatives voted to **impeach** Johnson in 1868. He escaped being removed from office by one vote. In 1869, the **Fifteenth Amendment** was passed. It forbids any state from denying suffrage on the grounds of race or color.

Review Questions

1. What were the main goals of the Reconstruction of the South?

_____

_____

2. Discuss Johnson's relationship with Congress.

_____

_____

READING CHECK

What was the goal of the Freedmen's Bureau?

_____

_____

_____

VOCABULARY STRATEGY

What does the word *stipulations* mean in the underlined sentence? Circle the word below that is a synonym for *stipulations*.

- requirements
- tests

READING SKILL

Identify Main Ideas What did Congress do to protect the rights of African Americans?

_____

_____

_____

CHAPTER
12
SECTION 2

Note Taking Study Guide

RECONSTRUCTION IN THE SOUTH

Focus Question: What were the immediate effects of Reconstruction?

A. *Use the chart below to record details about changes in the South during Reconstruction.*

Changes in the South		
Political	**Social**	**Economic**
•	•	•
•	•	•
•	•	•
•	•	•
•	•	
	•	

CHAPTER
12
SECTION 2

Note Taking Study Guide
RECONSTRUCTION IN THE SOUTH

Focus Question: What were the immediate effects of Reconstruction?

B. *Use the chart below to summarize the causes and effects of the Enforcement Acts.*

Effects

-
-
-
-

Event

- Congress passes Enforcement Acts.

Causes

-
-
-
-

CHAPTER 12 SECTION 2

Section Summary
RECONSTRUCTION IN THE SOUTH

Which system allowed landowners to dictate what crop was planted?

_____

_____

_____

What does the word *nevertheless* mean in the underlined sentence? Circle any words or phrases in the surrounding sentences that help you figure out what *nevertheless* means.

_____

_____

_____

Identify Main Ideas How did African Americans' lives change during Reconstruction?

_____

_____

_____

The era of Reconstruction brought many changes to the South. Millions of southern African American men were now voters, and many served as elected officials. They used their voting power to usher the Republican Party into the South. The Republican Party attracted people who sought change and challenge. **Scalawags** were white men who had been locked out of pre–Civil War politics by their wealthier neighbors. They found allies in **"carpetbaggers,"** or northern white or black men who relocated to the South.

Northern women, both white and black, had opportunities in the Reconstruction South that they could not pursue at home, including shaping the new public school system. Southerners opted for **segregation,** or separation of the races, in their school system. **Integration**—combining the schools—appealed to only the most radical white Republicans. Nevertheless, the beginning of a tax-supported public school system was a major Reconstruction success.

Many of the South's problems resulted from the uneven distribution of land. Wealth was defined by landownership. However, even owners of large tracts of land had no money with which to purchase supplies or pay workers. As a result, many southerners adopted one of three arrangements. Under the **sharecropping** system, a landowner dictated the crop and provided the sharecropper with a place to live and supplies in return for a "share" of the harvested crop. Under a **share-tenancy,** the farmworker chose what crop he would plant and bought his own supplies, then gave a share of the crop to the landowner. The most independent system was **tenant farming,** under which the tenant paid cash rent to the landowner and was free to choose his own crop and where to live.

The more progress African Americans made, the more hostile white southerners became. Dozens of loosely organized groups of white southerners emerged to terrorize African Americans. The best known of these was the **Ku Klux Klan.** Racial violence grew even more widespread after the Fifteenth Amendment guaranteed all American men the right to vote. Congress took action, passing **Enforcement Acts** in 1870 and 1871. These acts made it a federal offense to interfere with a citizen's right to vote.

Review Questions

1. How did Republicans gain control of elected government in the South?

_____

_____

2. What did Congress do to counteract racial violence?

_____

_____

CHAPTER 12 SECTION 3
Note Taking Study Guide
THE END OF RECONSTRUCTION

Focus Question: How and why did Reconstruction end?

A. *Use the chart below to record main ideas about the factors that led to the end of Reconstruction.*

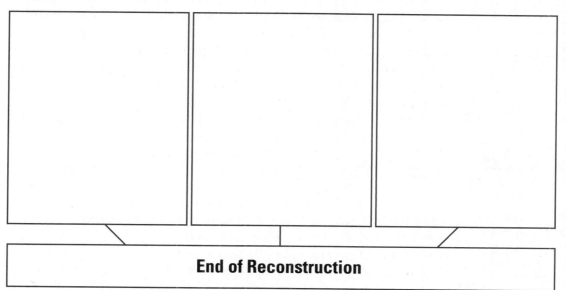

End of Reconstruction

B. *Fill in the chart below with information about the effects of Reconstruction.*

Effects of Reconstruction

African Americans	Women's Suffrage	State and National Parties
•	•	•
•	•	
•	•	
•		
•		

CHAPTER 12 SECTION 3 — Section Summary

THE END OF RECONSTRUCTION

Ulysses S. Grant was a popular war hero but a disappointing President. His ability to lead was marred by scandals involving members of his administration. Across the nation, local scandals also came to light. The most notorious involved a band of New York City Democratic politicians led by state senator William "Boss" Tweed. By 1873, when Tweed was convicted, the public's confidence in its leaders was at low ebb. When one of the nation's most influential banks failed in 1873, panic led to a depression. The uncertain economy preoccupied northerners, who lost the stamina necessary to keep pressure on the South.

The continued cost of military operations in the South worried many people. Beginning in 1871, troops were withdrawn from the South. In 1872, the Freedmen's Bureau was dissolved. The death of a Radical Republican leader in 1874 symbolized an important transition. A generation of white reformers, forged by abolitionist fervor, had passed away. Without such leaders, northern racial prejudice reemerged. In a series of landmark cases, the Supreme Court chipped away at African American freedoms in the 1870s. A group of southern Democrats put together a coalition to return the South to the rule of white men. The main focus of their strategy was compromise: finding common issues that would unite white southerners with the goal of regaining power in Congress. These compromisers have become known as **Redeemers.**

In the 1876 presidential election, the Democratic candidate received 51 percent of the popular vote. When the Republicans demanded a recount, they found enough mistakes to swing the election. **Rutherford B. Hayes** won by one electoral vote in what became known as the **Compromise of 1877.** In return, the remaining federal troops were withdrawn from the South and southern states were guaranteed federal subsidies to build railroads and improve their ports. Reconstruction was over. Although it fell short of its goals, Reconstruction opened new opportunities for black Americans, North and South. Constitutional amendments provided hope for full inclusion in American society, although it would take generations to use them to gain racial equality.

Review Questions

1. What kind of President was Ulysses S. Grant?

_____

_____

2. What were some of the successes of Reconstruction?

_____

_____

Name _____ Class _____ Date _____

Focus Question: How did industrialization and new technology affect the economy and society?

As you read, record the causes and effects of industrialization in the chart below.

Causes		Effects
•		•
•		•
•		•
•		•
•		•
•	**Event**	•
•	Industrialization	•
•		•
•		•
•		•

Name _____ Class _____ Date _____

READING CHECK

Name two inventions that changed Americans' lives.

_____

_____

_____

VOCABULARY STRATEGY

What does the word *stimulated* mean in the underlined sentence? Look for context clues in the surrounding words, phrases, and sentences.

_____

_____

_____

READING SKILL

Identify Causes and Effects
How did industrialization cause the United States to become more involved in world affairs?

_____

_____

_____

The Civil War encouraged industrial growth by challenging industries to make products more quickly and efficiently than they had been made before. The country's growth was also fueled by its vast supply of natural resources. In addition, industries had a huge workforce to fuel growth. After the Civil War, large numbers of Europeans, and some Asians, immigrated to the United States.

Entrepreneurs fueled industrialization. Capitalism is a system in which individuals own most businesses. The heroes of this system were **entrepreneurs,** or people who invest money in a product or enterprise in order to make a profit.

Government encouraged the success of businesses in the late 1800s. To encourage the buying of American goods, Congress enacted **protective tariffs,** or taxes that would make imported goods cost more than those made locally. The government also encouraged **laissez faire** policies, which allowed business to operate under minimal government regulation.

Thomas Edison received more than 1,000 **patents** for new inventions. Edison and his team invented the light bulb. George Westinghouse developed technology to send electricity over long distances. Electricity lit streets and powered homes and factories. Alexander Graham Bell patented the telephone. By 1900, there were more than one million telephones in the United States.

The **Bessemer process** created strong but lightweight steel that made possible innovations, including skyscrapers and **suspension bridges.** As railroads expanded, they stimulated new technology. To help trains set schedules, the globe was divided into twenty-four **time zones.** Electric streetcars, commuter trains, and subways appeared in major cities. As a result, American suburbs grew.

To meet the growing demand for goods, factory owners developed systems known as **mass production** for turning out large numbers of products quickly and inexpensively.

Industrialization touched every aspect of American life. Farms became mechanized. Mass production meant people had easy access to goods. As the United States grew as an economic power, it became more involved in the affairs of other nations.

Review Questions

1. How did entrepreneurs encourage industrialization?

_____

_____

2. What innovations were made possible by the Bessemer process?

_____

_____

CHAPTER 13 SECTION 2 Note Taking Study Guide
THE RISE OF BIG BUSINESS

Focus Question: How did big business shape the American economy in the late 1800s and early 1900s?

A. *Record supporting details about the rise of American big business in the chart below.*

Rise of Big Business

Corporations	Debates
•	•
•	•
•	•
•	•
•	•

B. *As you read, record details about how the government gradually became involved in regulating industry.*

Railroad industry controls economy.

↓ ↓ ↓

↓ ↓ ↓

↓ ↓ ↓

↓ ↓ ↓

CHAPTER
13
SECTION 2

Section Summary
THE RISE OF BIG BUSINESS

To take advantage of larger markets, investors developed a form of group ownership known as a **corporation.** In a corporation, a number of people share ownership of a business. Corporations had access to huge amounts of money, allowing them to fund new technology or enter new industries.

Corporations worked to maximize profits in several ways. Some corporations tried to gain a **monopoly,** or complete control of a product or service. Other corporations worked to eliminate competition by forming **cartels.** In this arrangement, businesses making the same product agreed to limit their production and thus keep prices high. Another way to increase profits was to create a giant company with lower production costs. This system of consolidating many firms in the same business is called **horizontal integration. John D. Rockefeller, Andrew Carnegie,** and other businessmen also increased their power by gaining control of the many different businesses that make up all phases of a product's development. This process, called **vertical integration,** allowed businessmen to reduce costs and charge higher costs to competitors.

Gradually, consumers, workers, and the federal government came to feel that systems like **trusts,** cartels, and monopolies gave powerful businessmen an unfair advantage. At the same time, many people believed that business leaders served the nation positively. Factories, steel mills, and railroads provided jobs. The development of efficient business practices and industrialists' support for developing technology benefited the nation's economy, shaping the United States into a strong international leader. Finally, many business leaders were important philanthropists.

Charles Darwin's theory of survival of the fittest was applied to the world of American capitalism and was called **Social Darwinism.** People used Social Darwinism to justify all sorts of beliefs and conditions, such as discrimination.

The federal government slowly became involved in regulating trusts. In 1890, the Senate passed the **Sherman Antitrust Act.** This act outlawed any trust that operated in restraint of trade or commerce among several states.

Review Questions

1. Name two methods that businesses used to increase their profits.

_____

_____

2. List two reasons some people had favorable opinions about the impact of big business.

_____

_____

Name _____ Class _____ Date _____

Focus Question: How did the rise of labor unions shape relations among workers, big business, and government?

Record the main ideas about the rise of organized labor in the concept web below.

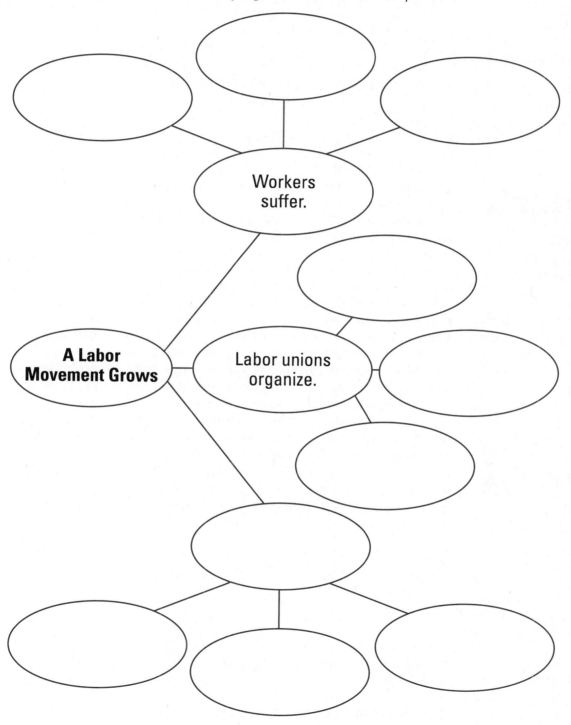

CHAPTER 13 SECTION 3

Section Summary
THE ORGANIZED LABOR MOVEMENT

Industrial growth produced wealth for business owners. However, factory workers toiled long hours in dirty workhouses known as **sweatshops.** Many miners were forced to live in communities near their workplace. The housing in these **company towns** was owned by the business and rented to employees. By the time workers received wages, most of the income was owed back to the company. As early as the 1820s, factory workers tried to gain more power against employers by using the technique of **collective bargaining.** One form of collective bargaining was the strike.

In the 1830s, a movement called **socialism** spread throughout Europe. Socialism is an economic and political philosophy that favors public, instead of private, control of property and income. Many labor activists borrowed ideas from socialism to support their goals.

The **Knights of Labor,** a labor union founded in 1869, included all workers of any trade, skilled or unskilled. The union sought broad social reform. In 1881, **Terrence V. Powderly** became its leader.

In 1886, **Samuel Gompers** formed the **American Federation of Labor (AFL).** Unlike the Knights of Labor, the AFL focused on specific workers' issues such as wages, working hours, and conditions.

On May 1, 1886, thousands of workers mounted a national demonstration for an eight-hour workday. Strikes erupted in several cities. At Haymarket Square in Chicago, frenzy broke out when a protester threw a bomb, killing a policeman. Dozens of people were killed. The result of the **Haymarket Riot** was that employers and many Americans associated union activities with violence.

The **Homestead Strike** was part of an epidemic of steelworkers' and miners' strikes that took place as economic depression crept across America. In each case, federal troops were called in.

In 1893, **Eugene V. Debs,** leader of the American Railway Union, called for a nationwide strike against the Pullman Company. By June 1894, nearly 300,000 railworkers had walked off their jobs. The **Pullman Strike** escalated, halting both railroad traffic and mail delivery. Federal troops were sent in to end the strike. Afterward, an important trend developed. The federal government regularly supported businesses over labor unions.

Review Questions

1. How did company towns negatively impact the workers who lived in them?

_____

_____

2. How did the goals of the Knights of Labor differ from those of the AFL?

_____

_____

CHAPTER 14 SECTION 1

Note Taking Study Guide
THE NEW IMMIGRANTS

Focus Question: Why did immigrants come to the United States, and what impact did they have upon society?

Record the main ideas of the section in the outline below.

I. **New Immigrants Come to America**

    A. _____

    B. _____

    C. _____

II. **Immigrants Decide to Leave Home**

    A. _____

        1. _____

        2. _____

    B. _____

        1. _____

        2. _____

III. _____

    A. _____

    B. _____

        1. _____

        2. _____

IV. _____

    A. _____

    B. _____

        1. _____

        2. _____

    C. _____

        1. _____

        2. _____

Name _____ Class _____ Date _____

<table>
<tr><td>CHAPTER
14
SECTION 1</td><td>**Section Summary**
THE NEW IMMIGRANTS</td></tr>
</table>

READING CHECK

How did most immigrants travel to America?

_____

_____

_____

VOCABULARY STRATEGY

What does the word *preliminary* mean in the underlined sentence? Use context clues in the surrounding words and phrases to help you figure out the meaning of *preliminary*.

_____

_____

_____

READING SKILL

Identify Main Ideas Discuss the challenges immigrants faced in America.

_____

_____

_____

Many early American immigrants were Protestants from northern and western Europe or German and Irish Catholics. Many were skilled and educated, and came as families to work on farms. In the 1870s, **"new" immigrants** from southern and eastern Europe came to America. They often came alone, were unskilled and poor, Catholic or Jewish, and settled in cities rather than on farms.

Two types of factors lead to immigration. Push factors compel people to leave their homes. These include famine, war, and persecution. Pull factors, such as economic opportunities or religious freedom, draw people to a new place. Land reform and low prices for grain pushed farmers in Mexico, Poland, China, and Italy to leave. Wars in China and eastern Europe, and religious persecution in eastern Europe were also push factors. Inexpensive land and employment opportunities were examples of pull factors.

Most immigrants traveled in **steerage,** the crowded and dirty lower decks of steamships. There, illness spread quickly. Shipowners did a preliminary medical screening before passengers boarded. Still, immigration officials met ships at American ports to determine who could stay. Immigrants had to be healthy and prove that they had money, a skill, or a sponsor. Beginning in 1892, most European immigrants were processed at **Ellis Island** in New York Harbor. Chinese and other Asian immigrants were processed at **Angel Island,** which opened in 1910, in San Francisco Bay.

Volunteer organizations tried to help immigrants blend into the **"melting pot"** of American society. Still, many immigrants held on to their traditions. Newcomers often faced **nativism,** the belief that native-born white Americans were superior to newcomers. Immigrants competed for jobs and housing, and their religious and cultural differences made native-born Americans suspicious. Hostility toward Chinese laborers led Congress to pass the **Chinese Exclusion Act** in 1882, limiting the civil rights of Chinese immigrants and forbidding their naturalization. Despite opposition, immigrants fueled industrial growth, elected politicians, and made their traditions part of American culture.

Review Questions

1. Describe the pull factors that drew immigrants to America.

_____

_____

2. What characteristics set new immigrants apart from earlier immigrants?

_____

_____

Note Taking Study Guide
CITIES EXPAND AND CHANGE

Focus Question: What challenges did city dwellers face, and how did they meet them?

Record the main ideas of this section in the following flowchart.

Cities Expand and Change		
Urbanization	**Technology**	**Problems**
•	•	•
•	•	•
•	•	•
•	•	•
•	•	•
		•

CHAPTER 14 SECTION 2 — Section Summary

CITIES EXPAND AND CHANGE

America went through **urbanization** in the late nineteenth century. The number of cities and of people living in them greatly increased. Major cities were clustered in the Northeast, on the Pacific Coast, and along Midwestern waterways. These centers of manufacturing and transportation were connected by new railroad lines.

In addition to immigrants looking for factory work, many **rural-to-urban migrants** moved to cities. Making a living by farming was increasingly difficult, and cities offered excitement and variety. Cities also offered greater job possibilities for women. Children had the opportunity to attend school.

To meet increased demands for water, sewers, schools, and safety in growing cities, Americans developed new technologies. These innovations included electric trolleys, subways, and **skyscrapers,** tall buildings that housed large numbers of offices. **Elisha Otis** developed a safety elevator that would not fall if the lifting rope broke. Streetcars powered by electricity revolutionized transportation, and **mass transit,** public transportation systems capable of carrying a large number of people inexpensively, reshaped the nation. Those who could afford it moved to cleaner and quieter streetcar **suburbs** on the outskirts of cities and rode mass transit into the city for work and entertainment.

Cities created different zones for heavy industry, financial institutions, and residences. They also built public places, such as libraries, government buildings, universities, and parks. Landscape engineer **Frederick Law Olmsted** was hired to design a number of parks including New York City's Central Park.

With the growth of cities came a number of problems. Cities were filthy and trash-filled. Most urban workers lived in over-crowded, low-cost multifamily housing called **tenements.** With few windows and little sanitation, they were unhealthy and dangerous places. Open fireplaces and gas lighting enabled fires to quickly rip through cities. Unlit streets also posed dangers to those coming from or going to work. In response, many cities created firefighting teams and police forces. City planners began regulating housing, sanitation, and sewers.

Review Questions

1. Describe the technologies that improved life in the city.

_____

_____

2. Why did people move to cities?

_____

_____

CHAPTER 14 SECTION 3

Note Taking Study Guide
SOCIAL AND CULTURAL TRENDS

Focus Question: What luxuries did cities offer to the middle class?

Record the main ideas of this section below.

Consumerism	Mass Culture	Entertainment
•	•	•
•	•	•
•	•	•
•	•	•
•		•
		•
		•
		•

CHAPTER 14 SECTION 3

Section Summary
SOCIAL AND CULTURAL TRENDS

In *The Gilded Age,* novelist **Mark Twain** depicted American society in the late 1800s as gilded, or having a rotten core covered with gold paint. Most Americans were not as cynical. More people worked for wages, and more products were available than ever before and at lower prices, leading to a culture of **conspicuous consumerism.**

Department stores opened in the late 1850s. They used advertising to sell high-quality goods at fair prices. The postal service lowered shipping rates and offered free rural delivery, leading to a mail-order boom. Companies began creating trademarks with distinctive logos and for the first time, consumers began buying brand-name goods.

Transportation, advertising, and communication helped create a **mass culture** in which Americans became more and more alike in their consumption patterns. Household gadgets, toys, and food preferences were often the same from house to house. Newspapers both reflected and helped create mass culture, including **Joseph Pulitzer**'s morning paper, the *World.* Pulitzer believed that newspapers should inform people and stir up controversy. **William Randolph Hearst** mimicked Pulitzer's sensationalist tactics in his newspaper, the *Morning Journal.* However, some novelists like **Horatio Alger** focused on moral issues. Ethnic and special-interest publications catered to urban dwellers, especially immigrants. Newspapers were successful, in part, because more people could read. Public education expanded rapidly, and by 1900, the literacy rate reached nearly 90 percent.

Urban areas became centers for new types of entertainment. Amusement parks were built close to cities around the country. Touring outdoor shows like "Buffalo Bill's Wild West Show" drew crowds. Religious-inspired entertainment, including the Chautauqua Circuit, also grew in popularity. **Vaudeville** shows, made up of musical drama, songs, and off-color comedy, were found throughout the country. Movie theaters introduced motion pictures, charging a nickel for admission. Baseball, horse racing, bicycle racing, boxing, and football became popular spectator sports.

Review Questions

1. Describe how a mass culture developed in America.

_____

_____

2. How did shopping change in America?

_____

_____

Name _____ Class _____ Date _____

Focus Question: How did the southern economy and society change after the Civil War?

As you read, fill in the concept web below with details about how the South changed after the Civil War.

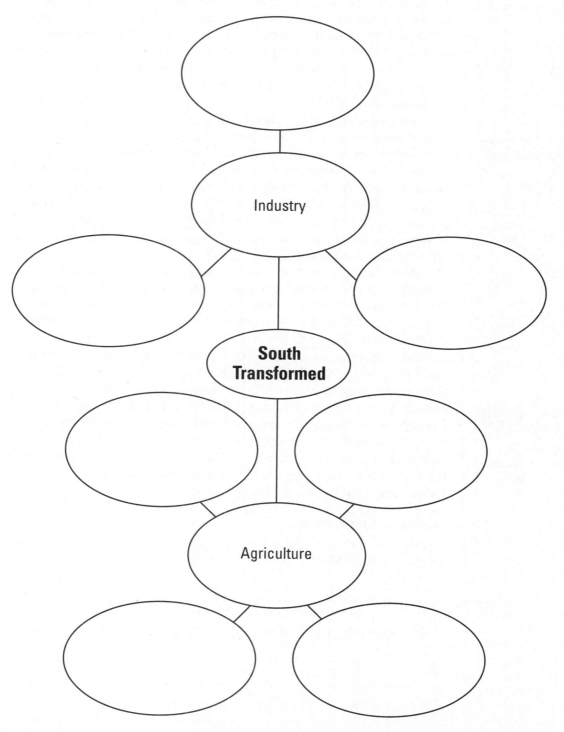

CHAPTER 15 SECTION 1

Section Summary
THE NEW SOUTH

What were the goals of the Farmers' Alliance?

_____

_____

_____

What does the word *component* mean in the underlined sentence? Use context clues in the surrounding sentences to help you figure out the meaning of *component*.

_____

_____

_____

Identify Supporting Details
Provide three examples of how the southern economy changed after the Civil War.

_____

_____

_____

Before the Civil War, the South had shipped its raw materials abroad or to the North for processing. In the 1880s, northern money helped the South to build its own factories. <u>Transportation was also a key component of industrialization.</u> As southern rail lines expanded, they joined rural areas with urban hubs. Despite these changes, the southern economy continued to lag behind the rest of the country. The South first had to repair the damages of war. Although the South had plenty of natural resources, it did not have enough skilled labor and capital investment. Wages were low and most of the region's wealth was in the hands of a few people.

Before the Civil War, most southern planters had concentrated on **cash crops** such as cotton and tobacco, which they grew to be sold. Cotton remained the centerpiece of southern agriculture, although many European textile factories had found other suppliers during the war, so the price had fallen. In the 1870s, Texas farmers began to organize and to negotiate as a group for lower prices for supplies. Local organizations joined to form the **Farmers' Alliance.** Alliance members tried to force railroads to lower freight prices. They also wanted the government to regulate the interest that banks could charge for loans.

Black southerners now had the right to vote. New opportunities opened up for them. Perhaps the most important goal was education. Hundreds of schools and dozens of teachers' colleges enabled African Americans to learn to read. However, some white southerners focused their own frustrations on trying to reverse the gains African Americans had achieved during Reconstruction. Groups such as the Ku Klux Klan used terror and violence to intimidate African Americans. Many African American freedoms were whittled away. Congress passed the **Civil Rights Act of 1875** to guarantee black patrons the right to ride trains and use public facilities. However, the Supreme Court ruled that decisions about who could use public accommodations was a local issue, to be governed by state or local laws. Southern municipalities took advantage of this ruling to further limit the rights of African Americans.

Review Questions

1. Why did the southern economy lag behind the rest of the country in the late 1800s?

_____

_____

2. How did the Civil Rights Act of 1875 affect African Americans?

_____

_____

CHAPTER 15 SECTION 2 — Note Taking Study Guide
WESTWARD EXPANSION AND THE AMERICAN INDIANS

Focus Question: How did the pressures of westward expansion impact Native Americans?

A. *As you read, fill in the concept web below with details about Native Americans west of the Mississippi.*

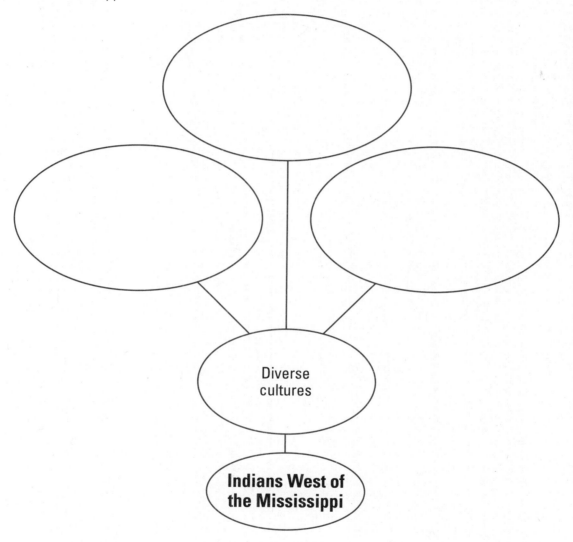

Diverse cultures

Indians West of the Mississippi

Name _____ Class _____ Date _____

Focus Question: How did the pressures of westward expansion impact Native Americans?

B. *Use the timeline below to record important dates and events in the Indian Wars.*

1864
Sand Creek
Massacre

1860

1870

1880

1890

Section Summary
WESTWARD EXPANSION AND THE AMERICAN INDIANS

By the end of the Civil War, about 250,000 Indians lived in the region west of the Mississippi River known as "The Great American Desert." Geography influenced their cultural diversity, but all Indian cultures saw themselves as part of nature and considered it sacred. By contrast, many whites viewed the land as a resource to produce wealth. In the early 1800s, the government began to move Native Americans out of the way of white settlers. Things changed when gold and silver were discovered in Indian Territory. In 1851, the government began to restrict Indians to smaller areas. By the late 1860s, they were forced to live on **reservations,** where they lacked adequate resources.

In 1864, Colorado militia attacked an unarmed camp of Cheyenne and Arapaho. The **Sand Creek Massacre,** as it came to be known, spawned more warfare between Plains Indians and white settlers. When gold was discovered in the Black Hills, the Sioux, led by chiefs Crazy Horse and **Sitting Bull,** tried to drive white prospectors out of Sioux lands. At the **Battle of Little Big Horn** in June 1876, the Sioux killed all the United States Army cavalry forces led by George Custer. In 1877, the Nez Percés tried to escape to Canada when the federal government wanted to relocate them to a smaller reservation. The Nez Percés were captured just short of the border and relocated to a barren reservation in Oklahoma. Their leader, **Chief Joseph,** traveled twice to Washington, D.C., to lobby for mercy for his people. In 1890, hostilities broke out at **Wounded Knee,** South Dakota, over a religious revival based on the Ghost Dance. The cavalry outgunned the Indians.

Policymakers hoped that Indians would become farmers and **assimilate** into national life by adopting the culture and civilization of whites. In 1887, Congress passed the **Dawes General Allotment Act.** It replaced the reservation system with a system under which each Indian family was granted a 160-acre farmstead. To help speed assimilation, missionaries and other reformers established boarding schools where Indian children were taught to live by the rules of white America.

Review Questions

1. What differing beliefs caused white settlers and Native Americans to clash over land use?

_____

_____

2. What measures were taken to assimilate Native Americans into national life?

_____

_____

READING CHECK

Who was Chief Joseph?

_____

_____

_____

VOCABULARY STRATEGY

What does the word *adequate* mean in the underlined sentence? Read the underlined sentence aloud, but leave out the word *adequate.* What word could you use in its place? Use this strategy to help you figure out the meaning of *adequate.*

_____

_____

_____

READING SKILL

Recognize Sequence How did life change for Native Americans after gold and silver were discovered in Indian Territory?

_____

_____

_____

Name _____ Class _____ Date _____

Focus Question: What economic and social factors changed the West after the Civil War?

Use the chart below to record details about changes in the West.

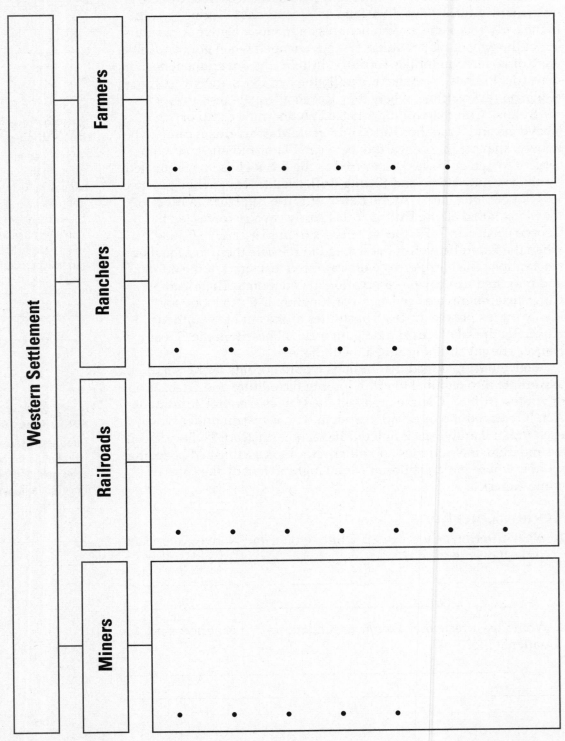

CHAPTER 15 SECTION 3

Section Summary

TRANSFORMING THE WEST

Mining was the first great boom in the West. Mining camps sprang up quickly. <u>To administer justice, miners set up rules of conduct and procedures for settling disputes.</u> At first, mining was done by individuals who found the minerals in the surface soil or a streambed. By the 1870s, big companies took over the industry. The federal government supported these companies by providing them with cheap land and patents for new inventions. Mining wealth helped fuel the nation's industrial development.

As industry in the West grew, the need for a **transcontinental railroad** linking the East and the West became apparent. Congress supported its construction in two ways: It provided money in the form of loans and made **land grants,** giving builders wide stretches of land, alternating on each side of the track route. Work on the railroad began in 1863 and was completed in 1869. Railroads had far-reaching effects. They tied the nation together, moved products and people across the continent, and spurred industrial development. They also stimulated the growth of towns and cities and intensified the demand for Indian land.

Cattle ranching was another western boom. With railroads to move meat to eastern markets, the race was on for land and water. At first, cattle were raised on the **open-range** system. Property was not fenced in, and cattle were branded to identify them. Cowboys learned much from the Mexican vaqueros. By the mid-1880s, the heyday of open-ranching came to an end.

The Great Plains was the last part of the country to be heavily settled by whites. Under the **Homestead Act,** passed in 1862, the government offered farm plots to homesteaders. Some new settlers were former slaves called **"Exodusters."** They followed an exodus out of bondage to a new "promised land" in Kansas and Oklahoma, where they planted crops and founded several all-black towns.

From the 1850s onward, the West had the widest diversity of people in the nation. Conflict came in many forms. There were ethnic tensions. Ranchers often belittled homesteaders. The last major land rush took place in 1889, when the federal government opened Oklahoma to homesteaders. The next year, the national census concluded that there was no longer a "frontier."

Review Questions

1. How did the railroads affect the settlement of the West?

_____

_____

2. How did ranching change over time?

_____

_____

READING CHECK

Who were the Exodusters?

_____

_____

_____

VOCABULARY STRATEGY

What does the word *administer* mean in the underlined sentence? Look for context clues in the surrounding words, phrases, and sentences. Circle the word below that is a synonym for *administer.*

• manage

• dispute

READING SKILL

Identify Main Ideas Why were early settlers attracted to the West?

_____

_____

_____

Note Taking Study Guide

SEGREGATION AND SOCIAL TENSIONS

Focus Question: How were the civil rights of certain groups in America undermined during the years after Reconstruction?

Record the ways in which different groups challenged Reconstruction.

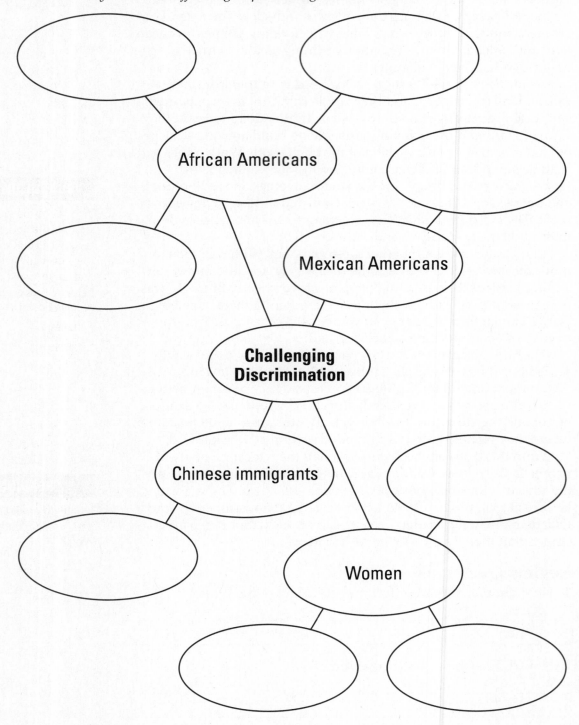

CHAPTER 16 SECTION 1

Section Summary
SEGREGATION AND SOCIAL TENSIONS

After federal troops were removed from the South, southern states enacted **Jim Crow laws** that segregated blacks and whites. There were Jim Crow railroad cars, cemeteries, and restaurants, among other things. The Supreme Court case *Plessy* v. *Ferguson* declared these laws constitutional as long as states maintained "separate but equal" facilities. In reality, facilities were rarely equal.

Southern states exploited a number of African Americans by passing restrictive measures that disqualified many of them as voters. They enacted a **poll tax,** requiring voters to pay a tax to vote. Voters also had to pass **literacy tests.**

Even during the darkest days of Jim Crow, African Americans refused to accept their status as second-class citizens. They established black newspapers, women's clubs, fraternal organizations, schools and colleges, and political associations with the goal of securing their freedom. Former slave **Ida B. Wells** published the newspaper *Free Speech.* She wrote articles condemning the treatment of blacks and criticizing lynching. **Booker T. Washington** argued that African Americans needed to accommodate themselves to segregation, build up economic resources, and establish reputations as hardworking and honest citizens. **W.E.B. Du Bois** criticized Washington and argued that blacks should demand full and immediate equality.

Chinese immigrants also faced racial prejudice. Congress passed the Chinese Exclusion Act, prohibiting Chinese laborers from entering the country. Chinese migrants turned to the federal courts. In 1898, the Supreme Court ruled that individuals of Chinese descent who were born in America could not be stripped of their citizenship.

Mexican Americans also struggled against discrimination. Despite guaranteed property rights, many Mexicans lost their lands after the Mexican-American War because they were unable to prove ownership. In the late 1880s and early 1890s, **Las Gorras Blancas** (the White Caps) fought back by engaging in guerrilla warfare against the railroads and large ranchers.

Women continued to fight for the right to vote, to own property, and to receive an education. Although women failed to gain the vote, the number of women attending college jumped dramatically.

Review Questions

1. Describe actions southern states took to limit the rights of African Americans.

_____

_____

2. How did African Americans respond to segregation?

_____

_____

READING CHECK

What act prohibited Chinese workers from entering the United States?

_____

_____

_____

VOCABULARY STRATEGY

What does the word *exploited* mean in the underlined sentence? Circle any words or phrases in the surrounding sentences that help you figure out what *exploited* means.

_____

_____

_____

READING SKILL

Summarize Booker T. Washington and W.E.B. Du Bois had different responses to discrimination. Describe those responses.

_____

_____

_____

Note Taking Study Guide

POLITICAL AND ECONOMIC CHALLENGES

Focus Question: Why did the political structure change during the Gilded Age?

As you read, describe the issues that dominated national politics in the 1870s and 1880s.

I. Politics and Economics

    A. Political Stalemate

    B. Corruption in Politics

        1. _____

        2. _____

        3. _____

    C. _____

        1. _____

        2. _____

            a. _____

            b. _____

CHAPTER 16 SECTION 2

Section Summary
POLITICAL AND ECONOMIC CHALLENGES

Inaction and political corruption characterized politics during the Gilded Age. Neither the Democrats nor the Republicans controlled the White House and both houses of Congress for more than two years in a row, making it difficult to pass new laws. Presidents during this era seemed weak and lacked integrity.

Political parties reached into nearly every ward and precinct in every city. Under the **spoils system,** politicians gave government jobs to loyal party workers without consideration of their qualifications. Government officials could and did use federal contracts to convince people to vote for their candidates.

A number of prominent figures promoted reforming the **civil service** system, a system that includes federal jobs in the executive branch. Under a reformed civil service, government workers would be offered jobs based on their expertise and keep those jobs regardless of which political party won the election. After President James Garfield was assassinated by a citizen who felt cheated out of a job, Vice President Chester Arthur signed the **Pendleton Civil Service Act** in 1883. This act established a civil service commission. The commission wrote an exam that all who sought government employment had to take before being hired. Getting a job was based on how well one did on the exam, not on one's political affiliation and connections.

Two economic issues created a political divide during the Gilded Age: the tariff and the monetary policy. Republicans favored a high tariff, arguing that it would promote job growth and allow American industry to grow. Democrats believed that high tariffs would raise prices and make it harder for American farmers to sell their goods abroad.

Disagreement flared over the **gold standard,** the use of gold as the basis of the nation's currency. Bankers and those in international trade feared that the use of silver for money would undermine the economy. Farmers argued that the rejection of silver money would lead to declining prices and financial ruin. Congress passed the Coinage Act of 1873, which ended the minting of silver coins, but after protest, it authorized minting of silver dollars.

Review Questions

1. How did the spoils system create government corruption?

_____

_____

2. Discuss how the civil service system was reformed after the assassination of President Garfield.

_____

_____

READING CHECK

What is the term for the use of gold as a nation's currency?

_____

_____

_____

VOCABULARY STRATEGY

What does the word *integrity* mean in the underlined sentence? The word "weak" earlier in the sentence has a negative meaning. Use this clue to help you figure out the meaning of *integrity*.

_____

_____

_____

READING SKILL

Identify Main Ideas Discuss two economic issues that were important to politics during the Gilded Age.

_____

_____

_____

Name _____ Class _____ Date _____

Focus Question: What led to the rise of the Populist movement, and what effect did it have?

As you read, list the reasons that farmers in the South and West felt the need to organize and the effects of their effort.

Causes		Effects
• Falling prices		•
•		
•		•
•		•
•	**Event** Farmers organize. →	•
•		•
•		•

Name _____ Class _____ Date _____

Between 1870 and 1895, farm prices fell sharply. At the same time, the cost of doing business increased. Many farmers mortgaged their farms to survive. Farmers blamed big business, especially the railroads and banks, for their problems. They believed that railroads charged whatever rates they wanted and that banks set interest rates too high.

In 1867, **Oliver H. Kelley,** a Minnesota farmer and businessman, organized the **Grange,** an organization of farmers that grew to nearly a million members. It was one of a network of organizations created to solve farmers' problems. The Grange provided education and called for the regulation of railroad and grain elevator rates. Grangers also prompted the federal government to establish the Interstate Commerce Commission (ICC) to oversee interstate transportation.

Farmers' Alliances took up the call for reform in the late 1870s. They formed cooperatives to collectively sell crops and called on the federal government to establish "sub-treasuries," or postal banks, to provide farmers with low-interest loans.

The spread of the Farmers' Alliances culminated with the creation of the **Populist Party,** or People's Party, in 1892. The party grew rapidly, putting pressure on the two major political parties to consider their demands. They called for the coinage of silver, or "free silver," to fight low prices. To combat high costs, they demanded government ownership of railroads. In the 1892 election, the Populists elected several governors and senators, and ten congressmen. Their presidential candidate received more than one million votes.

Following this success, Populists were forced to decide whether to nominate their own presidential candidate or to endorse Democratic Party nominee **William Jennings Bryan** for the 1896 election. They chose to endorse Bryan, who supported many Populist proposals.

Bryan lost the election to Republican candidate **William McKinley,** partly because his emphasis on monetary reform, especially free silver, did not appeal to urban workers. The Populist decision to endorse Bryan weakened the party at the local and state levels. The party never recovered, and by the early 1900s, it had disappeared as a viable alternative to the two major political parties.

Review Questions

1. What did the Populist Party hope to achieve?

_____

_____

2. Describe why the Populist Party waned in the late 1890s.

_____

_____

READING CHECK

What candidate did Populists endorse in the 1896 presidential election?

_____

_____

_____

VOCABULARY STRATEGY

Find the word *network* in the underlined sentence. Eliminate the word from the sentence and read it again. What word might you use in place of *network?* Use this strategy to help you figure out the meaning of *network.*

_____

_____

_____

READING SKILL

Identify Causes and Effects
Describe the problems that led farmers to create groups such as the Grange.

_____

_____

_____

CHAPTER 17 SECTION 1

Note Taking Study Guide
THE DRIVE FOR REFORM

Focus Question: What areas did Progressives think were in need of the greatest reform?

Fill in the chart below with details about Progressivism.

Progressivism		
Problems	**Muckrakers**	**Reforms**
• Industrial hazards	• Exposed conditions	• Factory laws
•	•	•
•	•	•
•	•	•
•		•
•		•
•		•
•		•
		•
		•
		•
		•
		•

CHAPTER 17 SECTION 1

Section Summary

THE DRIVE FOR REFORM

Industrialization, urbanization, and immigration brought many benefits to America, but they also produced challenging social problems. A movement called **Progressivism** arose in the 1890s to tackle these problems. Journalists whose stories dramatized the need for reform were called **muckrakers.** One leading muckraker was **Lincoln Steffens,** a magazine editor who published stories about political corruption. Another was **Jacob Riis,** a photographer whose pictures revealed life in urban slums. Novelist Frank Norris showed how the Southern Pacific Railroad kept a stranglehold on California farmers in *The Octopus.* Upton Sinclair's novel *The Jungle* revealed the unsafe and unsanitary conditions of Chicago meatpacking plants.

The work of the muckrakers increased popular support for Progressivism and helped the Progressives bring about reforms. Laws were passed to end child labor and break up monopolies and trusts. After a fire at a garment factory killed nearly 150 workers, Progressives were able to get laws passed to protect worker safety.

Many reformers thought that Christianity should be the basis of social reform. These followers of the **Social Gospel** believed that society would improve if people followed the Bible's teachings about charity and justice. One form of charity was the **settlement house,** which offered services for the poor such as child care and classes in English. Hull House in Chicago was a famous settlement house founded by **Jane Addams.** Her work inspired others to help solve the problems of the urban poor by becoming social workers.

In order to reform politics and remove corrupt governments, Progressives pushed for a number of new laws. <u>Dynamic leaders such as Governor Robert La Follette of Wisconsin created tools to limit the power of political bosses and business interests.</u> Reformers created the **direct primary** so citizens, not political bosses, could select nominees for upcoming elections. The **initiative** gave people the power to put a proposed new law directly on the ballot. The **referendum** allowed citizens to approve or reject laws passed by a legislature. The **recall** gave voters the power to remove elected officials from office before their terms ended. These reforms brought about by Progressives continue to affect society today.

Review Questions

1. Why were muckrakers important to Progressivism?

_____

_____

2. How did settlement houses help the poor?

_____

_____

READING CHECK

What were two examples of political reform?

_____

_____

_____

VOCABULARY STRATEGY

What does the word *dynamic* mean in the underlined sentence? Circle the words in the underlined sentence that could help you learn what *dynamic* means. Think about what kind of leader it would take to be a reformer.

_____

_____

_____

READING SKILL

Identify Details List four muckrakers whose work in the 1890s helped increase the public's awareness about social and political problems, and describe their work.

_____

_____

_____

_____

CHAPTER 17 SECTION 2

Note Taking Study Guide

WOMEN MAKE PROGRESS

Focus Question: How did women of the Progressive Era make progress and win the right to vote?

As you read this section, complete the outline below to capture the main ideas.

I. Women Expand Reforms

    A. Hardships for women

        1. _____

        2. _____

    B. _____

        1. _____

        2. _____

    C. _____

        1. _____

        2. _____

        3. _____

II. _____

    A. _____

        1. _____

        2. _____

    B. _____

        1. _____

        2. _____

    C. _____

        1. _____

        2. _____

CHAPTER 17 SECTION 2 — Section Summary

WOMEN MAKE PROGRESS

In the early 1900s, a growing number of women sought to do more than fulfill their roles as wives and mothers. Many went to college to prepare for careers in teaching and nursing. Women had already won a shorter workday, but reformers saw the need for more changes. **Florence Kelley** believed that unfair prices for household goods hurt women and their families, so she helped found the **National Consumers League (NCL).** The NCL labeled products made in safe workplaces. The NCL also asked the government to improve food and workplace safety and assist the unemployed.

Women also sought changes in the home. With the **temperance movement,** led by the Women's Christian Temperance Union (WCTU), women tried to reduce or end the consumption of alcohol. Members of the WCTU blamed alcohol for some men's abuse and neglect of their families. **Margaret Sanger** sought a different change. She thought that family life and women's health would improve if mothers had fewer children. Sanger opened the nation's first birth-control clinic. **Ida B. Wells** established the National Association of Colored Women, which helped African American families by providing childcare and education.

One of Progressivism's boldest goals was **suffrage**—the right to vote—for women. This fight was started in the 1860s but was reenergized by **Carrie Chapman Catt** in the 1890s. Catt toured the country encouraging women to join the **National American Woman Suffrage Association (NAWSA).** This group lobbied Congress for the right to vote and used the referendum process to try to get women the vote in individual states. By 1918, this strategy had helped women get the vote in several states. **Alice Paul** was more vocal in her efforts. In 1917, she formed the National Woman's Party (NWP), which staged protest marches and hunger strikes and even picketed the White House to demand the right to vote. When the United States entered World War I in 1917, the NAWSA supported the war effort. Its actions and those of the NWP convinced a growing number of legislators to support a woman suffrage amendment. This reform became official in 1920 as the **Nineteenth Amendment.** Women finally had the right to vote for President.

Review Questions

1. Why did many women want to end the drinking of alcohol?

_____

_____

2. What methods did reformers use to fight for women's suffrage?

_____

_____

READING CHECK

What is the Nineteenth Amendment?

_____

_____

_____

VOCABULARY STRATEGY

What does the word *strategy* mean in the underlined sentence? What clues can you find in the surrounding words, phrases, or sentences? Circle the words in the underlined sentence that could help you learn what *strategy* means.

_____

_____

_____

READING SKILL

Identify Main Ideas What goal did Margaret Sanger, Ida B. Wells, and Florence Kelley share?

_____

_____

_____

Focus Question: What steps did minorities take to combat social problems and discrimination?

Outline the section's main ideas and details.

I. The Struggle Against Discrimination

   A. _____

      1. _____

      2. _____

      3. _____

      4. _____

   B. _____

      1. _____

      2. _____

      3. _____

   C. _____

      1. _____

      2. _____

      3. _____

      4. _____

CHAPTER 17 SECTION 3 — Section Summary
THE STRUGGLE AGAINST DISCRIMINATION

The Progressive Era was not so progressive for nonwhite and immigrant Americans. Most Progressives were white Anglo-Saxon Protestant reformers who were indifferent or hostile to minorities.

Settlement houses and other civic groups played a big role in the **Americanization** efforts of many Progressives. Americanization occurred when Progressives encouraged everyone to follow white, middle-class ways of life.

Many Progressives shared the same prejudices against nonwhites as other Americans. They agreed with so-called scientific theories that said that dark-skinned peoples had less intelligence than whites. They also supported segregation, or separation of the races, and laws to limit minority voting.

African American reformers responded in different ways to formal segregation and discrimination. For example, **Booker T. Washington** told blacks that the best way to win their rights was to be patient and to earn the respect of white Americans. **W.E.B. Du Bois,** on the other hand, said that blacks should demand immediately all the rights guaranteed by the Constitution.

W.E.B. Du Bois was a member of the **Niagara Movement,** a group that called for rapid progress and more education for blacks. After a race riot broke out in Illinois, its members joined with white reformers to form the **National Association for the Advancement of Colored People (NAACP).** The NAACP planned to use the court system to fight for the civil rights of African Americans, including the right to vote. The efforts of the NAACP mostly helped middle-class blacks, but the **Urban League** focused on poorer urban workers. It helped families buy clothes and books and helped factory workers and maids find jobs.

African Americans were not alone in seeking their rights. Individuals and organizations of diverse ethnic groups spoke out against injustice and created self-help agencies. Jews in New York City formed the **Anti-Defamation League** to defend themselves against verbal attacks and false statements. Mexican Americans in several states formed **mutualistas,** groups that gave loans and provided legal assistance to the poor.

Review Questions

1. Why did Progressives not fight for the civil rights of minorities?

_____

_____

2. How did the Urban League differ from the NAACP?

_____

_____

READING CHECK

Who organized the Anti-Defamation League?

_____

_____

_____

VOCABULARY STRATEGY

What does the word *so-called* mean in the underlined sentence? Two synonyms for *so-called* are *supposed* and *presumed.* Use the meanings of the synonyms to help you determine the meaning of *so-called.*

_____

_____

_____

READING SKILL

Main Idea and Details How did Booker T. Washington differ from W.E.B. Du Bois in his approach to civil rights?

_____

_____

_____

Name _____ Class _____ Date _____

Focus Question: What did Roosevelt think government should do for citizens?

A. *As you read this section, use the concept web below to record the main ideas.*

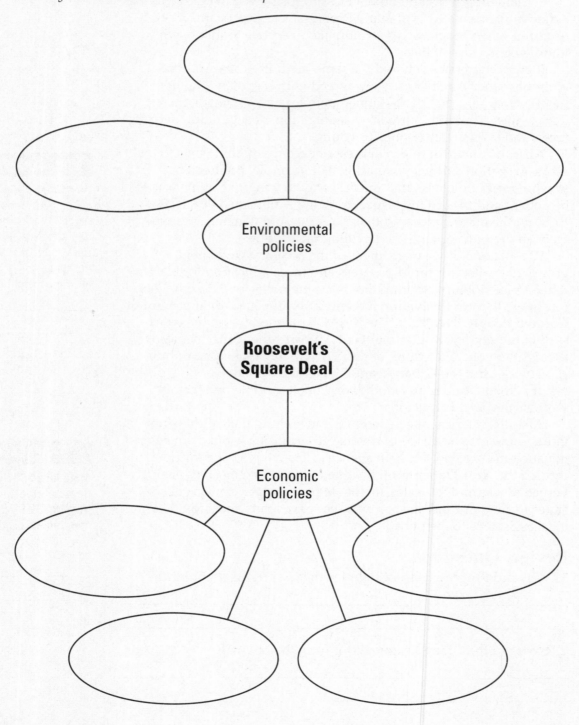

Name _____ Class _____ Date _____

CHAPTER
17
SECTION 4

Note Taking Study Guide
ROOSEVELT'S SQUARE DEAL

Focus Question: What did Roosevelt think government should do for citizens?

B. *As you read, fill in the Venn diagram with similarities and differences between Roosevelt and Taft.*

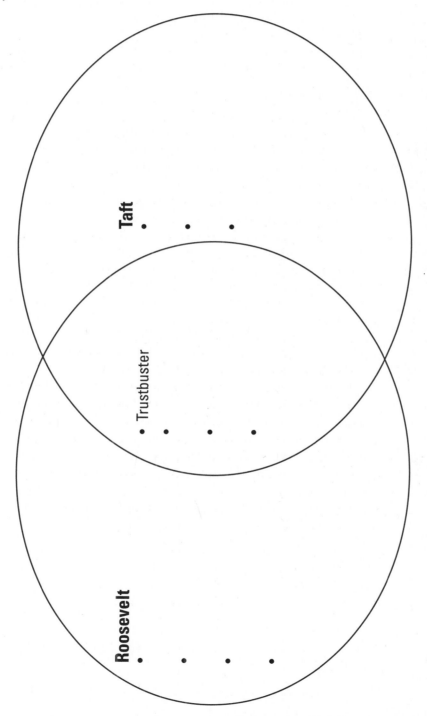

CHAPTER **17** SECTION 4	**Section Summary** ROOSEVELT'S SQUARE DEAL

READING CHECK

What was New Nationalism?

_____

_____

_____

VOCABULARY STRATEGY

What does the word *dominating* mean in the underlined sentence? What clues can you find in the surrounding words, phrases, or sentences? Circle the words in the underlined sentence that could help you learn what *dominating* means.

_____

_____

_____

READING SKILL

Identify Main Ideas How were the Square Deal and the New Nationalism programs similar?

_____

_____

_____

Theodore Roosevelt was a war hero, seasoned politician, and a dedicated reformer when he became President in 1901. He quickly pushed Congress to approve the Square Deal, a program of reform aimed at stopping the wealthy and powerful from dominating small business owners and the poor. Roosevelt used the power of the federal government to take on big business, breaking up trusts he considered abusive. In 1906, Roosevelt convinced Congress to pass the **Hepburn Act,** which limited what railroads could charge for shipping. This helped farmers in the West who had been at the mercy of the railroads.

After reading Upton Sinclair's novel *The Jungle,* Roosevelt pushed Congress to pass the **Meat Inspection Act.** This law gave the government power to inspect meat and meat-processing plants to ensure the meat was safe to eat. The **Pure Food and Drug Act** banned interstate shipment of impure food and the mislabeling of food and drugs.

Roosevelt loved nature, and he respected naturalist **John Muir,** whose efforts had led to the creation of Yosemite National Park. Following Muir's advice, Roosevelt put millions of acres of forests under federal control. However, he did not agree with Muir that it should all remain untouched. Like the head of the Division of Forestry, **Gifford Pinchot,** Roosevelt believed in the "rational use" of forests. The forests would be protected as future sources of lumber. To help settle fights over sources of water in the West, Roosevelt pushed for passage of the **National Reclamation Act.** That law gave the government power to build and manage dams and to control where and how water was used.

After two terms in office, Roosevelt wanted William Howard Taft to follow him because Taft shared his belief in regulating businesses. However, Taft did not follow the course Roosevelt had set, and Roosevelt became disappointed and, later, angry. He began to speak out against Taft, promoting what he called **New Nationalism,** a program to restore the government's trustbusting power. As another election neared, the Taft-Roosevelt battle split the Republican Party. A group of Progressives created the **Progressive Party** and nominated Roosevelt as its candidate for President.

Review Questions

1. How did the Meat Inspection Act protect consumers?

_____

_____

2. Why did President Roosevelt and Gifford Pinchot want to protect forests?

_____

_____

Name _____ Class _____ Date _____

Focus Question: What steps did Wilson take to increase the government's role in the economy?

As you read this section, fill in the concept web below to record details from the section.

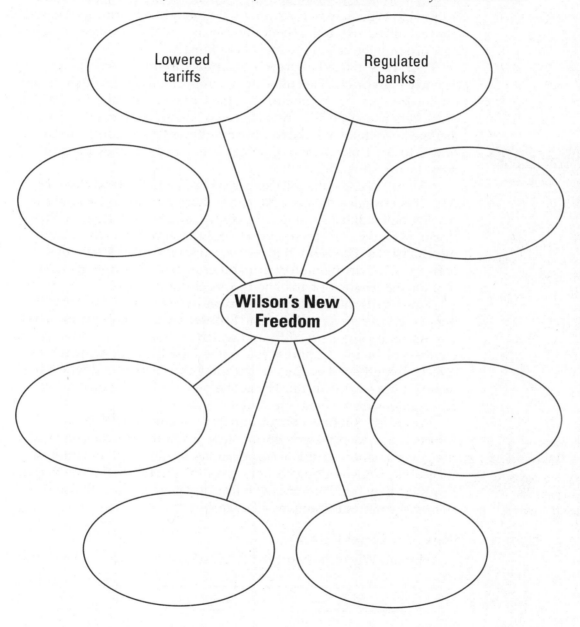

CHAPTER 17 SECTION 5

Section Summary
WILSON'S NEW FREEDOM

During the 1912 election, Roosevelt and Taft split the Republican Party vote, allowing Democrat **Woodrow Wilson** to win the election. Wilson was an intellectual man from Virginia who had taught college as a professor before becoming governor of New Jersey. Like Roosevelt, Wilson was a reformer who thought government should play an active role in the economy. He shaped his ideas into a three-part program he called the **New Freedom.**

First, Wilson tried to prevent manufacturers from charging unfairly high prices. He cut tariffs on imported goods, which made foreign goods more competitive in the United States and forced U.S. producers to charge fair prices. He also pushed for creation of an income tax, which the **Sixteenth Amendment** gave Congress the power to do. This tax more than made up for the money the government lost by lowering tariffs.

Second, Wilson pushed Congress to pass the **Federal Reserve Act.** This law gave the government authority to supervise banks by placing national banks under the control of a Federal Reserve Board. Regional banks were then set up to hold reserve funds from commercial banks. The Federal Reserve also set the interest rate that banks pay to borrow money from other banks. This system ensured that no one person or bank had too much control over the economy.

Third, Wilson made sure that trusts did not behave unfairly. He persuaded Congress to create the **Federal Trade Commission (FTC)** to monitor business practices and watch out for false advertising and dishonest labeling. Congress also passed the **Clayton Antitrust Act,** which strengthened earlier antitrust laws by spelling out which business activities were illegal. The act helped workers by protecting labor unions from being attacked as trusts.

Progressivism had a major impact on the nation. Political reforms expanded the power of voters. Economic reforms enabled the government to regulate corporations and banks in the interest of the public. Consumer protections gave the public confidence that the products they bought were not harmful. The government also began to manage natural resources all over the nation.

Review Questions

1. Why did Wilson support the Federal Reserve Act?

_____

_____

2. What were three ways Wilson wanted to regulate the economy?

_____

_____

Name _____ Class _____ Date _____

Note Taking Study Guide
THE ROOTS OF IMPERIALISM

Focus Question: How and why did the United States take a more active role in world affairs?

As you read, fill in the concept web below with the key events that marked America's first steps toward world power.

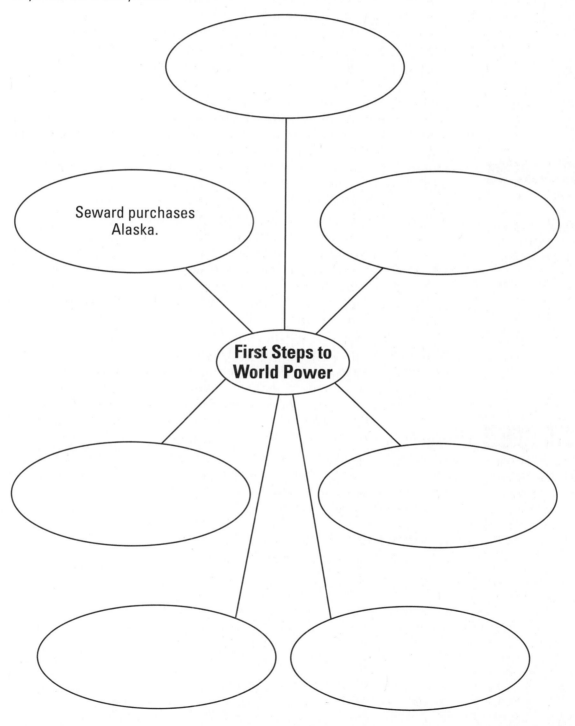

Seward purchases Alaska.

First Steps to World Power

CHAPTER 18 SECTION 1

Section Summary
THE ROOTS OF IMPERIALISM

During the late 1800s, the United States began to acquire influence and territory outside of its continental borders. It pursued a policy of **imperialism,** or the use of economic, political, and military control over weaker territories. Many imperialist nations wanted colonies to serve as **extractive economies.** Raw materials would be removed from these colonies and sent to the home country. In America there was a surplus of goods. American industrialists would benefit because they could sell their commodities in new colonial markets around the world.

Alfred T. Mahan, a historian and officer in the United States Navy, called upon the government to build a large navy in order to protect American interests around the world. To justify imperialism, many imperialists used ideas of racial, national, and cultural superiority. One of these ideas was **Social Darwinism,** the belief that life is a competitive struggle and that some races are superior to others and more fit to rule. Historian **Frederick J. Turner** wrote that America needed a large amount of unsettled land to succeed. Some Americans felt that the nation should expand into foreign lands.

In 1853, Commodore **Matthew Perry** sailed a large naval force to Japan. Perry won the Japanese emperor's favor by showering him with lavish gifts. Within a year, Japan agreed to trade with the United States. In 1867, Secretary of State William Seward bought Alaska from Russia. The purchase almost doubled the size of the United States and provided timber, oil, and other natural resources. In Latin America, U.S. businessmen sought to expand their trade and investments, which expanded the U.S. sphere of influence.

The Hawaiian Islands had been economically linked to the United States for almost a century. American sugar planters owned much of the Hawaiian land. They used their influence to exclude many Hawaiians from the voting process. **Queen Liliuokalani,** the ruler of Hawaii, tried to limit the political power of the white minority. In 1893, the planters overthrew the queen and set up a new government. The United States annexed Hawaii in 1898. The United States was abandoning isolationism and emerging as a new power on the global stage.

Review Questions

1. How did Social Darwinism contribute to imperialism?

_____

_____

2. What led to the annexation of Hawaii?

_____

_____

READING CHECK

How did Commodore Matthew Perry win the Japanese emperor's favor?

_____

_____

_____

VOCABULARY STRATEGY

What does the word *commodities* mean in the underlined sentence? What clues can you find in the surrounding words, phrases, or sentences?

_____

_____

_____

_____

READING SKILL

Identify Main Ideas Locate the sentence that identifies the main idea of the summary. Write the sentence below.

_____

_____

Focus Question: What were the causes and effects of the Spanish-American War?

As you read, note the causes, key events, and effects of the Spanish-American War.

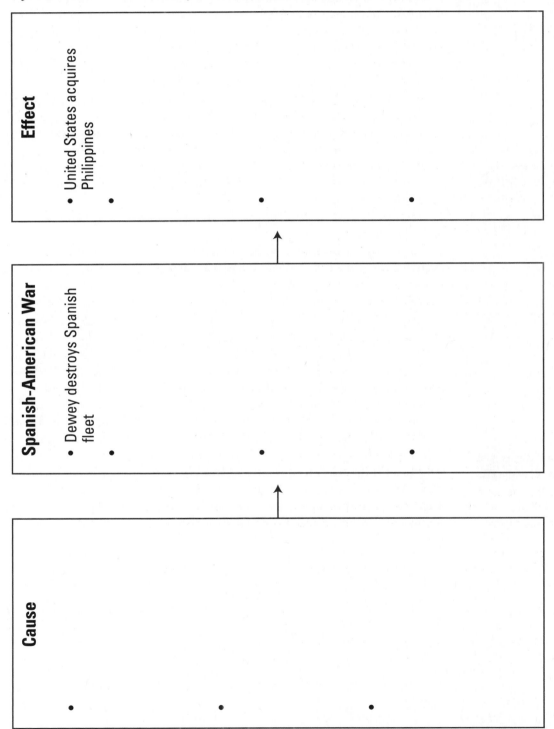

Effect
- United States acquires Philippines
-
-
-

Spanish-American War
- Dewey destroys Spanish fleet
-
-
-

Cause
-
-
-

CHAPTER 18 SECTION 2

Section Summary
THE SPANISH-AMERICAN WAR

READING CHECK

What was the Yellow Press?

_____
_____
_____

VOCABULARY STRATEGY

What does the word *obsolete* mean in the underlined sentence? What clues can you find in the surrounding words, phrases, or sentences?

_____
_____
_____

READING SKILL

Identify Causes and Effects
What was the effect of the Yellow Press on the American public?

_____
_____
_____

At the end of the nineteenth century, tensions were rising between Spain and its colony in Cuba. Cuban patriot **José Martí** launched a war for independence from Spain in 1895. Many Americans supported the Cubans, whose struggle for freedom and democracy reminded Americans of their own struggle for independence.

Newspaper publishers Joseph Pulitzer and **William Randolph Hearst** heightened the public's dislike of the Spanish government. Their publications, known as the **Yellow Press,** pushed for war with Spain by printing exaggerated stories of Spanish atrocities. In February 1898, Hearst's *New York Journal* published a letter written by Spain's ambassador, which called McKinley a weak and stupid politician. The letter fueled American **jingoism,** or aggressive nationalism. Soon after, the American battleship *Maine* exploded in Havana harbor. The Yellow Press promptly accused Spain of blowing up the battleship. In April 1898, the U.S. Congress declared war on Spain, beginning the Spanish-American War.

In the Spanish-held Philippines, Commodore **George Dewey** quickly destroyed a large part of the Spanish fleet. While Dewey was defeating the Spanish navy, Filipino nationalists led by **Emilio Aguinaldo** were defeating the Spanish army. In August, Spanish troops surrendered to the United States.

Meanwhile, American troops landed in Cuba in June 1898. Although the troops were poorly trained, wore unsuitable uniforms, and carried old, obsolete weapons, they were successful. Spanish forces in Cuba surrendered to the United States. Future President Theodore Roosevelt organized a force known as the **Rough Riders.** Joined by African American soldiers from the Ninth and Tenth Cavalry regiments, the Rough Riders played a key role in the war.

In December 1898, Spain and the United States signed the **Treaty of Paris,** officially ending the Spanish-American War. Spain gave up control of Cuba, Puerto Rico, and the Pacific island of Guam. It also sold the Philippines to the United States. While many were happy with America's expanded role in world affairs, some Americans argued that imperialism was unjust and un-American. The Spanish-American War marked a turning point in the history of American foreign policy.

Review Questions
1. How did some Americans feel about Cuba's war for independence?

_____
_____

2. What territories did Spain give up in the Treaty of Paris?

_____
_____

CHAPTER
18
SECTION 3

Note Taking Study Guide
THE UNITED STATES AND EAST ASIA

Focus Question: How did the United States extend its influence in Asia?

As you read, use the timeline to trace events and developments in East Asia that tested America's new global power.

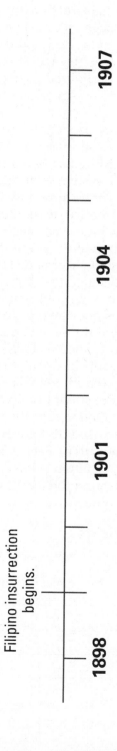

1907

1904

1901

Filipino insurrection
begins.

1898

CHAPTER 18 SECTION 3

Section Summary
THE UNITED STATES AND EAST ASIA

During the Spanish-American War, Filipino nationalist Emilio Aguinaldo viewed America as an ally in the Filipino struggle for independence. However, when the United States kept possession of the Philippines after the war, Aguinaldo grew disillusioned. He helped organize an **insurrection,** or rebellion, against U.S. rule.

The Filipino insurgents relied on **guerrilla warfare** tactics, including surprise raids and hit-and-run attacks. In turn, the U.S. military used extraordinary measures to crush the rebellion. The war in the Philippines highlighted the rigors of fighting against guerrilla insurgents. Nearly 5,000 Americans and 200,000 Filipinos were killed in the fighting.

The United States also wanted to increase trade with China. By 1899, Britain, France, Germany, and Russia had carved China into distinct **spheres of influence,** or zones. Because the United States did not have a zone, this system of privileged access to Chinese markets threatened to limit American trade. U.S. Secretary of State **John Hay** made it clear that America demanded equal trade access.

In May 1900, a Chinese nationalist group launched the **Boxer Rebellion** in objection to the presence of foreigners. As the rebellion engulfed China, Secretary of State Hay reasserted America's **Open Door Policy,** which stated that the United States wanted free trade, not colonies, in China. A multinational force of European, American, and Japanese troops put down the uprising.

In 1905, President Roosevelt negotiated an end to the **Russo-Japanese War.** The President's intervention displayed America's growing role in world affairs. However, in 1906, the segregation of Japanese children in San Francisco schools drew Japan's immediate wrath. President Roosevelt negotiated a **"Gentlemen's Agreement"** with Japan to ease the tension.

While Roosevelt used diplomacy with Japan, he also promoted military preparedness to protect U.S. interests in Asia. In 1907, Roosevelt sent a force of navy ships, known as the **Great White Fleet,** on a cruise around the world to demonstrate America's increased military power.

Review Questions

1. What problem did U.S. forces face in the Philippines?

_____

_____

2. What was the purpose of proclaiming the Open Door Policy?

_____

_____

| CHAPTER **18** SECTION 4 | **Note Taking Study Guide** |
| THE UNITED STATES AND LATIN AMERICA | |

Focus Question: What actions did the United States take to achieve its goals in Latin America?

A. *Complete the table below to note how the United States dealt with Puerto Rico and Cuba.*

American Policy After Spanish-American War	
Puerto Rico	**Cuba**
• Foraker Act establishes civil government in 1900 • •	• • •

CHAPTER 18 SECTION 4

Note Taking Study Guide
THE UNITED STATES AND LATIN AMERICA

Focus Question: What actions did the United States take to achieve its goals in Latin America?

B. *As you read, compare Wilson's moral diplomacy with the foreign policies of Roosevelt and Taft by completing the flowchart below.*

United States Foreign Policy

Roosevelt	Taft	Wilson
•	•	• "Moral diplomacy" •
•	•	•
• Supported rebellion in Panama •		•

CHAPTER 18 SECTION 4 — Section Summary

THE UNITED STATES AND LATIN AMERICA

After the Spanish-American War, the United States assumed control of Puerto Rico and Cuba. In 1900, the U.S. Congress passed the **Foraker Act,** which established a civil government in Puerto Rico. Later, in 1917, Puerto Ricans gained more citizenship rights and greater control over their own legislature.

Before the United States Army withdrew from Cuba in 1902, Congress forced Cuba to add the **Platt Amendment** to its constitution. The amendment restricted the rights of newly independent Cubans, gave the United States the right to intervene in Cuba, and made Cuba a protectorate of the United States.

After assuming the presidency, Theodore Roosevelt promoted **"big stick" diplomacy,** which relied on a strong U.S. military to achieve America's goals. Roosevelt used this forceful approach to intimidate Colombia and gain control over the "Canal Zone" in Panama. America then built the **Panama Canal,** a waterway that connected the Atlantic and Pacific oceans.

In 1904, President Roosevelt announced the **Roosevelt Corollary,** which updated the Monroe Doctrine for an age of economic imperialism. The policy stated that the United States would serve as the policing power in Latin America and would restore order when necessary. Many Latin Americans resented America's role as the hemisphere's police force.

President William Howard Taft shared Roosevelt's basic foreign policy objectives. However, Taft stressed **"dollar diplomacy,"** which aimed to increase American investments throughout Central America and the Caribbean. In 1913, President Woodrow Wilson, who had criticized imperialism, promoted his policy of **"moral diplomacy."** Wilson promised that America would work to promote "human rights, national integrity, and opportunity."

Although he intended to take U.S. policy in a different direction, President Wilson nevertheless used the military on a number of occasions. During the Mexican Revolution, Wilson sent marines to help Venustiano Carranza, a reformer, to assume the presidency. Wilson also sent troops to capture **Francisco "Pancho" Villa,** whose raid into New Mexico left 18 Americans dead. America's triumph over Spain and U.S. actions in Asia and Latin America demonstrated that America had emerged as a global power.

Review Questions

1. What did "big stick" diplomacy rely on?

_____

_____

2. How was Wilson's foreign policy different from Roosevelt's?

_____

_____

_____

READING CHECK

Why might Cubans have resented the Platt Amendment?

_____

_____

_____

VOCABULARY STRATEGY

What does the word *nevertheless* mean in the underlined sentence? Circle the words in the underlined passage that could help you learn what *nevertheless* means.

_____

_____

_____

READING SKILL

Identify Supporting Details
What details support the idea that Wilson did not always follow "moral diplomacy"?

_____

_____

_____

CHAPTER 19 SECTION 1

Note Taking Study Guide

FROM NEUTRALITY TO WAR

Focus Question: What caused World War I, and why did the United States enter the war?

As you read, identify the causes of World War I, the conditions facing soldiers, and the reasons for U.S. involvement.

World War I

Reasons for U.S. involvement
- •
- •
- •
- •

Nature of warfare
- •
- •
- •

Causes of the war
- •
- •
- •
- •
- •

CHAPTER 19 SECTION 1

Section Summary

FROM NEUTRALITY TO WAR

Although there had been no major wars, the 50 years before World War I were not tranquil. Nationalism renewed old grudges among countries. **Militarism,** or glorification of the military, eventually produced an arms race between Germany and Britain at sea and among Germany, France, and Russia on land.

In addition to strengthening their military power, European leaders prepared for war by forming alliances. Germany, Austria-Hungary, and Italy formed the Triple Alliance. Opposing them were France, Russia, and Great Britain, which formed the Triple Entente. In 1914, a Serbian youth assassinated **Francis Ferdinand,** the archduke of Austria-Hungary. <u>War spread as European countries entered the fighting to help their allies.</u> Russia came to the aid of Serbia against Austria. Germany declared war on Russia. France, Russia's ally, declared war on Germany. After Germany declared war on Belgium, Great Britain declared war on Germany. World War I had begun.

Although fighting went on in Eastern Europe, the Middle East, and other parts of the world, the **Western Front** in France became the critical battle front. German soldiers settled onto high ground, dug trenches, and fortified their position. The French and British then dug their own trenches. A stalemate developed and the war dragged on for years. New military technology, including machine guns and poison gas, led to millions of **casualties.**

As the war continued in Europe, President Woodrow Wilson called for Americans to remain impartial. However, the brutal German invasion of Belgium swayed American opinion against Germany. Americans also protested when a German submarine, or **U-boat,** sank the British passenger liner *Lusitania.*

In January 1917, German Foreign Minister Arthur Zimmermann sent a telegram to Mexico proposing an alliance between Germany and Mexico. The **Zimmermann note** was intercepted by the British, who gave it to American authorities. When the telegram was published, Americans were shocked by its contents. Next, Germany announced unrestricted submarine warfare against Britain. On April 6, 1917, the United States Congress declared war on Germany.

Review Questions

1. How did the alliances between European countries lead to war?

_____

_____

2. Why did the United States get involved in the war?

_____

_____

READING CHECK

Who was Francis Ferdinand?

_____

_____

_____

VOCABULARY BUILDER

What does the word *allies* mean in the underlined sentence? What clues can you find in the surrounding words, phrases, or sentences? Circle the words that could help you learn what *allies* means.

_____

_____

_____

READING SKILL

Identify Causes Identify the causes of World War I.

_____

_____

Note Taking Study Guide
THE HOME FRONT

Focus Question: How did the war affect Americans at home?

As you read, summarize the key points made in the section in the chart below.

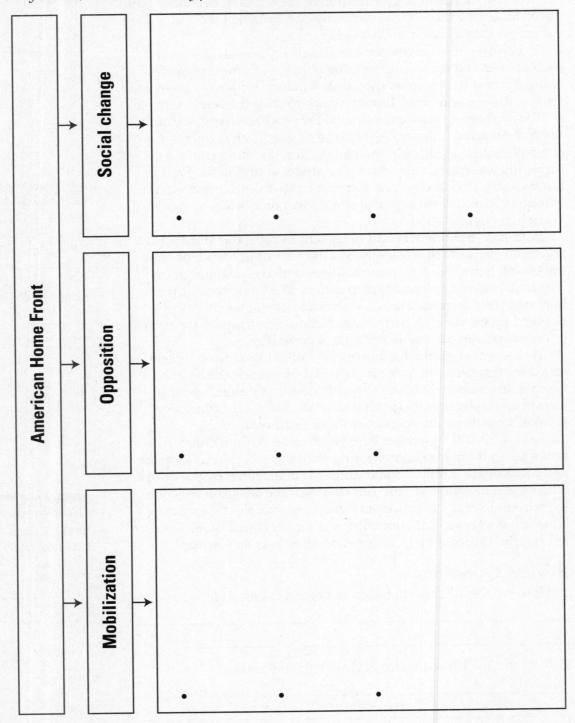

When the United States entered World War I, its army was only a fraction of the size of European armies. To build the army, Congress passed the **Selective Service Act,** which authorized a draft of young men for military service in Europe.

While the Selective Service Commission raised an army, the War Industries Board (WIB), headed by **Bernard Baruch,** regulated all industries engaged in the war effort. <u>The WIB also urged Americans to conserve food as a patriotic gesture.</u> As head of the Food Administration, future U.S. President Herbert Hoover set high prices for food to encourage farmers to increase production.

In 1917, many Americans questioned U.S. involvement in the war. The **Committee on Public Information (CPI)** worked to convince the American public that the war effort was a just cause. **George Creel,** the director of the CPI, combined education and a widespread advertising campaign to "sell America."

Still, not all Americans favored America's entry into the war. German Americans and Irish Americans tended to oppose the Allies. Opposition also came from **conscientious objectors,** people whose moral or religious beliefs forbid them to fight in wars.

During the war, the U.S. government restricted individual rights. In June 1917, Congress passed the **Espionage Act,** which banned subversive newspapers, magazines, or printed materials. Congress further limited freedom of speech with the Sedition Act. In *Schenck* v. *United States* (1919), the Supreme Court ruled that there are times when the First Amendment protections on speech do not apply.

The war also brought substantial social changes. It created jobs for women while men were serving in the military and ushered in the Nineteenth Amendment, which gave women the right to vote. Meanwhile, a great movement of African Americans from the rural South to the industrial North was taking place. The **Great Migration** saw more than 1.2 million African Americans move to the North to escape racism and find better jobs. Many Mexicans also sought to improve their lives. Some crossed the border into the United States, where they looked for jobs. World War I had opened up new opportunities for women, African Americans, and Mexican Americans.

Review Questions

1. What was the purpose of the Committee on Public Information (CPI)?

_____

_____

2. Why did conscientious objectors oppose the war?

_____

_____

READING CHECK

Why did many African Americans move to the North during the Great Migration?

_____

_____

_____

VOCABULARY BUILDER

What does the word *conserve* mean in the underlined sentence? An antonym for *conserve* is *squander*. Use the antonym to help you figure out the meaning of *conserve*.

_____

_____

_____

READING SKILL

Summarize Summarize how the American government mobilized the public to support the war effort.

_____

_____

_____

CHAPTER 19 SECTION 3
Note Taking Study Guide
WILSON, WAR, AND PEACE

Focus Question: How did Americans affect the end of World War I and its peace settlements?

A. *As you read, sequence the events leading to the end of World War I in the timeline below.*

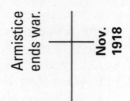

Armistice ends war.

Nov. 1918

U-boat war intensifies.

March 1917

Focus Question: How did Americans affect the end of World War I and its peace settlements?

B. *As you read, summarize Wilson's goals for peace and whether or not each goal was fulfilled.*

Wilson's Ideas for Peace	Decision Made at Paris Peace Conference
Peace without victory	Great Britain and France make Germany pay reparations.
Open diplomacy	
Freedom of seas and free trade	
Move toward ending colonialism	
Self-determination	
League of Nations	

Section Summary
WILSON, WAR, AND PEACE

READING CHECK

Why did the "irreconcilables" oppose the treaty to end World War I?

_____

_____

_____

When the United States entered World War I in 1917, the conflict had become a deadly stalemate. Hoping to end the conflict before the Americans could make a difference, Germany renewed unrestricted submarine warfare. <u>British and American **convoys** provided mutual safety by sending warships to protect the merchant ships.</u> As a result, shipping losses from U-boat attacks fell sharply.

In November 1917, radical communists led by **Vladimir Lenin** gained control of Russia. Fighting stopped between Russia and Germany, which allowed Germany to launch an all-out offensive on the Western Front. American troops under the command of **John J. Pershing** helped stop the German offensive and launch successful counteroffensives. On November 11, 1918, Germany surrendered, officially ending World War I.

In what became known as the **Fourteen Points,** President Woodrow Wilson promoted openness, encouraged independence, and supported freedom. Wilson also advocated **self-determination,** or the right of people to choose their own form of government. Finally, he asked for a **League of Nations,** a world organization where countries could gather and peacefully resolve their quarrels.

VOCABULARY BUILDER

What does the word *mutual* mean in the underlined sentence? What clues can you find in the surrounding words, phrases, or sentences?

_____

_____

_____

In 1919, the victorious Allies held a peace conference in France. Although Wilson's hope for the League of Nations was fulfilled, the various peace treaties created almost as many problems as they solved. The other Allied leaders insisted that Germany make **reparations,** or payment for war damages. When the map of Europe was redrawn, national self-determination was violated many times.

In the United States, many people opposed the treaty. A handful of senators known as the **"irreconcilables"** believed that the United States should not get entangled in world organizations such as the League of Nations. A larger group of senators, led by **Henry Cabot Lodge** and known as the **"reservationists,"** was opposed to the treaty as it was written. Wilson and his opponents refused to put aside their differences and compromise, and the Senate did not ratify the treaty. Without full American support, the League of Nations proved unable to maintain peace among nations.

READING SKILL

Sequence Sequence the events that led the U.S. Senate to not ratify the treaty ending World War I.

_____

_____

_____

Review Questions

1. Describe the aims of the Fourteen Points.

_____

_____

2. How did convoys contribute to the success of the Allies?

_____

_____

Name _____ Class _____ Date _____

Focus Question: What political, economic, and social effects did World War I have on the United States?

As you read, identify and record the main ideas of this section in the concept web below.

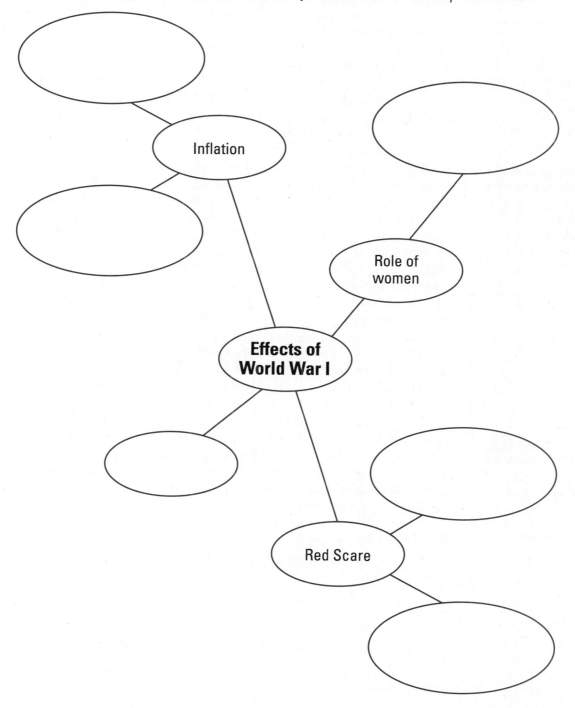

CHAPTER **19** SECTION 4	**Section Summary**
	EFFECTS OF THE WAR

World War I produced significant economic, social, political, and cultural changes in America. An **influenza** virus that killed millions worldwide made the movement from war to peace even more difficult. The flu pandemic created a sense of doom and dread.

The end of the war spelled the end of wartime economic opportunities for women and African Americans. Adding to this crisis atmosphere were normal postwar adjustments. Falling agricultural prices made it difficult for farmers to pay their debts. **Inflation,** or rising prices, meant industrial workers' wages did not buy as much as they had bought during the war. All around the country, workers struck for higher wages and shorter workdays. They won some of the strikes, but they lost far more.

The violence of some strikes was often attributed to the presence of radicals among the strike leaders. The emergence of the Soviet Union as a communist nation compounded the fear of radicals and communists. Communist ideology called for an international workers' revolution, and communist revolts in Central and Eastern Europe made it seem like the worldwide revolution was starting.

Widespread fear of suspected communists and radicals thought to be plotting revolution within the United States prompted the first American **Red Scare.** In early 1920, Attorney General A. Mitchell Palmer mounted a series of raids, known as the **Palmer Raids.** Police arrested thousands of people, some who were radicals and some who were simply immigrants from southern or Eastern Europe. To many, these actions seemed to attack the liberties that Americans held most dear. By the summer of 1920, the Red Scare hysteria had run its course. **Warren G. Harding** campaigned for President calling for a return to "normalcy." Harding won in a landslide.

By 1920, the United States was the richest, most industrialized country in the world. The United States was also the largest **creditor nation** in the world, meaning that other countries owed the United States more money than the United States owed them. As a result of World War I, America's economic and political standing in the world had fundamentally changed.

Review Questions

1. Describe the problems Americans faced immediately after the war.

_____

_____

2. How did the war change America's role in world affairs?

_____

_____

CHAPTER **20** SECTION 1	**Note Taking Study Guide**
	A BOOMING ECONOMY

Focus Question: How did the booming economy of the 1920s lead to changes in American life?

As you read, note specific examples that support the idea that the economy changed during the 1920s.

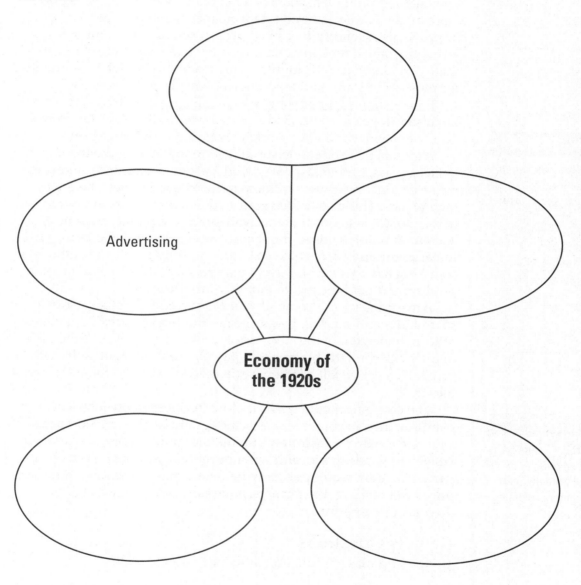

CHAPTER 20 SECTION 1

Section Summary
A BOOMING ECONOMY

During the 1920s, revolutionary **mass-production** techniques enabled American workers to produce more goods in less time. Because of this, the economy boomed. The automobile industry played a major role in the boom. Carmaker **Henry Ford** introduced new methods and ideas that changed the way manufactured goods were made. Ford also hired **scientific management** experts to improve his **assembly-line** mass production of automobiles. In two years, the time it took to build an automobile dropped from more than 12 hours to just 90 minutes. This made the **Model T** affordable for most Americans, and automobile ownership skyrocketed.

Ford also used innovation in managing his employees. In 1914, he raised wages from $2.35 to $5 a day. He cut the workday from 9 hours to 8 hours and gave workers Saturday and Sunday off.

Automobile production stimulated many other industries, such as steel, glass, rubber, asphalt, wood, gasoline, insurance, and road construction. The growth of these industries led to new, better-paying jobs. This also helped spur national prosperity. A flood of new, affordable goods became available to the public, creating a **consumer revolution.** At the same time, a new kind of credit called **installment buying** enabled consumers to buy goods they otherwise could not have afforded. Buyers made a small down payment on a product and paid the rest in monthly installments.

Americans were also buying stock on credit. As stock prices soared in a **bull market,** people began **buying on margin,** paying as little as 10 percent of the stock price upfront to a broker. If the price of the stock rose, the buyer could pay off the broker and still made a profit. If the price fell, the buyer still owed the broker the full price of the stock.

The economic boom was felt more in cities, where jobs were plentiful, than in rural areas. As cities grew, people moved out to suburbs and drove their new automobiles into the city to work. However, America's wealth was unevenly distributed. Farmers, in particular, suffered under growing debt, while at the same time crop prices were falling. For farmers, and many others, it was not a decade of prosperity.

Review Questions

1. How did mass production influence the economy?

_____

_____

2. What was installment buying?

_____

_____

Name _____ Class _____ Date _____

Focus Question: How did domestic and foreign policy change direction under Harding and Coolidge?

As you read, note similarities and differences between the characters and policies of Presidents Harding and Coolidge.

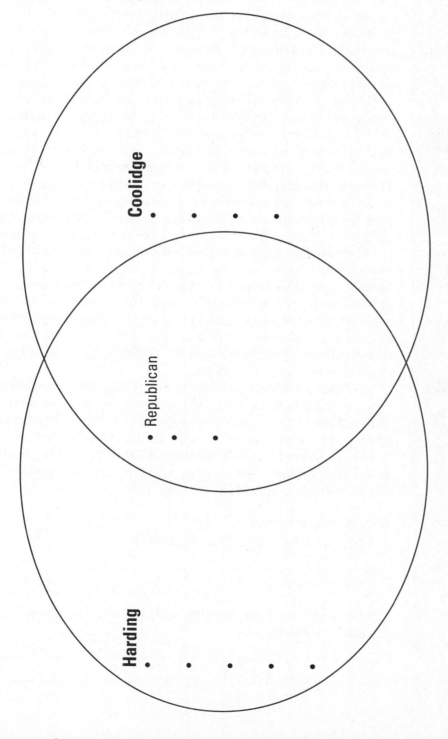

Section Summary
THE BUSINESS OF GOVERNMENT

What was the purpose of the Kellogg-Briand Pact?

_____

_____

_____

Find the word *incentives* in the underlined sentence. Money, rewards, and praise are sometimes used as incentives. What is the meaning of *incentives*?

_____

_____

_____

Compare and Contrast Look at the diagram comparing similarities and differences between Presidents Harding and Coolidge. How did their differences influence their presidencies?

_____

_____

_____

In 1920, fun-loving Warren G. Harding was elected President. Preferring a laissez-faire approach to business, Harding named banker **Andrew Mellon** as Secretary of the Treasury. Together they worked to reduce regulations on businesses and to raise protective tariff rates. This made it easier for U.S. producers to sell goods at home. In response, Europeans also raised tariffs, making U.S. products more expensive there. Laws had been previously passed to break up monopolies and protect workers, but Harding favored less restriction on businesses. His Secretary of Commerce, **Herbert Hoover,** asked business leaders to voluntarily make advancements.

Harding admitted that he preferred playing golf or poker to governing. He trusted his friends with important government positions. One friend, Charles Forbes, wasted millions of dollars while running the Veterans' Bureau. Another, Secretary of the Interior Albert Fall, created the biggest scandal of Harding's administration. In the **Teapot Dome scandal,** Fall took bribes to transfer control of oil reserves from the United States Navy to private oilmen. Fall was later forced to return the oil and sentenced to a year in jail. Harding died in 1923, before the full extent of the scandal came to light.

The new President, **Calvin Coolidge,** was quiet and honest. He put his administration in the hands of men who held to the simple virtues of an older generation. Like Harding, he mistrusted the use of legislation to achieve social change. He favored big business. He reduced the national debt and lowered taxes to give incentives to businesses. However, Coolidge said and did nothing about the country's many problems, such as low prices for farm crops, racial discrimination, and low wages.

In foreign policy, Coolidge pushed European governments to repay war debts to the United States. In 1924, an agreement known as the **Dawes Plan** was arranged to help Germany, France, and Great Britain repay those debts. In 1928, exhausted by World War I, 62 nations signed the **Kellogg-Briand Pact,** a treaty that outlawed war. Unfortunately, there was no way for nations to enforce the treaty, and it was quickly forgotten.

Review Questions

1. What was the Teapot Dome scandal?

_____

_____

2. How did Presidents Harding and Coolidge feel about laws that restricted businesses?

_____

_____

_____

Note Taking Study Guide
SOCIAL AND CULTURAL TENSIONS

Focus Question: How did Americans differ on major social and cultural issues?

As you read, look for issues that divided Americans in the 1920s.

Differing Viewpoints	
Education	• Viewpoint 1: • Viewpoint 2:
Evolution	• Viewpoint 1: • Viewpoint 2:
	• Viewpoint 1: • Viewpoint 2:
	• Viewpoint 1: • Viewpoint 2:
	• Viewpoint 1: • Viewpoint 2:

Name _____ Class _____ Date _____

READING CHECK

What did the Eighteenth Amendment forbid?

_____

_____

_____

VOCABULARY STRATEGY

What does the word *imperial* mean in the underlined sentence? Look for context clues in the surrounding words and phrases. Circle any words or phrases in the paragraph that help you figure out what *imperial* means.

_____

_____

_____

READING SKILL

Contrast Select an issue that divided Americans. Contrast the ways rural and urban Americans felt about this issue.

_____

_____

_____

As the 1920s began, striking differences arose between urban and rural America. Urban Americans enjoyed a rising standard of living and embraced a modern view of the world. City dwellers tended to value education and to be advocates of science and social change.

By contrast, in rural America times were hard. Formal education was considered less important than keeping the farm going. People tended to be conservative about political and social issues, preferring to keep things the way they were. Many rural Americans believed that the Bible was literally true. This belief was called **fundamentalism.** It opposed modernism, which stressed science.

The two beliefs clashed head-on in the 1925 **Scopes Trial.** That year, Tennessee passed a law making it illegal to teach the theory of evolution in the state's public schools. The most celebrated defense attorney in the country, **Clarence Darrow,** defended John Scopes for teaching this scientific theory to his high school class. Scopes was found guilty of breaking the law and fined $100.

A wave of immigration inspired nativist politicians to pass laws forcing immigrants to pass a literacy test, and to create a **quota system.** The quota system set limits on the number of new immigrants allowed into the United States. Although many Americans appreciated the nation's growing diversity, many did not. In 1915, the **Ku Klux Klan** was reorganized in Georgia. This violent group, whose leaders had titles such as Grand Dragon and Imperial Wizard, promoted hatred of African Americans, Jews, Catholics, and immigrants.

Another divisive issue of the 1920s was **Prohibition.** In 1919 the states ratified the **Eighteenth Amendment** to the Constitution, which forbade the manufacture, distribution, and sale (but not consumption) of alcohol. Congress then passed the **Volstead Act** to enforce the amendment. Police often turned a blind eye to illegal drinking establishments, which left room for **bootleggers** to not only sell alcohol but also to expand into other illegal activities, such as prostitution, drugs, robbery, and murder. Thus, Prohibition unintentionally led to the growth of organized crime.

Review Questions

1. What were some of the issues and beliefs that rural and urban America clashed over in the 1920s?

_____

_____

2. How did nativists feel about immigration?

_____

_____

CHAPTER
20
SECTION 4

Note Taking Study Guide
A NEW MASS CULTURE

Focus Question: How did the new mass culture reflect technological and social changes?

A. *As you read, look for examples of the ways in which American culture changed during the 1920s.*

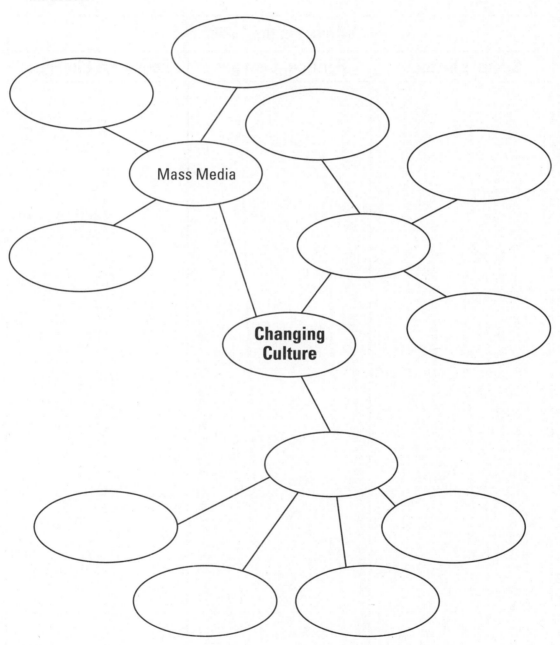

Note Taking Study Guide

A NEW MASS CULTURE

Focus Question: How did the new mass culture reflect technological and social changes?

B. *As you read, classify the various types of changes that took place in women's lives in the 1920s.*

Women in the 1920s		
Social Changes	**Political Changes**	**Economic Changes**
•	•	•
•	•	•
•		
•		

Section Summary
A NEW MASS CULTURE

As urban Americans' wages rose in the 1920s, workers also enjoyed shorter workweeks. For the first time, a large city-dwelling population had free time and money to spend on entertainment. One of the most popular forms of entertainment was movies, which were attended by 60 to 100 million Americans each week. Actors such as comedian **Charlie Chaplin,** heartthrob Rudolf Valentino, and cowboy William S. Hart became silent film stars. Then in 1927, the movie *The Jazz Singer* startled audiences when Al Jolson said, "You ain't seen nothin' yet." *The Jazz Singer* became the first movie to include sound matched to the action on the screen, and the era of "talkies" was born.

For entertainment at home, Americans bought millions of phonographs and radios. By 1923, almost 600 licensed radio stations broadcast to more than 600,000 radio sets. Americans across the continent listened to the same songs, learned the same dances, and shared a popular culture as never before. People admired the same heroes, such as baseball player **Babe Ruth,** the home-run king, and aviator **Charles Lindbergh,** who was the first to fly solo and non-stop across the Atlantic Ocean.

American women challenged political, economic, social, and educational boundaries. With passage of the Nineteenth Amendment, they won the right to vote. Many ran for political office and more joined the workforce. Some women, known as **flappers,** shocked society by wearing short skirts and bobbed hair. At home, new electric appliances made housework easier. Popular magazines, sociological studies, novels, and movies all featured the "New Woman" of the 1920s prominently.

A spirit of modernism grew, especially in cities. Austrian psychologist **Sigmund Freud** contributed to modernism with his theory that human behavior is driven by unconscious desires rather than by rational thought. Painters rejected artistic norms. Writers, including **F. Scott Fitzgerald** and **Ernest Hemingway,** wrote about the meaning of life and war. Their literary masterpieces examined subconscious desires and the dark side of the American dream.

Review Questions

1. What technological advances led to cultural change during the 1920s?

_____

_____

2. What changes in the 1920s allowed urban Americans to enjoy more entertainment?

_____

_____

READING CHECK

Who developed a theory about behavior and the unconscious?

_____

_____

_____

VOCABULARY STRATEGY

What does the word *sociological* mean in the underlined sentence? The term *socio* means "relating to society." The term *–ology* usually refers to a type of study. Use these definitions to help you figure out the meaning of *sociological.*

_____

_____

_____

READING SKILL

Summarize List three ways American culture changed in the 1920s.

_____

_____

_____

Note Taking Study Guide
THE HARLEM RENAISSANCE

Focus Question: How did African Americans express a new sense of hope and pride?

As you read, identify the main ideas.

I. New "Black Consciousness"

    A. New Chances, New Challenges

        1. Migration to North continues

        2. _____

        3. _____

    B. _____

        1. _____

        2. _____

        3. _____

II. _____

    A. _____

        1. _____

        2. _____

    B. _____

        1. _____

III. _____

    A. _____

        1. _____

    B. _____

        1. _____

Name _____ Class _____ Date _____

CHAPTER 20 SECTION 5	Section Summary
	THE HARLEM RENAISSANCE

Millions of African Americans left the South after World War I to find freedom and economic opportunity in the North. In the South, they faced low-paying jobs, substandard schools, Jim Crow oppression, and the threat of lynching. However, they found well-paying jobs, a middle class of African American professionals, and a growing political voice in cities such as New York, Chicago, and Detroit.

Harlem in New York City became a haven for about 200,000 African Americans from the South as well as black immigrants from the Caribbean. One immigrant was **Marcus Garvey,** a Jamaican who had traveled widely. After seeing that blacks were treated poorly, Garvey organized a "Back to Africa" movement that urged black unity and separation of the races.

It was F. Scott Fitzgerald who called the 1920s the "Jazz Age." However, it was African Americans who gave the age its **jazz.** A truly indigenous American musical form, jazz emerged in the South as a combination of African American and European musical styles. African Americans migrating north brought the new musical style with them. Musicians such as trumpet player **Louis Armstrong** took jazz to the world. Singer **Bessie Smith,** nicknamed the "Empress of the Blues," was so popular she became the highest-paid African American entertainer of the 1920s.

The decade also saw the **Harlem Renaissance,** an outpouring of art and literature that explored the African American experience. Among its most famous writers was **Claude McKay,** whose novels and poems were militant calls for action. **Langston Hughes** celebrated African American culture, and **Zora Neale Hurston** wrote about women's desire for independence.

The Great Depression ended the Harlem Renaissance. However, the pride and unity it created provided a foundation for the future civil rights movement.

Review Questions

1. Why did many African Americans migrate north?

_____

_____

2. What was the "Back to Africa" movement?

_____

_____

READING CHECK

What did F. Scott Fitzgerald name the 1920s?

_____

_____

_____

VOCABULARY STRATEGY

Find the word *indigenous* in the underlined sentence. What do you think it means? Circle words, phrases, or sentences in the surrounding paragraph to help you define *indigenous.*

_____

_____

_____

READING SKILL

Identify Main Ideas What was the Harlem Renaissance?

_____

_____

Name _____ Class _____ Date _____

Focus Question: How did the prosperity of the 1920s give way to the Great Depression?

A. *Identify the causes of the Great Depression.*

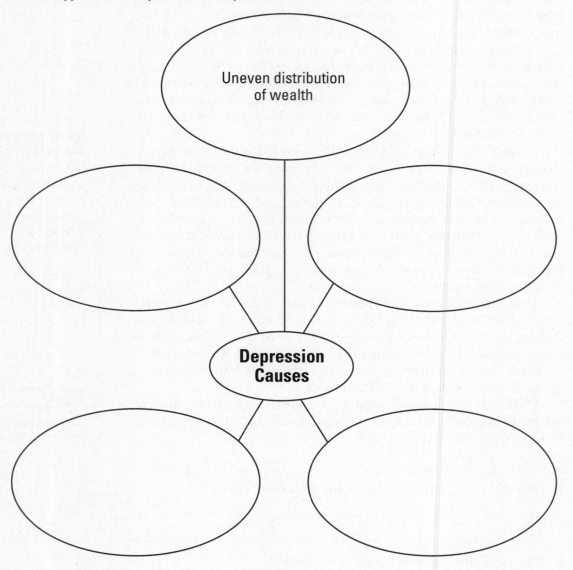

CHAPTER
21
SECTION 1

Note Taking Study Guide
CAUSES OF THE DEPRESSION

Focus Question: How did the prosperity of the 1920s give way to the Great Depression?

B. *Use a flowchart to note what happened in the wake of the stock market crash.*

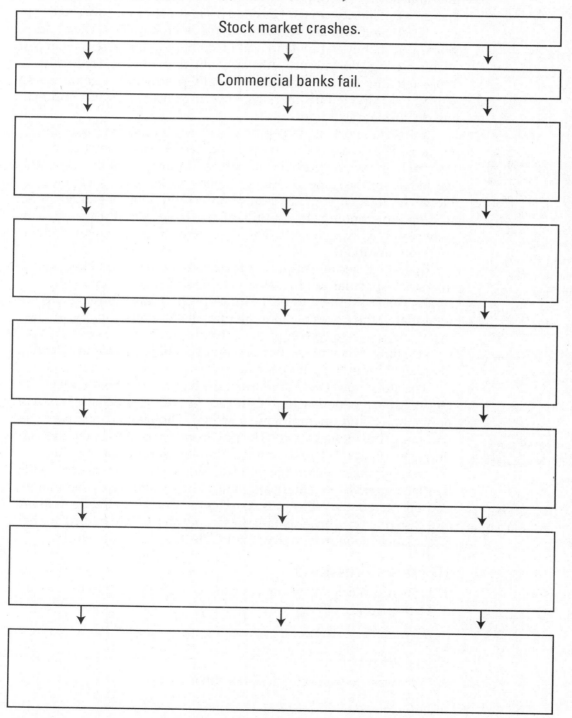

Stock market crashes.

Commercial banks fail.

CHAPTER 21 SECTION 1

Section Summary
CAUSES OF THE DEPRESSION

READING CHECK

In 1928, how did Americans show their approval for the way Republicans handled the economy?

_____

_____

_____

The Roaring Twenties were a Republican decade. Beginning in 1920, Republican Presidents led the nation and took credit for the good economic times. In 1928, the country continued to support the Republicans by electing **Herbert Hoover** President. However, the nation's prosperity was not as deep or as sturdy as it appeared.

American farmers faced difficult times in the 1920s. They had borrowed money to buy land and machinery to increase the harvest yields during World War I. Although the demand for American crops fell after the war, farmers were still producing large harvests. Cheap food flooded the markets, lowering farmers' profits and making debt repayment hard.

Industrial workers, whose wages rose steadily, did better than farmers. The owners of companies did even better. They became very rich. In fact, in 1929, the wealthiest 0.1 percent of the population earned about the same amount of money as the bottom 42 percent. However, the people with great wealth could not buy enough goods to keep the economy strong. Still, many workers took advantage of easy credit to buy products. This disguised the problem and helped the economy to grow.

By 1929, it became clear that too much money was being poured into stock **speculation.** Investors often borrowed money to buy stocks, then sold them to turn a quick profit. Frantic buying and selling inflated the prices of stocks to unrealistic levels. <u>Finally, all the problems began to converge.</u> A sharp drop in stock prices led to panicked selling. Stock prices bottomed out on **Black Tuesday,** October 29, 1929, wiping out whole fortunes in hours.

The stock market crash marked the beginning of the **Great Depression,** a period lasting from 1929 to 1941 in which the U.S. economy faltered and unemployment soared. Thousands of banks closed and many businesses failed. The government tried to boost the sale of American goods by passing the **Hawley-Smoot Tariff,** which placed high taxes on foreign goods. Foreign governments responded by placing tariffs on American goods. The result was closed markets and unsold goods, which destroyed international trade. Economists still disagree on what was the most important factor leading to the Great Depression, which eventually affected the whole world.

VOCABULARY STRATEGY

What does the word *converge* mean in the underlined sentence? What context clues can you find in the surrounding words or phrases? Circle any words or phrases in the paragraph that help you figure out what *converge* means.

_____

_____

_____

READING SKILL

Recognize Causes Look over the concept web. Select a cause of the Great Depression. Explain how it contributed to the depression.

_____

_____

Review Questions

1. How did World War I affect farmers and help lead to the Great Depression?

_____

_____

2. Why was stock speculation a problem?

_____

_____

CHAPTER
21
SECTION 2

Note Taking Study Guide

AMERICANS FACE HARD TIMES

Focus Question: How did the Great Depression affect the lives of urban and rural Americans?

As you read, use the Venn diagram below to note how the depression affected both urban and rural America.

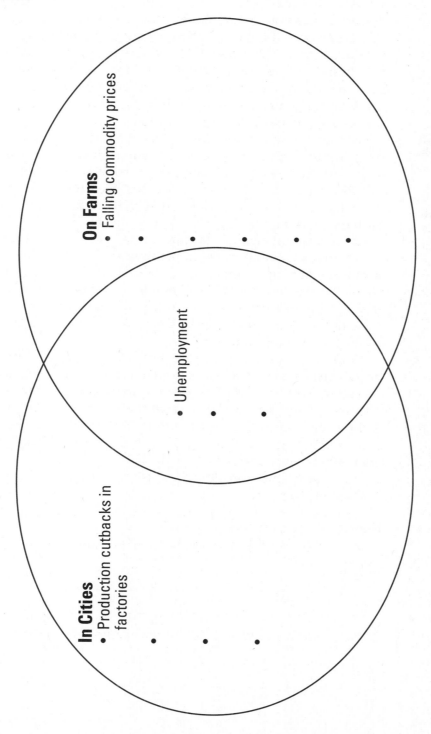

On Farms
• Falling commodity prices

Unemployment

In Cities
• Production cutbacks in factories

CHAPTER 21 SECTION 2

Section Summary
AMERICANS FACE HARD TIMES

READING CHECK

In what part of the country did the Dust Bowl occur?

_____

_____

_____

VOCABULARY STRATEGY

What does *drastic* mean in the underlined sentence? Read the underlined sentence aloud, but leave out the word *drastic*. What word could you use in its place? Use this strategy to help you figure out the meaning of *drastic*.

_____

_____

_____

READING SKILL

Categorize Which of the following were present in both urban and rural America? Circle your answer.

• Hoovervilles

• Unemployment

• Farm foreclosures

The Great Depression deeply affected Americans. Some lost everything they had while others struggled simply to survive. In the cities, Americans faced rampant unemployment. Between 1921 and 1929, annual average unemployment rates never rose above 3.7 percent. By 1933, almost 25 percent of workers were without jobs. As unemployed families ran out of money, their hardship deepened. Drastic necessity forced them to sell their belongings. Sometimes a family's only food came from a **bread line,** where people lined up for handouts from charities or public agencies. Many people were evicted from their homes. With no place else to go, they sometimes grouped together in **Hoovervilles**—makeshift shantytowns of tents and shacks built on public land or vacant lots.

Conditions were bad in rural America, too. Before the depression, farmers had already been struggling. During the depression, their problems worsened. Crop prices dropped lower. Between 1930 and 1934, nearly one million farmers lost their homes for failure to pay their mortgages. Some farmers stayed on the land as **tenant farmers,** working for bigger landowners rather than for themselves. A severe drought and overfarming on the Great Plains turned the soil to dust, making farming impossible and creating huge dust storms. High plains regions in Texas, Oklahoma, Kansas, New Mexico, and Colorado became known as the **Dust Bowl.** Many farmers left the area and moved to California to look for work. Because some of these people were from Oklahoma, Dust Bowl refugees became known as **Okies.**

Minorities were hit the hardest by the depression. African American sharecroppers were thrown off the land they had farmed and migrated north. In 1932, unemployment among African Americans was nearly double the national rate. In the Southwest, many white Americans urged **repatriation** of Mexican Americans. Repatriation involved government efforts to send Mexican immigrants and their American children back to Mexico.

For many Americans, the depression was a time of great hopelessness and despair.

Review Questions

1. What were some of the problems that farmers faced during the depression?

_____

_____

2. What was repatriation, and who was most affected by it?

_____

_____

Focus Question: Why did Herbert Hoover's policies fail to solve the country's economic crisis?

As you read, fill in the outline with details about President Hoover's response to the depression.

Hoover's Response to the Depression

I. Cautious Response Fails

    A. Hoover Tries Volunteerism

        1. Calls on business leaders to maintain employment, wages, prices

        2. _____

        3. _____

    B. Volunteerism Fails

        1. _____

        2. _____

II. More Activist Policies

    A. _____

        1. _____

        2. _____

    B. _____

        1. _____

        2. _____

        3. _____

        4. _____

    C. _____

        1. _____

        2. _____

        3. _____

Section Summary
HOOVER'S RESPONSE FAILS

Who led army troops against protesters in Washington, D.C., during the summer of 1932?

_____

_____

_____

VOCABULARY STRATEGY

What does the word *simultaneously* mean in the underlined sentence? Look for clues in the surrounding words, phrases, and sentences. Circle the phrase below that has the same meaning as *simultaneously*.

• done at the same time
• done one after the other

READING SKILL

Identify Supporting Details List the details that support the conclusion that Hoover's policy of volunteerism failed.

_____

_____

_____

From big cities to small towns, the Great Depression spread misery across America. As the crisis deepened, Herbert Hoover struggled to respond to the nation's problems.

At first, Hoover felt that government should not interfere with what he thought was the natural downswing of the business cycle. Soon, however, Hoover tried a different approach, called volunteerism. Hoover asked business leaders not to cut prices and wages. He called for the government to simultaneously reduce taxes, lower interest rates, and create public-works programs. He also asked the wealthy to give to the poor through charities. Finally, Hoover called for a policy of **localism.** This policy asked state and local governments to provide more jobs and relief measures. However, businesses cut wages and laid off workers, towns and states did not have the resources to respond to the crisis, and charities ran low on money. The crisis demanded federal action.

Next, the President decided to adopt a policy of **trickle-down economics.** The idea was that the government would provide loans to bankers so they in turn could lend money to businesses. Businesses would then hire workers, leading to increased production and consumption, and the end of the depression. At Hoover's urging, Congress created the **Reconstruction Finance Corporation (RFC)** to provide loans to businesses. However, businesses that did receive loans did not always use them to hire workers. Hoover did have one success in the building of **Hoover Dam.** Construction of the dam on the Colorado River brought much-needed employment to the Southwest in the early 1930s.

Americans became increasingly unhappy with Hoover's handling of the depression. A group of almost twenty thousand unemployed World War I veterans known as the **Bonus Army** marched in protest and set up camps in Washington, D.C. They wanted early payment of a bonus promised them. Congress agreed, but Hoover vetoed the plan. When riots broke out in July 1932, Hoover called in the military. General **Douglas MacArthur** led army troops against the veterans. Many of the veterans were hurt, a situation that angered many Americans. Hoover had little hope of reelection.

Review Questions
1. What was President Hoover's first response to the depression?

_____

_____

2. What was the Bonus Army?

_____

_____

CHAPTER 22 SECTION 1

Note Taking Study Guide
FDR OFFERS RELIEF AND RECOVERY

Focus Question: How did the New Deal attempt to address the problems of the depression?

Fill in the chart below with the problems that FDR faced and the steps he took to overcome them.

FDR Tackles Tough Problems	
Problem	**FDR's Policy**
Failing banks	•
	•
	• •
	•
	• • • •

Section Summary
FDR OFFERS RELIEF AND RECOVERY

In November 1932, **Franklin D. Roosevelt** won the presidency by more than 7 million votes. FDR had lost the use of his legs to polio in 1921. Because of his disability, he relied heavily on his wife, **Eleanor Roosevelt.** She served as his "eyes and ears" during his presidency.

In his first hundred days in office, FDR proposed and Congress passed 15 bills known as the First **New Deal.** These measures had three goals: relief, recovery, and reform. "Relief" referred to improving the immediate hardships of the depression; "recovery" was aimed at achieving a long-term economic recovery; and "reforms" were designed to prevent future depressions. One immediate relief effort involved the government paying farmers subsidies to reduce production, a move that would help raise farm prices.

Other relief efforts included establishment of the **Tennessee Valley Authority (TVA)** to build dams in the Tennessee River valley to control floods and generate electric power, and the creation of the **Civilian Conservation Corps (CCC).** The CCC provided jobs for more than 2 million young men. They replanted forests, built trails, dug irrigation ditches, and fought fires. Recovery efforts included the **National Recovery Administration (NRA)** and the **Public Works Administration (PWA).** The NRA developed industry codes that set minimum wages for workers and minimum prices for goods. The PWA created millions of new jobs constructing bridges, dams, power plants, and government buildings. Additionally, FDR sought to reform the nation's financial institutions. The **Federal Deposit Insurance Corporation (FDIC)** insured bank deposits, and the Securities Exchange Commission (SEC) regulated the stock market.

Some Americans thought the New Deal made the government too powerful. Others thought that the New Deal did not provide enough help to citizens. The strongest criticism from this second group came from individuals with roots in the Populist movement. Father **Charles Coughlin** was a Roman Catholic priest who aired increasingly angry views on a weekly radio show. Roman Catholic officials eventually forced Coughlin to stop his broadcasts. Senator **Huey Long** of Louisiana proposed placing high taxes on wealthy Americans so that their income could be redistributed to the poor.

Review Questions

1. What were the three main goals of the New Deal?

_____

_____

2. How did critics respond to FDR's New Deal policies?

_____

_____

CHAPTER
22
SECTION 2

Note Taking Study Guide
THE SECOND NEW DEAL

Focus Question: What major issues did the second New Deal address?

Complete the table below to record problems and the second New Deal's solutions.

The Second New Deal	
Problem	**Solution**
Unemployment	

CHAPTER 22 SECTION 2

Section Summary

THE SECOND NEW DEAL

READING CHECK

What were the immediate and long-term results of the sit-down strike against General Motors?

_____

_____

_____

VOCABULARY STRATEGY

What does the word *upsurge* in the underlined sentence mean? Look for clues in the surrounding words, phrases, and sentences. Circle the word below that is a synonym for *upsurge.*

• gain

• loss

READING SKILL

Connect Ideas How did the policies of the second New Deal improve the standard of living of Americans?

_____

_____

_____

President Franklin D. Roosevelt's goals for the first New Deal were relief, recovery, and reform. He used legislation passed by the **second New Deal** to accomplish the goals of promoting the general welfare and protecting citizens' rights.

In the spring of 1935, Congress created the **Works Progress Administration (WPA)** to provide new jobs doing public works. The WPA even provided programs to employ displaced artists. The government paid for WPA programs by spending money it didn't have. British economist **John Maynard Keynes** argued that such deficit spending was needed to end the depression.

The **Social Security Act** created a pension system for retirees, as well as unemployment insurance for workers who lost their jobs and aid for the disabled. New programs aided farmers. The Rural Electrification Administration (REA) helped bring electricity to farms. New laws also aided industrial workers. The **Wagner Act** gave workers the right to **collective bargaining.** This meant that employers had to negotiate with unions about hours, wages, and other working conditions. The **Fair Labor Standards Act** of 1938 established a minimum wage and a maximum number of hours for the workweek. It also outlawed child labor.

During the Great Depression, there was an upsurge in union activity. The **Congress of Industrial Organizations (CIO)** was established to organize workers in major industries. In 1936, CIO members staged a **sit-down strike** against General Motors, refusing to leave the workplace until a settlement had been reached. Their success led to other strikes, which improved wages and working conditions for union members.

FDR faced challenges from the Supreme Court, which struck down a number of the key laws of the New Deal. To dilute the power of the sitting Justices, FDR asked Congress to add six new Justices to the nine-member court, a plan that became known as **court packing.** After 1937, the Supreme Court became more willing to accept New Deal legislation. After a new economic downturn in 1938, FDR chose not to try to force more reforms through Congress.

Review Questions

1. Describe one New Deal program that promoted the general welfare.

_____

_____

2. Explain how New Deal legislation promoted the well-being of workers.

_____

_____

_____

Focus Question: How did the New Deal change the social, economic, and political landscape of the United States for future generations?

As you read, identify the lasting effects of the New Deal upon American society.

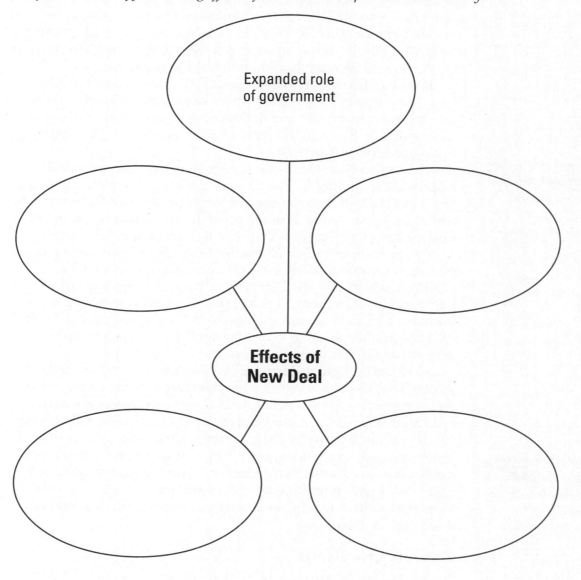

CHAPTER 22 SECTION 3

Section Summary
EFFECTS OF THE NEW DEAL

READING CHECK

How did the New Deal lead to the rise of a welfare state?

_____

_____

_____

VOCABULARY STRATEGY

What does the word *gender* mean in the underlined sentence? The paragraph it appears in discusses the role of women in the New Deal. Use the subject of the paragraph to help you figure out the meaning of *gender*.

_____

_____

_____

READING SKILL

Identify Main Ideas How did the New Deal benefit different groups in American society?

_____

_____

_____

The New Deal brought fundamental changes to the nation. Some women were provided with the opportunity to increase their political influence. Eleanor Roosevelt transformed the office of First Lady to a politically active position. She traveled extensively and advocated equal justice for all. The first female Cabinet member was Secretary of Labor Frances Perkins, who played a leading role in establishing Social Security and a minimum wage. Despite this, the New Deal did not fight to end gender discrimination in the workplace.

President Roosevelt invited African American leaders to advise him. These unofficial advisers became known as the **Black Cabinet.** One member, **Mary McLeod Bethune,** was a powerful champion of racial equality. Even so, racial discrimination and injustice continued to plague African Americans.

The **Indian New Deal** was a program to help American Indians by providing funding for the construction of new schools and hospitals. In 1934, the Indian Reorganization Act restored tribal control of American Indian lands. The Bureau of Indian Affairs also stopped discouraging the practice of traditional American Indian customs.

By his death in 1945, FDR had united a culturally diverse group of Americans into a strong political force called the **New Deal coalition,** which gave the Democratic Party a sizable majority in both houses of Congress. FDR and the New Deal also helped to unify the nation. Programs such as the WPA allowed people of varied backgrounds to get to know one another, breaking down regional and ethnic prejudices.

New Deal programs increased the size and scope of the federal government like never before. The government assumed responsibility for providing for the welfare of children and the poor, elderly, sick, disabled, and unemployed. This led to the rise of a **welfare state.**

The expanding role of the government, including the creation of many new federal agencies, gave the executive branch much more power. Roosevelt was elected President four times. After his death, there was a call for limiting the President's term of office. In 1951, the Twenty-second Amendment limited the President to two consecutive terms in office.

Review Questions

1. What effect did the New Deal coalition have on American party politics?

_____

_____

2. How did Franklin D. Roosevelt expand the role of the federal government?

_____

_____

Focus Question: How did the men and women of the depression find relief from their hardships in the popular culture?

As you read, complete the table below to record examples of cultural or popular media.

Cultural or Popular Media	Example
Movies	

CHAPTER
22
SECTION 4

Section Summary
CULTURE OF THE 1930s

Entertainment became big business during the 1930s, creating a golden age in American culture. Large radio networks dominated the airwaves, while a cluster of film companies ruled the silver screen. Radio ownership grew during the decade, and nearly two thirds of all Americans attended at least one movie a week.

The movies were a form of escapism during the Great Depression as Americans sought relief from their concerns. Movies like *The Wizard of Oz* promised weary audiences that their dreams really could come true. In the early 1930s, many films reflected the public's distrust of big business and government. Others, such as the films of **Frank Capra,** celebrated American idealism and the triumph of the common man over adversity.

Radio brought news and entertainment into American homes. FDR used fireside radio chats to explain his New Deal programs. National radio networks broadcast dramas, comedies, soap operas, and variety shows. Episodes from *The Lone Ranger* began running in 1933 and lasted for more than 20 years. Sometimes the lines between news and entertainment were blurred. When the Mercury Theatre broadcast a drama called *War of the Worlds* on October 30, 1938, many people panicked, believing that Martians were actually invading.

Music also provided a diversion from hard times, whether on the radio at home or in nightclubs. Americans enjoyed "swing" music played by "big bands." Blues singers focused on the harsh conditions faced by African Americans. Woody Guthrie wrote ballads about the Okies, farmers who fled the Dust Bowl.

The federal government funded the arts for the first time through programs such as the **Federal Art Project.** Artists painted huge **murals** on public buildings across the nation. **Dorothea Lange** and other photographers documented the plight of America's farmers.

Many writers produced novels featuring working-class heroes. **John Steinbeck's** *The Grapes of Wrath* traces the fictional Joad family from the Oklahoma Dust Bowl to California. **Lillian Hellman** wrote several plays featuring strong roles for women as well as screenplays for movies. Americans also enjoyed comic strips and comic books.

Review Questions

1. How did popular culture change during the 1930s?

_____

_____

2. What were some of the major themes of literature in the 1930s?

_____

_____

CHAPTER
23
SECTION 1

Note Taking Study Guide
DICTATORS AND WAR

Focus Question: Why did totalitarian states rise after World War I, and what did they do?

A. *As you read, summarize the actions in the 1930s of each of the countries listed in the table below.*

1930s Actions	**Japan**	• •
	Germany	• • • •
	Italy	• • •
	Soviet Union	• •

Focus Question: Why did totalitarian states rise after World War I, and what did they do?

B. *Use the concept web below to record the main ideas about the policies of Great Britain, France, and the United States toward aggressive nations.*

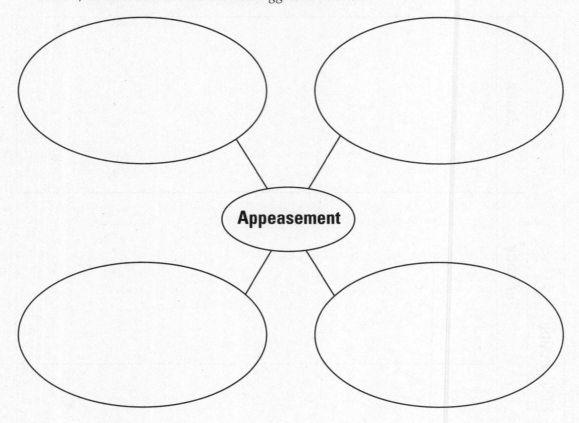

Appeasement

Name _____ Class _____ Date _____

CHAPTER 23 SECTION 1

Section Summary
DICTATORS AND WAR

In the 1920s, some nations moved toward democracy. Others moved toward repressive dictatorships and **totalitarianism,** a type of government in which a single party or leader controls the economic, social, and cultural lives of its people.

The 1917 communist revolution in the Soviet Union produced the first totalitarian state, headed by Vladimir Lenin. In 1924, **Joseph Stalin** took his place as the Communist Party's head.

A postwar economic depression troubled Italy. In 1922, the king asked the founder of the Fascist Party, **Benito Mussolini,** to form a government. Mussolini turned Italy into a fascist country, with a controlled press, secret police, and no political parties.

Following World War I, Germany became a democracy. However, the Great Depression caused severe economic troubles in the 1930s. The National Socialist German Workers' Party (Nazi Party) led by **Adolf Hitler** rose to power. <u>Hitler criticized many people, political programs, and ideologies, but his sharpest assaults were against communists and Jews.</u> Hitler was violently **antisemitic,** or prejudiced against Jewish people. He was appointed chancellor in 1933 and became president of Germany within two years.

In Japan, the Great Depression ended a period of increased democracy and peaceful change. Military leaders argued that expansion throughout Asia would solve Japan's problems. Japan attacked Manchuria and established a puppet state in 1931. Six years later, Japan attacked China again, raiding the capital city with such brutality that it became known as the "Rape of Nanjing."

In the 1930s, Italy and Germany resorted to acts of aggression similar to those of Japan in Asia. Hitler reclaimed the Saar region from French control and sent troops into the Rhineland, while Mussolini led an invasion into Ethiopia. The League of Nations did almost nothing to stop the aggression.

France, Britain, and the United States pursued the policy of **appeasement** toward the fascist leaders. Appeasement means granting concessions to a potential enemy to maintain peace. However, this approach only encouraged the leaders to become bolder and more aggressive.

Review Questions

1. After World War I, what kind of government was set up in Germany? Who became the country's leader?

_____

_____

2. How did the military leaders of Japan want to solve the country's problems?

_____

_____

READING CHECK

How did Benito Mussolini come to rule Italy?

_____

_____

_____

VOCABULARY STRATEGY

What does the word *ideologies* mean in the underlined sentence? What context clues can you find in the surrounding words or phrases? Circle any words or phrases in the paragraph that help you figure out what *ideologies* means.

_____

_____

_____

READING SKILL

Summarize Name the countries and leaders discussed in this section.

_____

_____

_____

Name _____ Class _____ Date _____

Focus Question: How did Americans react to events in Europe and Asia in the early years of World War II?

Sequence the major events described in the section using the timeline below.

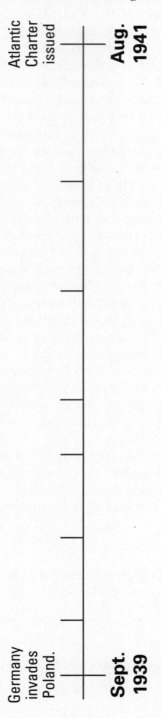

Atlantic Charter issued

Aug. 1941

Germany invades Poland.

Sept. 1939

CHAPTER 23 SECTION 2 — Section Summary

FROM ISOLATION TO INVOLVEMENT

After Japan's violent attack on China in 1937, President Roosevelt criticized the Japanese aggression. The United States, however, continued to back away from intervention in foreign conflicts.

Despite a military alliance among France, Britain, and Poland, Germany invaded Poland in 1939. Britain and France declared war on Germany, and World War II had begun. The **Axis Powers** would come to include Germany, Italy, Japan, and several other nations. The Axis Powers fought the **Allies,** which included Britain, France, and eventually the Soviet Union, China, and the United States.

Germany used a new technique called **blitzkrieg,** or "lightning war." <u>Tanks and planes attacked in a coordinated effort and quickly conquered Poland.</u> In April 1940, Denmark and Norway fell to the German blitzkrieg. In May, Germany took the Netherlands, Belgium and Luxembourg, and then invaded France. The next month, Germany attacked Britain from the air.

Winston Churchill, the prime minister of Britain, hoped to convince America to join the Allies. Reports by news reporter Edward R. Murrow on the bombing of London shocked the American public. Murrow emphasized that the Germans were bombing civilians, not armies or military sites. Despite its isolationist policies, the United States moved slowly toward involvement. Congress passed the **Neutrality Act of 1939.** This law helped the Allies buy goods and munitions from the United States. Isolationists, however, believed that getting involved in a bloody European war would be wasteful and dangerous.

Even though most Americans wanted to remain neutral, President Roosevelt constantly argued for helping Britain. In early 1941, Congress approved the **Lend-Lease Act.** This act gave the President the power to sell, give, or lease weapons to protect the United States. In 1941, Roosevelt also met with Churchill to discuss the war. They signed the **Atlantic Charter,** a document that endorsed national self-determination and an international system of "general security." The agreement signaled the deepening alliance between the two nations. Hitler was not blind to American support of the Allies. In the fall of 1941, he ordered German U-boats to attack American ships. U.S. involvement in the war seemed inevitable.

Review Questions

1. What nations made up the Axis Powers?

_____

_____

2. What was President Roosevelt's position on the war in Europe?

_____

_____

READING CHECK

What is a blitzkrieg?

_____

_____

_____

VOCABULARY STRATEGY

What does the word *coordinated* mean in the underlined sentence? What clues can you find in the surrounding words, phrases, or sentences? Circle the words in the underlined passage that could help you learn what *coordinated* means.

_____

_____

_____

READING SKILL

Sequence List the countries Germany conquered by order of date.

_____

_____

_____

Name _____ Class _____ Date _____

Focus Question: How did the United States react to the Japanese attack on Pearl Harbor?

A. *As you read, record the causes and effects of the attack on Pearl Harbor, as well as details about the attack itself, in the chart below.*

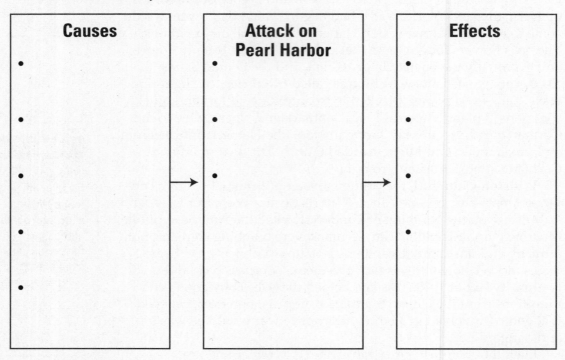

Causes	Attack on Pearl Harbor	Effects
•	•	•
•	•	•
•	•	•
•		•
•		•

B. *Sequence the fighting that followed Pearl Harbor in the timetable below.*

Early War in the Pacific	
May 1942	The Philippines fall to the Japanese.

CHAPTER 23 SECTION 3 — Section Summary

AMERICA ENTERS THE WAR

As Japan expanded its empire throughout Asia, its relationship with the United States worsened. Japan needed resources such as oil, steel, and rubber to maintain its military. The United States began to withhold these goods to limit Japan's expansion. The United States also instituted a trade embargo against Japan.

At first, **Hideki Tojo,** the Japanese prime minister, tried to keep the United States neutral. However, when a trade agreement with the United States failed, Tojo decided on a decisive military strike. On December 7, 1941, hundreds of Japanese airplanes bombed the site of the United States Navy's main base in the Pacific at **Pearl Harbor,** Hawaii. Nearly 2,500 people were killed in this devastating surprise attack. Many ships were sunk, and hundreds of aircraft were destroyed or damaged.

Congress immediately declared war on Japan. Germany and Italy then declared war on the United States. Men joined the military by the millions. Thousands of women joined the **Women's Army Corps (WAC)** as clerical workers, truck drivers, instructors, and lab technicians. The government also created agencies to ensure the production of military equipment. <u>These agencies allocated scarce materials to the proper industries.</u>

In Asia, United States Army General **Douglas MacArthur** struggled unsuccessfully to hold the Philippines against the Japanese forces. U.S. forces finally had to retreat, and MacArthur evacuated to Australia. Some 75,000 U.S. troops fell back to the Bataan Peninsula and Corregidor Island where, in May 1942, they had to surrender. Japanese troops forced these sick and malnourished men to march many miles. More than 7,000 American and Filipino troops died on the march, which is known as the **Bataan Death March.**

By the summer of 1942, Japan controlled Southeast Asia and the western Pacific. Then in May 1942, the United States Navy finally began to stop the Japanese advance. At the **Battle of Coral Sea,** the United States Navy prevented Japan from taking a key spot in New Guinea. The impressive Japanese offensive was over.

Review Questions

1. Why did the United States begin a trade embargo against Japan?

_____

_____

2. What happened to U.S. forces in the Philippines?

_____

_____

READING CHECK

Why was the Battle of Coral Sea so important to the United States?

_____

_____

_____

VOCABULARY STRATEGY

What does the word *allocated* mean in the underlined sentence? What clues can you find in the surrounding words, phrases, or sentences? Circle the words in the underlined passage that could help you learn what *allocated* means.

_____

_____

_____

READING SKILL

Identify Causes and Effects
What was the United States' immediate reaction to the attack on Pearl Harbor?

_____

_____

_____

Name _____ Class _____ Date _____

Focus Question: How did the Allies turn the tide against the Axis?

List the ways in which the Allies turned back the Axis advance.

Turning Back the Axis	
In Europe	**In the Pacific**
• Battle against U-boats in Atlantic	•
•	
	•
•	
	•
•	
•	
•	

CHAPTER 24 SECTION 1 — Section Summary
THE ALLIES TURN THE TIDE

The attack on Pearl Harbor brought the United States into World War II. <u>The Allies' ultimate goal was to fight and win a two-front war.</u> Their first objective, however, was to defeat Hitler. The United States was producing millions of tons of guns, tanks, and other war supplies. German U-boats, however, had sunk over 3,500 merchant ships bound for Britain. By mid-1943, using radar, bombers, and underwater depth charges, Allied forces were sinking U-boats faster than Germany could manufacture them. The Allies had begun to win the war in the North Atlantic.

In 1941, Germany attacked Russia, and Stalin wanted Roosevelt and Churchill to open a second front in France. Instead, in early 1942, British planes began **saturation bombing,** dropping large numbers of bombs on German cities. American bombers used **strategic bombing,** targeting key political and industrial centers. The **Tuskegee Airmen,** an African American fighter squadron, played a key role in the bombing campaign. In January 1943, after the long, bitter Battle of Stalingrad, the Russians turned back the German invasion of their country. During the same month, FDR announced that only the **unconditional surrender** of the Axis Powers would end the war. That is, they had to give up completely.

To help pave the way for an invasion of Italy, the Allies decided to push the Germans out of North Africa, where they had been fighting British troops since 1940. In February 1942, American General **Dwight Eisenhower** commanded the Allied invasion. After difficult battles, General **George S. Patton, Jr.** took charge of American forces. In May 1943, German and Italian forces in North Africa surrendered. Two months later, Allied forces invaded Sicily, two miles off the mainland of Italy. From there, they launched their invasion of Italy, and in September, Italy surrendered.

In spite of its "Europe first" strategy, the United States did not ignore the Pacific where Japanese forces had continued to advance. In June 1942, the Japanese attacked Midway, a vital American naval base in the central Pacific. The American naval commander, Admiral **Chester Nimitz,** had learned of the Japanese plans, and the **Battle of Midway** was a decisive American victory. It ended Japanese expansion in the Pacific and put Japan on the defensive.

Review Questions

1. What tactics did the Allies use to weaken Germany?

_____

_____

2. Why was it so important for the United States to defeat the Japanese at Midway?

_____

_____

READING CHECK

Who were the Tuskegee Airmen?

_____

_____

_____

VOCABULARY STRATEGY

What does the word *ultimate* mean in the underlined sentence? Circle the word below that is a synonym for *ultimate.*

- first
- final

READING SKILL

Summarize How did the Allies prepare for the invasion of Italy?

_____

_____

CHAPTER 24 SECTION 2

Note Taking Study Guide

THE HOME FRONT

Focus Question: How did the war change America at home?

As you read, identify the major effects of World War II on the home front.

The Home Front, World War II		
Economy	**Effects on Women**	**Effects on Minorities**
• War bonds • Wage controls • • •	• • • • •	• • • • •

CHAPTER 24 SECTION 2

Section Summary
THE HOME FRONT

World War II fears and tensions tested civil liberties, but the war also provided new opportunities for women and minorities. Many women found jobs, especially in heavy industry. They gained confidence, knowledge, organizational experience, and a paycheck. However, few African Americans found meaningful employment with defense employers. In response, African American labor leader **A. Philip Randolph** planned a massive march on Washington, D.C., to protest employment discrimination. Under pressure, FDR issued **Executive Order 8802.** It assured fair hiring practices in any job funded with government money.

Wartime needs encouraged people to move to the South and Southwest to find jobs in defense industries. <u>To alleviate the rural population drain, the United States initiated the **bracero program.**</u> This program brought Mexican laborers to work on American farms. Although they often faced discrimination, braceros contributed greatly to the war effort.

After the attack on Pearl Harbor, the federal government moved 100,000 Japanese Americans living on the West Coast to camps in isolated locations under a policy of **internment.** There, they were held in jail-like conditions for the duration of the war. Some Japanese Americans went to court to seek their rights. In the 1944 case of *Korematsu v. United States,* the Supreme Court upheld the government's wartime internment policy. When the government lifted a ban on Japanese Americans serving in the armed forces, many enlisted. The Japanese American **442nd Regimental Combat Team** fought in the Italian campaign and became the most decorated military unit in American history.

The war cost Americans $330 billion. To help pay for it, Congress levied a tax on all working Americans. To ensure that there would be adequate raw materials, such as oil and rubber, for war production, **rationing** was instituted. The federal **Office of War Information (OWI)** worked with the media to encourage support of the war effort. Millions of Americans bought war bonds and contributed to the war effort in many other ways, large and small.

Review Questions

1. How did World War II change women's lives?

_____

_____

2. How did World War II affect Japanese Americans?

_____

_____

READING CHECK

What was the bracero program?

_____

_____

_____

VOCABULARY STRATEGY

What does the word *initiated* mean in the underlined sentence? Read the underlined sentence and the sentence that follows aloud, but leave out the word *initiated.* Think about what word could be used in its place. Use this strategy to help you figure out the meaning of *initiated.*

_____

_____

_____

READING SKILL

Identify Main Ideas How did the workplace change as a result of World War II?

_____

_____

Name _____ Class _____ Date _____

CHAPTER 24 SECTION 3

Note Taking Study Guide
VICTORY IN EUROPE AND THE PACIFIC

Focus Question: How did the Allies defeat the Axis Powers?

Identify the steps that led to the Allied victory.

Europe	**The Pacific**
• Allies land at Normandy on D-Day. • • • •	• • • • •

Allies Win World War II

Section Summary
VICTORY IN EUROPE AND THE PACIFIC

In 1943, the Allied leaders agreed to open a second front in France. On June 6, 1944, known as **D-Day,** British and American forces invaded France from the west, across the English Channel. More than 11,000 planes prepared the way, followed by more than 4,400 ships and landing crafts. By the end of the day, they had gained a toehold in France. By July 1, more than one million Allied troops had landed.

Germany now faced a hopeless two-front war, as the Soviets advanced from the east. In December 1944, Hitler ordered a counterattack, known as the **Battle of the Bulge.** <u>Hitler's scenario called for German forces to capture communication and transportation hubs.</u> The attack almost succeeded. However, with help from their bombers, the Allies managed to push the Germans out of France. By January 1945, the Soviet Army had reached the Oder River outside Berlin, and in April, the United States Army was just 50 miles west of Berlin. Hitler committed suicide on April 30, and on May 7, Germany surrendered.

American forces in the Pacific followed an **island-hopping** strategy in a steady path toward Japan. Japanese troops fought hard, and Japanese **kamikaze** pilots deliberately crashed their planes into American ships. By April 1945, American pilots finally made their way to Okinawa, 340 miles from Japan. From Okinawa, American pilots could bomb the Japanese home islands. American bombers hit factories, military bases, and cities.

Advances in technology helped determine the final outcome of the war. **Albert Einstein,** a famous scientist, had alerted FDR to the need to proceed with atomic development. Physicist **J. Robert Oppenheimer** was in charge of the scientific aspect of the program, known as the **Manhattan Project.** On the morning of July 16, 1945, the first atomic bomb was tested. In order to save American lives and to end the war, President **Harry S. Truman** decided to use the atomic bomb against Japan. On August 6, 1945, U.S. pilots dropped an atomic bomb on Hiroshima. Three days later, the United States dropped a second atomic bomb on Nagasaki. Emperor Hirohito made the decision to surrender, and on August 15, the Allies celebrated V-J (Victory in Japan) Day. World War II had been the most costly war in history. As many as 60 million people—mostly civilians—had died in the conflict.

Review Questions

1. What was involved in the D-Day invasion of France?

_____

_____

2. How did the Allies bring about the surrender of Japan?

_____

_____

READING CHECK

What was the Manhattan Project?

_____

_____

_____

VOCABULARY STRATEGY

What does the word *scenario* mean in the underlined sentence? Circle any words or phrases in the paragraph that help you figure out what *scenario* means.

_____

_____

_____

READING SKILL

Recognize Sequence Number the following events in chronological order.

_____ Japan surrenders.

_____ The first atomic bomb is tested.

_____ Germany surrenders.

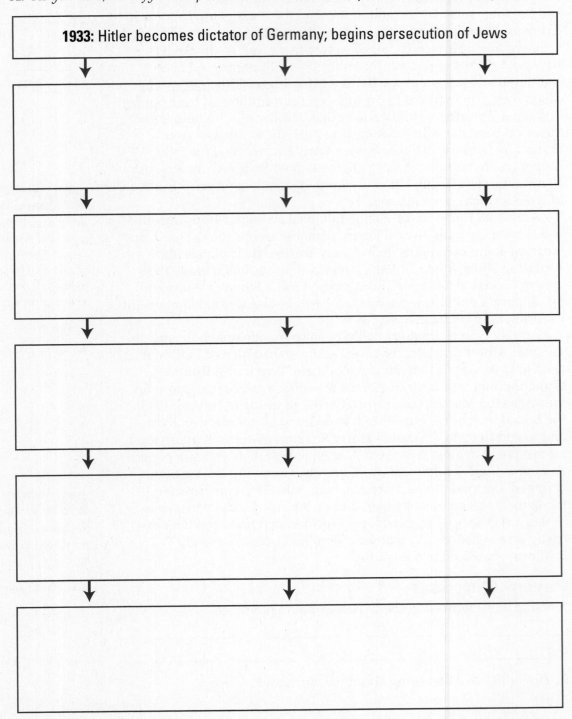

Note Taking Study Guide

THE HOLOCAUST

Focus Question: How did the Holocaust develop and what were its results?

A. *As you read, identify the steps that led to Hitler's attempt to exterminate European Jews.*

> **1933:** Hitler becomes dictator of Germany; begins persecution of Jews

CHAPTER
24
SECTION 4

Note Taking Study Guide
THE HOLOCAUST

Focus Question: How did the Holocaust develop and what were its results?

B. *As you read, identify different ways in which the United States and other nations responded to the treatment of Jews in Nazi Germany before, during, and after the war.*

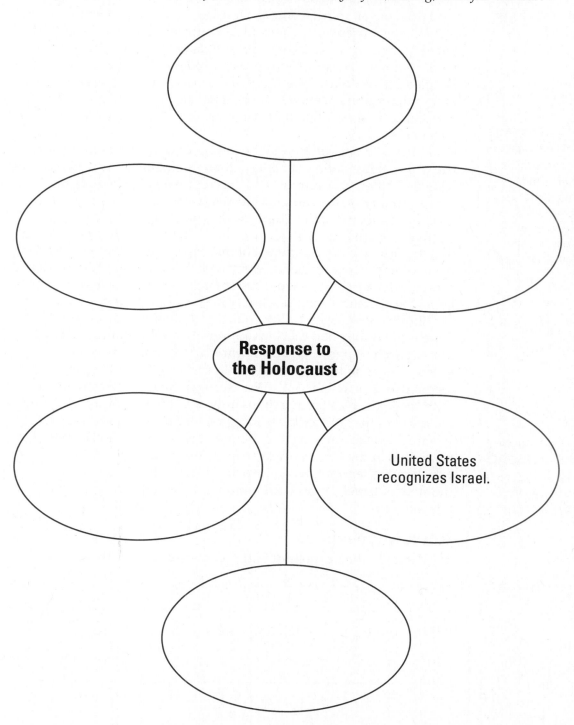

Response to the Holocaust

United States recognizes Israel.

Name _____ Class _____ Date _____

READING CHECK

What was Kristallnacht?

_____

_____

_____

VOCABULARY STRATEGY

What does the word *restraints* mean in the underlined sentence? Note that the word is a noun, and that it contains the verb *restrain*, which means "hold back." Use this information to help you figure out what *restraints* means.

_____

_____

_____

READING SKILL

Recognize Sequence What happened to Jews in Germany after Hitler came to power?

_____

_____

In 1945, there was no word for the **Holocaust,** the most horrific event of World War II. It was the Nazi attempt to kill all Jews, as well as other "undesirables," under their control. This was part of a racist Nazi ideology that considered Aryans—white Northern European gentiles—superior to other people.

Hitler began to persecute the Jews as soon as he came to power. In 1935, the **Nuremberg Laws** denied citizenship to Jews and segregated them at every level of society. Acts of violence against Jews were common. The most serious occurred on November 9, 1938, and is called **Kristallnacht,** the "Night of Broken Glass." Secret police and military units destroyed more than 200 synagogues and 7,500 Jewish businesses, killed more than 200 Jews, and injured more than 600 others.

Hitler's "Final Solution to the Jewish question" was **genocide,** the willful annihilation of all Jews living in regions under his control. Jews and other "undesirables" were confined in **concentration camps.** In theory, the camps were designed to turn prisoners into "useful members" of the Third Reich. There were, however, no restraints on guards, who tortured and killed prisoners without fear of reprisals. Doctors conducted bogus experiments that killed prisoners or left them deformed. Many concentration camps were **death camps,** where prisoners were systematically exterminated. The largest death camp was Auschwitz in southern Poland.

Before the war, the United States and other countries could have done more if they had relaxed immigration policies and accepted more Jewish refugees. Once the war started, news of the mass killings began to filter to the West. In early 1944, FDR began to respond and established the **War Refugee Board,** which worked with the Red Cross to save thousands of Eastern European Jews. The enormity of the Nazi crime became real for most Americans only when Allied soldiers began to liberate the concentration camps. The revelation of the Holocaust increased American support for a Jewish homeland. Therefore, when Jewish settlers in Palestine proclaimed the state of Israel, President Truman immediately recognized the new nation.

Review Questions

1. What was the purpose of Hitler's concentration camps?

_____

_____

2. How did the United States respond to the Holocaust?

_____

_____

CHAPTER
24
SECTION 5

Note Taking Study Guide
EFFECTS OF THE WAR

Focus Question: What were the major immediate and long-term effects of World War II?

As you read, look for various developments in the postwar world that resulted from World War II.

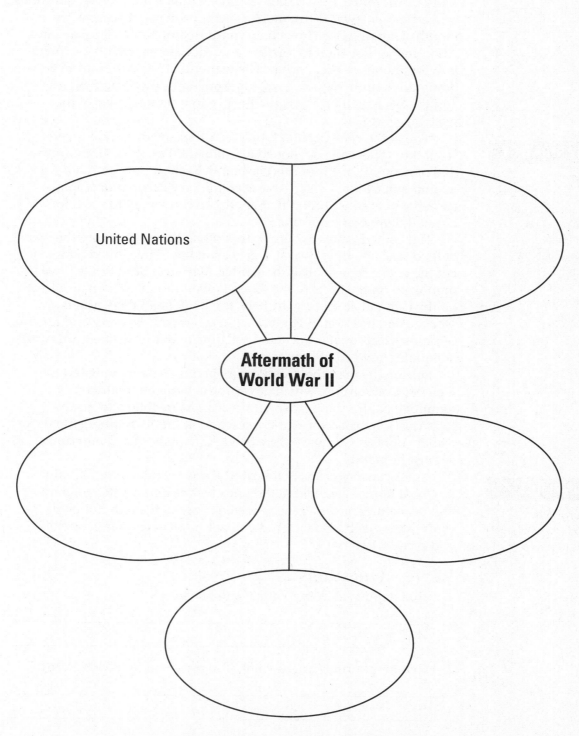

CHAPTER 24 SECTION 5 — Section Summary

EFFECTS OF THE WAR

As World War II drew to an end, Japan and Germany kept fighting long after their defeat was certain. The protracted fighting gave the Allies time to make plans for a postwar world. In February 1945, Roosevelt, Churchill, and Stalin met at Yalta on the Black Sea. At the **Yalta Conference,** they discussed final strategy and crucial questions concerning postwar Germany, Eastern Europe, and Asia. A few months later, the Big Three, now composed of Stalin, Truman, and Atlee, met at Potsdam to formalize the decision to divide Germany into four zones of occupation. The war ended Western European domination of the world. Two **superpowers**—the United States and the Soviet Union—became the predominant nations of the postwar world.

Not all the changes that took place after the war ended were what the Allies had envisioned at Yalta and Potsdam. Communist and noncommunist interests clashed in Eastern Europe. Civil war resumed in China. Under American military occupation, Japan gained a new constitution that abolished the armed forces and enacted democratic reforms.

The United States, where industry had boomed during the war, helped to shape the postwar world economy. The United States also led the charge to establish the **United Nations (UN).** While it was organized on the basis of the Great Powers, all member nations sat on the General Assembly. In 1948, the UN issued the **Universal Declaration of Human Rights,** which condemns slavery and torture, upholds freedom of speech and religion, and affirms the right to an adequate standard of living.

During the war, the Axis Powers had repeatedly violated the **Geneva Convention,** which governs the humane treatment of wounded soldiers and prisoners of war. More than a thousand Japanese were tried for war crimes, and at the **Nuremberg Trials** key leaders of Nazi Germany were brought to justice for their crimes against humanity.

Americans had closely followed the war and learned to think in global terms. They defined themselves as democratic, tolerant, and peaceful. The war gave renewed vigor to the fight for civil rights at home. It also ushered in a period of economic growth and prosperity.

Review Questions

1. What happened at the Yalta Conference?

_____

_____

2. What long-term changes were brought about by World War II?

_____

_____

CHAPTER
25
SECTION 1

Note Taking Study Guide
THE COLD WAR BEGINS

Focus Question: How did U.S. leaders respond to the threat of Soviet expansion in Europe?

A. *As you read, contrast the conflicting goals of the United States and the Soviet Union.*

American Goals	Soviet Goals

Name _____ Class _____ Date _____

Focus Question: How did U.S. leaders respond to the threat of Soviet expansion in Europe?

B. *As you read, trace events and developments in Europe that contributed to the growth of Cold War tensions.*

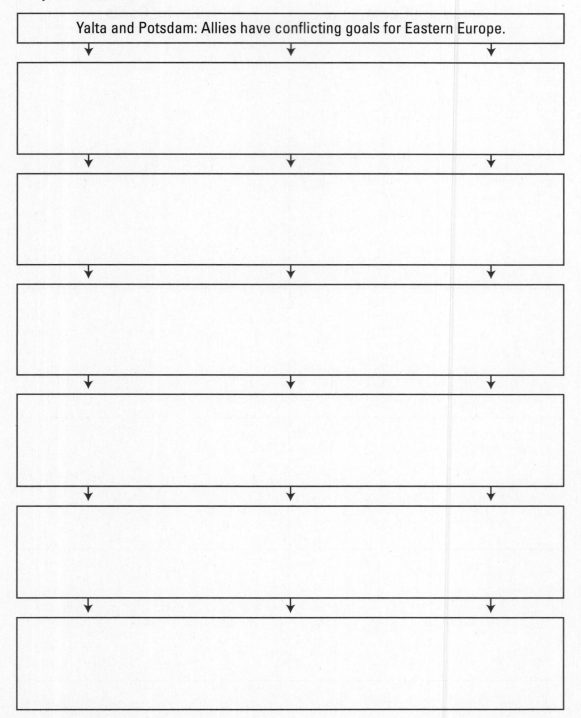

Yalta and Potsdam: Allies have conflicting goals for Eastern Europe.

CHAPTER 25 SECTION 1

Section Summary

THE COLD WAR BEGINS

When Roosevelt, Stalin, and Churchill met at Yalta in February 1945, it was clear that the Allies would defeat Germany. The United States and Great Britain wanted a united Germany and independent nations in Eastern Europe after the war. Soviet dictator Stalin wanted a weak, divided Germany and an Eastern Europe under communist control. Despite Stalin's promises, Poland, Czechoslovakia, Hungary, Romania, and Bulgaria became **satellite states** of the Soviet Union, along with the eastern part of Germany. After another meeting that summer at Potsdam, Harry S. Truman, who was now President, became convinced that the Soviet Union had aspirations toward world domination. Thus began the 46-year-long **Cold War.**

Churchill agreed with President Truman and said an **iron curtain** had descended upon Europe. East of the curtain, Stalin was tightening his grip and trying to spread communism to other countries. Truman asked Congress for money to help Turkey and Greece fight communism. His promise of aid became known as the **Truman Doctrine.** It set a new course for American foreign policy.

The goal of another American policy, called **containment,** was to use American power to help nations resist communism. Containment's first success was based on Secretary of State George C. Marshall's economic recovery plan for Europe. Under the **Marshall Plan,** the United States gave about $13 billion in grants and loans to Western European nations, starting in 1948.

In June 1948, Stalin decided to block all shipping from western Germany into West Berlin—deep inside communist East Germany—hoping that would make the city fall to the communists. The United States and Britain stopped his plan by airlifting supplies, including food, fuel, and clothing, into West Berlin.

The **Berlin airlift** showed that communism could be contained. To continue to block Soviet expansion, the **North Atlantic Treaty Organization, NATO,** formed in 1949. Twelve Western European and North American nations agreed to act together to defend Western Europe. In 1955, West Germany joined NATO. In response, the Soviet Union and its satellite states formed the **Warsaw Pact.** All communist states of Eastern Europe except Yugoslavia promised to defend one another if attacked.

Review Questions

1. What was Truman's promise of aid to countries fighting communism called?

_____

_____

2. Which event proved that the policy of containment worked?

_____

_____

READING CHECK

President Truman asked Congress for aid for which two countries?

_____

_____

_____

VOCABULARY STRATEGY

What does the word *aspirations* mean in the underlined sentence? Circle the words in the underlined sentence that could help you learn what *aspirations* means.

_____

_____

_____

READING SKILL

Contrast After World War II, what were the differences in goals between Stalin and the Soviets and Truman and the United States?

_____

_____

_____

Note Taking Study Guide

THE KOREAN WAR

Focus Question: How did President Truman use the power of the presidency to limit the spread of communism in East Asia?

As you read, note problems and the steps that President Truman took to solve them. Use the problem-solution table below.

Problem	Solution
Communists threaten takeover of China.	

Since the Russian Revolution, the Soviets had tried to export communism around the world, sure that it would reach worldwide influence. Events in China in 1949 seemed to prove them right.

Chinese Nationalist leader **Jiang Jieshi** (known as Chiang Kai-shek in the United States) and communist leader **Mao Zedong** had been allies against Japan during World War II, but once the war ended, they became enemies. The United States supported Jiang, while the Soviet Union aided Mao. In 1949, Mao's communists took over the Chinese mainland, calling their government the People's Republic of China.

From there, the conflict over communism moved to Korea. After World War II, the United States and the Soviet Union had split Korea into two nations divided by the **38th parallel** of latitude. On June 25, 1950, about 90,000 North Korean troops armed with Soviet weapons crossed the 38th parallel to attack South Korea.

President Truman sent American troops to join South Korean and United Nations forces. Under the World War II hero General **Douglas MacArthur,** they attacked the port city of Inchon in September 1950. By October, they drove the North Koreans back north.

Truman worried what China might do if the war continued, but MacArthur told him China would not intervene and he continued to push northward. Then, on November 26, 1950, around 300,000 Chinese soldiers attacked. Truman did not want the United States to enter into a major war that would involve huge numbers of troops and maybe even atomic weapons, but MacArthur distrusted Truman's policy of a **"limited war."** When MacArthur sent a letter to Congress condemning the policy, Truman fired him.

By the spring of 1951, the war settled into a stalemate. To achieve a cease-fire in 1953, Dwight D. Eisenhower, now President, hinted he might use nuclear weapons.

No side won the Korean War, and the two Koreas remain divided today. But two things did change: Truman's use of American forces enlarged the power of the presidency, and a new alliance called the **Southeast Asia Treaty Organization (SEATO)** was formed to prevent the spread of communism. It was the Asian version of NATO.

Review Questions

1. What is the significance of the 38th parallel?

_____

_____

2. What was President Eisenhower's role in the cease-fire that ended the Korean War?

_____

_____

READING CHECK

What did China do that MacArthur insisted would not happen?

_____

_____

_____

VOCABULARY STRATEGY

What does the word *intervene* mean in the underlined sentence? Look at the context clues in the sentence to help you figure out what the word means. Circle the words that could help you learn what *intervene* means.

_____

_____

_____

READING SKILL

Categorize What idea and event led directly to Truman's firing of MacArthur?

_____

_____

_____

Name _____ Class _____ Date _____

Focus Question: What methods did the United States use in its global struggle against the Soviet Union?

Identify the tactics used to wage the Cold War.

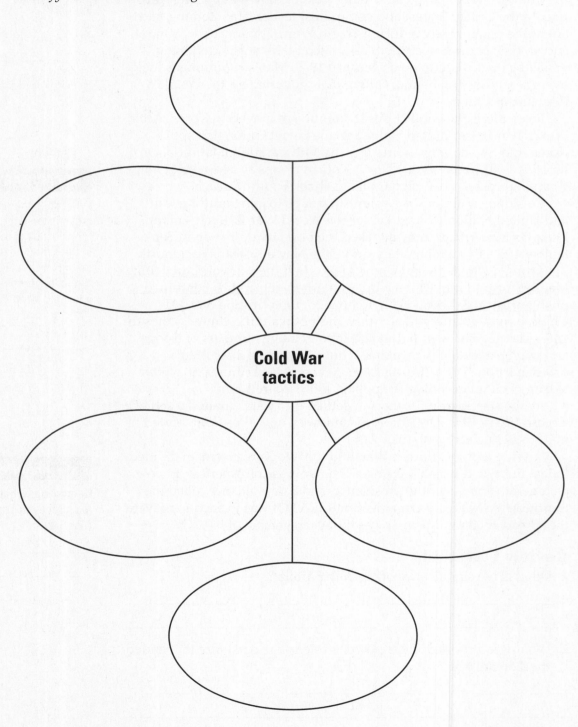

CHAPTER 25 SECTION 3

Section Summary
THE COLD WAR EXPANDS

On September 2, 1949, America learned that the Soviets now had an atomic bomb. The following month, communists took over China. For Americans, the world had suddenly become more threatening.

Truman soon ordered the development of a hydrogen bomb. Some scientists warned that developing the H-Bomb would lead to a perpetual **arms race.** For the next four decades, the United States and the Soviet Union stockpiled nuclear weapons. Each hoped this program of **mutually assured destruction** would prevent the other from actually using the weapons.

President Dwight D. Eisenhower continued to stockpile nuclear weapons. His foreign policy emphasized **massive retaliation.** Eisenhower's Secretary of State, **John Foster Dulles,** believed that only by going to the brink of war—an approach called **brinkmanship** —could the United States discourage communist aggression.

Nikita Khrushchev, who became leader of the Soviet Union in 1953, continued to try to spread communism. In 1956, workers in Poland rioted against Soviet rule and won greater control of their government. But when students and workers in Hungary tried the same thing, Khrushchev crushed the revolt.

In the Middle East, Egypt's president, Gamal Abdel Nasser, wanted to build a dam on the Nile River. When he opened relations with communist China and the Soviet Union, the United States withdrew its offer to help. Nasser then **nationalized** the Suez Canal. In response, Britain, France, and Israel invaded Egypt in October 1956. Using the **Suez crisis** as an excuse, Britain and France took control of the canal but withdrew when Eisenhower would not support them.

Eisenhower then announced the United States would use force to help any nation threatened by communism. This **Eisenhower Doctrine** was used in 1958 to put down a revolt against a pro-American government in Lebanon. The Eisenhower administration also used the **Central Intelligence Agency (CIA)** to help return pro-American governments to Iran and Guatemala.

On October 4, 1957, the Soviets launched the satellite *Sputnik 1.* Alarmed, Congress passed legislation to educate more scientists and created the **National Aeronautics and Space Administration (NASA).**

Review Questions

1. How were brinkmanship and massive retaliation supposed to deter communist aggression?

   _____

   _____

2. What three countries were the focus of the Eisenhower Doctrine?

   _____

   _____

READING CHECK

What did each side do to ensure the likelihood of mutually assured destruction?

_____

_____

_____

VOCABULARY STRATEGY

What does the word *perpetual* mean in the underlined sentence? Look at the sentence that comes before it for connections to people and things. Then, look for context clues in the sentence to help you figure out why *perpetual* was used in this sentence.

_____

_____

_____

READING SKILL

Identify Main Ideas Describe the ways the United States and the Soviet Union competed with each other for supremacy.

_____

_____

_____

Note Taking Study Guide

THE COLD WAR AT HOME

Focus Question: How did fear of domestic communism affect American society during the Cold War?

A. *List efforts taken to protect Americans from communism and how these policies affected rights.*

Anticommunist Policy	Effect on Rights

B. *As you read, identify similarities and differences between the Hiss case and the Rosenberg case. Consider both the facts and the impact of the two spy cases.*

Alger Hiss
• Accused of stealing government documents

•

•

Rosenbergs
• Accused of passing on atomic secrets

•

•

CHAPTER 25 SECTION 4

Section Summary

THE COLD WAR AT HOME

The **Red Scare**—public fear that communists were working to destroy America both from within and without—spurred President Truman in 1947 to investigate federal employees. About 3,000 people were dismissed or resigned. The Truman administration also used the 1940 **Smith Act,** a law against advocating violent overthrow of the government, to send 11 U.S. Communist Party members to prison.

Meanwhile, the **House Committee on Un-American Activities (HUAC)** investigated subversive activities throughout American life, including academic institutions, labor unions, and city halls. In 1947, HUAC targeted the **Hollywood Ten,** a group of left-wing writers, directors, and producers. They refused to testify against themselves but were sent to prison. Movie executives then circulated a **blacklist** that named entertainment figures suspected of communist ties, shattering many careers.

Two sensational spy trials increased the country's suspicion of communists. The first one concerned **Alger Hiss,** a government employee who had helped organize the United Nations. In 1948, Whittaker Chambers, a former member of the Communist Party and an espionage agent, named Hiss as one of his government contacts. Hiss denied everything before HUAC but was sentenced to five years in prison. The second trial involved **Julius and Ethel Rosenberg,** who were accused of passing secret information about nuclear science to Soviet agents. The Rosenbergs claimed that they were being persecuted because they were Jewish and held unpopular beliefs. They were convicted in a highly controversial trial and executed in 1953.

Joseph R. McCarthy, a senator from Wisconsin, also fanned Americans' fears. He claimed he had a long list of communists in the State Department, but each time he was asked to give specific names and numbers, his figures changed. Still, with the outbreak of the Korean War in 1950, McCarthy's popularity soared. **McCarthyism** became a catchword for the senator's vicious style of reckless charges. McCarthy's targets grew bigger, and in 1954, he went after the United States Army. After viewers saw him badger witnesses and twist the truth during televised hearings, he lost his strongest supporters. The end of the Korean War in 1953 and McCarthy's downfall in 1954 signaled the decline of the Red Scare.

Review Questions

1. How were the Smith Act and HUAC supposed to discourage communism in the United States?

_____

_____

2. What events led to the decline of the Red Scare?

_____

_____

READING CHECK

What happened to the Hollywood Ten?

_____

_____

_____

VOCABULARY STRATEGY

What does the word *academic* mean in the underlined sentence? Use context clues and your prior knowledge to help you figure out what *academic* means.

_____

_____

_____

READING SKILL

Identify Causes and Effects
Discuss the events that led to McCarthyism and the popularity of the senator from Wisconsin.

_____

_____

_____

CHAPTER 26 SECTION 1
Note Taking Study Guide
AN ECONOMIC BOOM

Focus Question: How did the nation experience recovery and economic prosperity after World War II?

List the problems raised by the shift to a peacetime economy and the steps taken to solve them.

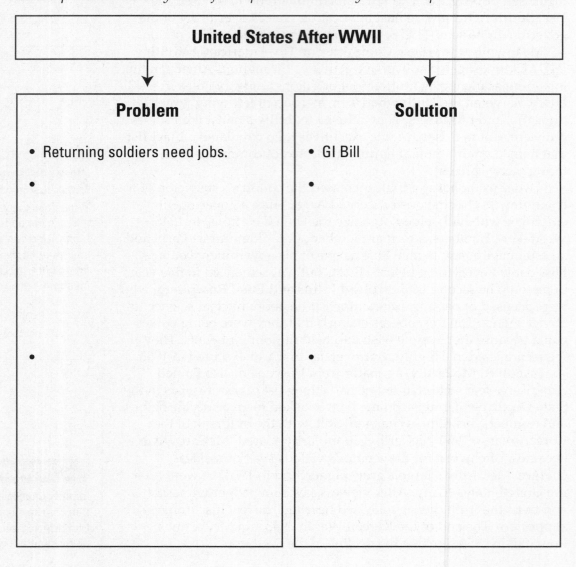

United States After WWII	
Problem	**Solution**
• Returning soldiers need jobs.	• GI Bill
•	•
•	•

CHAPTER 26 SECTION 1

Section Summary
AN ECONOMIC BOOM

The production of military supplies halted at the end of World War II. Millions of Americans initially lost their jobs, but soon the nation experienced the longest period of economic growth in American history.

President Harry Truman brought soldiers home by starting the **demobilization,** or sending home members of the army. To calm fears about the economy, the government passed the law known as the **GI Bill of Rights.** The GI Bill provided veterans with unemployment benefits, financial aid for college, and loans to start businesses. Veterans also received home loans, fueling an upsurge in home construction, which led to explosive growth in the suburbs.

Many veterans started families upon returning home. This **baby boom** peaked in 1957 when 4.3 million babies were born. Between 1940 and 1955, the U.S. population grew by 27 percent.

Soaring demand for consumer products caused skyrocketing prices and inflation. Businesses employed more people to produce goods. The United States soon dominated the world economy, producing nearly 50 percent of the world's total output. However, the inflation rate prompted several trade unions to demand pay increases. When employers refused, millions of workers went on strike. Congress then enacted the **Taft-Hartley Act** to outlaw the closed shop—a workplace that hired only union members.

By 1951, Truman's executive order to desegregate the military had been mostly implemented. However, his support of civil rights caused Southern Democrats to leave the party and establish the States' Rights Party. Another split in the Democratic Party led to the creation of the new Progressive Party. The splits seemed to give the 1948 presidential election to Republican Candidate Thomas Dewey. However, Truman won by a narrow margin.

After the election, Truman introduced the **Fair Deal,** a program to strengthen New Deal reforms and establish programs such as national health insurance. Most of the Fair Deal failed in Congress.

In 1952, Republican Dwight Eisenhower won the presidency by a landslide. He helped create an interstate highway system and gave financial support to education.

Review Questions

1. What is the Taft-Hartley Act? Why was it passed?

_____

_____

2. How did President Truman's late-term legislative efforts compare with those of President Eisenhower?

_____

_____

READING CHECK

How much did the U.S. population grow between 1940 and 1955?

_____

_____

_____

VOCABULARY STRATEGY

What does the word *upsurge* mean in the underlined sentence? The word *decrease* is an antonym of *upsurge*. Use the meaning of the antonym and context clues such as "fueling" and "explosive growth" to help you figure out the meaning of *upsurge*.

_____

_____

_____

READING SKILL

Understand Effects How did the GI Bill benefit the American economy?

_____

_____

_____

Name _____ Class _____ Date _____

Note Taking Study Guide

A SOCIETY ON THE MOVE

Focus Question: What social and economic factors changed American life during the 1950s?

A. *Complete the chart below to capture the main ideas.*

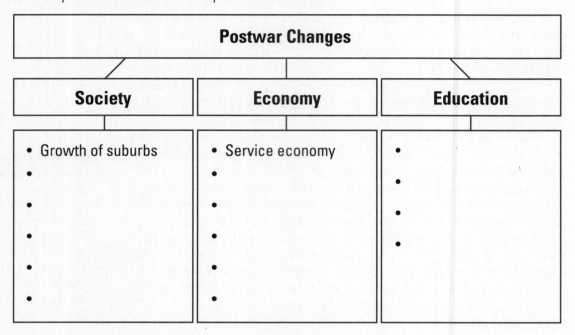

Postwar Changes

Society	Economy	Education
• Growth of suburbs	• Service economy	•
•	•	•
•	•	•
•	•	•
•	•	
•	•	

B. *As you read, identify the effects of the population shift to the Sunbelt.*

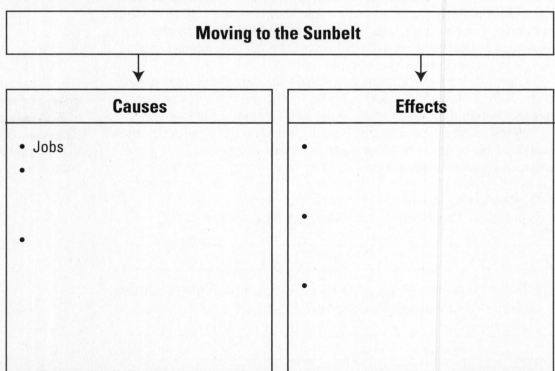

Moving to the Sunbelt

Causes	Effects
• Jobs	•
•	
	•
•	
	•

CHAPTER 26
SECTION 2

Section Summary
A SOCIETY ON THE MOVE

Between 1940 and 1960, more than 40 million Americans moved to the suburbs, one of the largest mass migrations in history. Developers began quickly building affordable housing in the suburbs to fill the gap left by a shortage of urban housing. Government-backed low-interest loans enabled more people to purchase homes.

Suburban growth would not have been possible had Congress not passed the **Interstate Highway Act** in 1956. This act authorized funds to build 41,000 miles of highway, consisting of multilane expressways that would connect the nation's major cities. The new highways eased the commute from suburbs to cities and boosted the travel and vacation industries.

Southern and western states, known as the **Sunbelt,** also experienced rapid growth. These states had appealing climates and a large number of jobs in the defense, aerospace, and electronics industries. As people moved, their political power moved with them. The Sunbelt and suburbs gained representation while urban areas in the Northeast and the Midwest lost political power.

The American economy was also shifting. Fewer people worked in manufacturing or farming. Employment grew in the **service sector,** businesses that provided services rather than manufactured goods, and **information industries,** businesses that provided informational services. **Franchise businesses** allowed companies to distribute their products and services through retail outlets owned by independent operators. **Multinational corporations,** companies that produced and sold their goods and services across the globe, thrived.

Unions also experienced change. The AFL and the CIO joined in 1955 to form the **AFL-CIO,** bringing them more political clout. However, new white-collar workers generally did not join unions.

Educational opportunities grew as well. By the early 1960s, close to 40 percent of college-age Americans attended college, up from about 15 percent in 1940. The federal government increased education funds, in part to produce more scientists and science teachers. Many states undertook improvement of their public universities. Accessibility to ordinary Americans also increased. California created a **California Master Plan,** creating three tiers of higher education: research universities, state colleges, and community colleges.

Review Questions

1. Discuss the factors that fostered suburban growth.

_____

_____

2. What industries and types of businesses saw job growth in the postwar period?

_____

_____

Why did people move to the Sunbelt?

_____

_____

_____

VOCABULARY STRATEGY

What does *undertook* mean in the underlined sentence? Read the underlined sentence aloud but leave out the word *undertook*. Think about what word you could use in its place. Use this strategy to help you figure out the meaning of *undertook*.

_____

_____

_____

READING SKILL

Identify Main Ideas Discuss changes in American education in the postwar period.

_____

_____

_____

Note Taking Study Guide
MASS CULTURE AND FAMILY LIFE

Focus Question: How did popular culture and family life change during the 1950s?

Identify postwar changes in daily life and popular culture.

I. The Culture of Consumerism
   A. Americans spend more
      1. Increased family income
      2. _____
   B. _____
      1. _____
      2. _____

II. _____
   A. _____
      1. _____
      2. _____
   B. _____
      1. _____
      2. _____
   C. _____
      1. _____
      2. _____
   D. _____
      1. _____
      2. _____

III. _____
   A. _____
   B. _____

IV. _____
   A. _____
   B. _____
      1. _____
      2. _____

CHAPTER
26
SECTION 3

Section Summary
MASS CULTURE AND FAMILY LIFE

Name the medical advancement that helped control infectious diseases.

_____

_____

_____

As the U.S. economy began to boom in the postwar era, Americans were caught up in a wave of **consumerism,** buying as much as they could, much of it on credit. **Median family income** refers to average family income. Median family income rose dramatically during the 1950s. With money to spend, easy credit, and new goods to buy, shopping became a new pastime for Americans.

During the 1950s, the ideal family was one in which men worked and women stayed home. Popular magazines of the era described the **nuclear family,** or a household consisting of a mother and father and their children, as the backbone of American society. Nevertheless, as the 1950s progressed, more women were willing to challenge the view that a woman should not have a career.

More so than in the past, family life revolved around children. Dr. **Benjamin Spock,** a best-selling author of the era, emphasized the importance of nurturing children, from their earliest days as infants through their teen years. Parents were also spending more money on their children. Some parents even defended their spending by arguing that it would prevent the recurrence of economic depression.

The 1950s also witnessed a revival of religion in the United States. Regular church attendance rose. At the same time, numerous advances in medicine were made, including the widespread use of antibiotics to help control many infectious diseases.

Television had a profound impact on American society, particularly among children. Sitcoms, which rarely discussed real-life problems, were popular. These shows reflected and reinforced the ideal of the 1950s family. Television also eroded distinct regional and ethnic cultures, helping to develop a national culture.

Like television, **rock-and-roll** captured the attention of Americans. Rock music originated in the rhythm and blues traditions of African Americans. **Elvis Presley** made rock music popular when he integrated African American gospel tunes into the music he played. Although some Americans complained about rock music, it nonetheless became a symbol of the emerging youth culture and of the growing power of youth on mass culture.

VOCABULARY STRATEGY

What does the word *nevertheless* mean in the underlined sentence? Circle any words or phrases in the paragraph that help you figure out what *nevertheless* means.

_____

_____

_____

READING SKILL

Identify Main Ideas How did television and rock-and-roll impact postwar American society?

_____

_____

_____

Review Questions
1. Why did shopping become a new pastime for Americans?

_____

_____

2. Who was Dr. Benjamin Spock?

_____

_____

CHAPTER
26
SECTION 4

Note Taking Study Guide
DISSENT AND DISCONTENT

Focus Question: Why were some groups of Americans dissatisfied with conditions in postwar America?

Record the main ideas and supporting details.

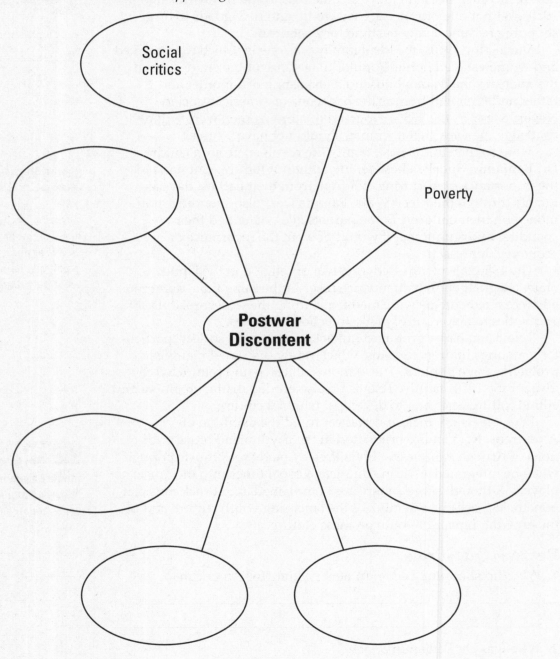

CHAPTER 26 SECTION 4

Section Summary

DISSENT AND DISCONTENT

Despite the prosperity of the 1950s, not everyone benefited from it. <u>Some Americans were dissatisfied with the changes brought by affluence.</u> Social critics and a small group of writers and artists known as **beatniks** criticized what they viewed as the crass materialism and conformity of the American middle class. The theme of alienation, or the feeling of being cut off from mainstream society, dominated many of the era's popular novels.

Hidden behind this prosperity were urban slums, desperate rural poverty, and discrimination. Michael Harrington's influential book *The Other America* (1962) opened America's eyes to the fifty million people, one fourth of the nation, living in poverty. Many of the "invisible" poor were inner-city African Americans, rural whites, and Hispanics in migrant farm camps and urban barrios.

As the middle class moved from cities to the suburbs, cities lost revenue and political clout. Minorities moved in great numbers to cities in search of better economic opportunities. Strained city services such as garbage removal deteriorated. Crime increased in what was now called the **inner city,** further encouraging middle-class Americans to flee. Government-funded **urban renewal** projects tried to reverse this trend by creating developments they hoped would revitalize downtowns. Many failed, pushing people from their homes into already overcrowded areas. To ease the overcrowding and provide affordable housing, the federal government constructed public housing, often in poor neighborhoods. Poverty and associated problems such as crime became further concentrated.

Many of the rural poor also relocated to cities. Small farmers slipped into poverty when they could not compete with the corporations and large-farm owners dominating farm production.

Efforts to overcome housing and employment discrimination became central to the struggle for civil rights. Latinos and Native Americans struggled with many of the same problems. In 1953, the federal government enacted the **termination policy,** a law that sought to end tribal government and to relocate Native Americans to the nation's cities. Proponents of the policy argued that it would free American Indians to assimilate into American society.

Review Questions

1. List three problems that many minorities faced in the postwar era.

_____

_____

2. Discuss how cities changed during this period.

_____

_____

READING CHECK

Who were the beatniks?

_____

_____

_____

VOCABULARY STRATEGY

What does the word *affluence* mean in the underlined sentence? The terms *prosperity* and *material comfort* are synonyms of *affluence*. Use the synonyms to help you figure out the meaning of *affluence*.

_____

_____

_____

READING SKILL

Identify Main Ideas Why did government efforts fail to improve life for minorities?

_____

_____

_____

Focus Question: How did African Americans challenge segregation after World War II?

Fill in the timeline below with events of the early civil rights movement. When you finish, write two sentences that summarize the information in your timeline.

_____

_____

CHAPTER 27 SECTION 1

Section Summary

EARLY DEMANDS FOR EQUALITY

After World War II, Jim Crow laws in the South continued to enforce strict separation of the races. Segregation that is imposed by law is known as **de jure segregation.** African Americans faced segregation in the North, too, even where there were no explicit laws. **De facto segregation,** or segregation by unwritten custom, was a fact of life.

Thurgood Marshall, an African American lawyer, worked with civil rights organizations to challenge segregation in the courts. In 1954, *Brown v. Board of Education* challenged segregated public education at all grade levels. Chief Justice **Earl Warren** wrote the *Brown* decision in which the Supreme Court agreed that segregated public schools violated the United States Constitution. The *Brown* decision overturned the principle of "separate but equal." It also lent support to the view that all forms of segregation were wrong.

In Little Rock, Arkansas, the governor ordered the National Guard to block nine African American students from entering the high school. President Eisenhower sent federal troops to protect the students and to enforce the Court's decision. However, southern states continued to resist compliance with the law.

Congress passed the **Civil Rights Act of 1957.** This act established the U.S. Civil Rights Commission. The law's main significance was that it was the first civil rights bill passed by Congress since Reconstruction. It was a small, but important, victory.

In 1955, in Montgomery, Alabama, an African American woman named **Rosa Parks** refused to give up her bus seat to a white passenger. She was arrested. A core of civil rights activists in Montgomery organized a one-day bus boycott to express opposition to Park's arrest and to segregation in general.

The next evening, Dr. **Martin Luther King, Jr.,** a Baptist minister, gave an inspirational speech in which he called upon African Americans to protest segregation and oppression in a nonviolent manner. The **Montgomery bus boycott** continued for more than a year. In 1956, the Supreme Court ruled that the Montgomery city law that segregated buses was unconstitutional. The boycott revealed the power African Americans could have if they joined together. It also helped King and his philosophy of nonviolence to gain prominence within the civil rights movement.

Review Questions

1. Explain the importance of *Brown* v. *Board of Education.*

_____

_____

2. How did the Montgomery bus boycott strengthen the civil rights movement?

_____

_____

READING CHECK

What action did the governor of Arkansas take to prevent the desegregation of schools in Little Rock?

_____

_____

_____

VOCABULARY BUILDER

What does the word *compliance* mean in the underlined sentence? Here is a clue: an antonym for *compliance* is *disobedience.* Use this clue to figure out what *compliance* means.

_____

_____

_____

READING SKILL

Summarize List three key events of the 1950s that helped to end segregation.

_____

_____

_____

Focus Question: How did the civil rights movement gain ground in the 1960s?

Use the concept web below to record information about the civil rights protests of the 1960s.

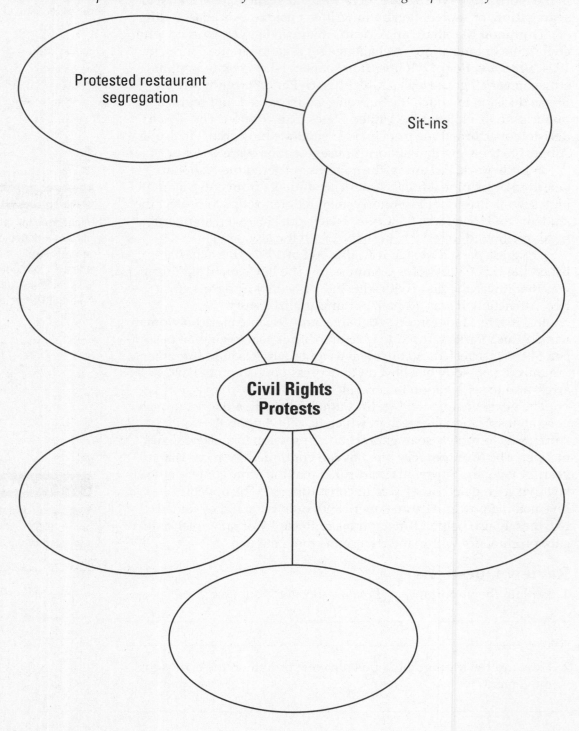

Protested restaurant segregation

Sit-ins

Civil Rights Protests

CHAPTER 27 SECTION 2

Section Summary

THE MOVEMENT GAINS GROUND

Despite some victories, activists continued to struggle for civil rights for African Americans. In North Carolina, four college students started a **sit-in** to protest discrimination. This sit-in sparked a wave of similar protests across the nation. Young African American activists established the **Student Nonviolent Coordinating Committee,** or **SNCC,** to create a grass-roots movement to gain equality.

The next battleground was interstate transportation. The Supreme Court had ruled that segregation on interstate buses was illegal. In the spring of 1961, the Congress of Racial Equality (CORE) staged a **"freedom ride"** through the Deep South to test the federal government's willingness to enforce the law. After the freedom riders met with violence, President John F. Kennedy intervened. Mississippi's leaders agreed to send police to protect the riders.

In September 1962, **James Meredith** won a federal court case that allowed him to enroll at the all-white University of Mississippi. Civil rights activist **Medgar Evers** was instrumental in this effort. Although full-scale riots erupted the night before his arrival, Meredith went on to graduate from the university in 1963.

In the spring of 1963, Martin Luther King, Jr., and the Southern Christian Leadership Conference (SCLC) targeted Birmingham, Alabama, for a major civil rights campaign. The campaign began nonviolently with protest marches and sit-ins. However, Birmingham's Public Safety Commissioner refused to tolerate the demonstrations. He used police dogs and fire hoses on the peaceful protesters. News coverage of the violence shocked many Americans.

To put pressure on Congress to pass a new civil rights bill, supporters organized a massive demonstration in Washington, D.C. More than 200,000 Americans gathered for the **March on Washington** on August 28, 1963. The highlight of the day came when King gave his "I Have a Dream" speech.

On November 22, 1963, President Kennedy was assassinated. Vice President Lyndon B. Johnson assumed the presidency. Johnson used his political skills to gain the passage of the **Civil Rights Act of 1964,** which banned segregation in public accommodations. The surge in support for the civil rights movement had produced a dramatic shift in race relations and set the stage for future reforms.

Review Questions

1. What was the purpose of the March on Washington?

_____

_____

2. Describe the Civil Rights Act of 1964.

_____

_____

READING CHECK

What was the highlight of the March on Washington?

_____

_____

_____

VOCABULARY BUILDER

What does the word *tolerate* mean in the underlined sentence? The word *forbid* is an antonym of *tolerate*. It means "to not permit." Use the meaning of *forbid* to figure out the meaning of *tolerate*.

_____

_____

_____

READING SKILL

Summarize Summarize the significance of James Meredith's actions in 1962.

_____

_____

_____

CHAPTER 27 SECTION 3

Note Taking Study Guide

NEW SUCCESSES AND CHALLENGES

Focus Question: What successes and challenges faced the civil rights movement after 1964?

Complete the outline below to summarize the contents of this section.

I. Push for Voting Rights

    A. Freedom Summer

    B. _____

II. _____

    A. _____

    B. _____

III. _____

    A. _____

    B. _____

IV. _____

    A. _____

    B. _____

V. _____

    A. _____

    B. _____

Although the civil rights movement had made progress, the southern political system still prevented African Americans from voting. In 1964, the SNCC mounted a major voter registration project, known as **Freedom Summer.** About 1,000 volunteers flooded Mississippi to register African Americans to vote.

In Selma, Alabama, Martin Luther King, Jr., and the SCLC organized a campaign to pressure the government to enact voting rights legislation. The protests climaxed in a series of confrontations, as heavily armed state troopers attacked the marchers. Spurred by the actions of the protesters, Congress passed the **Voting Rights Act** of 1965, which banned literacy tests. Another legal landmark was the **Twenty-fourth Amendment,** ratified in 1964. This amendment banned the poll tax, which had been used to prevent poor African Americans from voting.

Still, for some African Americans, things had not changed much. In many urban areas, anger over continuing discrimination and poverty erupted into violence and race riots. To determine the causes of the riots, President Johnson established the **Kerner Commission.** The commission concluded that long-term racial discrimination was the single most important cause of violence.

The riots coincided with the radicalization of many young urban African Americans. **Malcolm X** was the most well-known African American radical. Malcolm X became the most prominent minister of the **Nation of Islam,** a religious sect that demanded separation of the races. In February 1965, however, he was assassinated.

Many young African Americans considered themselves heirs of Malcolm X and moved away from the principle of nonviolence. SNCC leader Stokely Carmichael thought that African Americans should use their economic and political muscle, which he termed **"black power,"** to gain equality. Not long after, militants formed the Black Panther Party. Almost overnight, the **Black Panthers** became the symbol of young militant African Americans.

On April 4, 1968, Martin Luther King, Jr., was assassinated. In the wake of his murder, Congress passed the Fair Housing Act, which banned discrimination in housing. Although African Americans had made significant gains, the radicalism of the times left a bitter legacy.

Review Questions

1. Explain the significance of the march in Selma.

_____

_____

2. Why did violence erupt in many American cities in the 1960s?

_____

_____

READING CHECK

Which group became the symbol for young militant African Americans?

_____

_____

_____

VOCABULARY BUILDER

What does the word *confrontations* mean in the underlined sentence? Circle any words or phrases in the paragraph that help you figure out what *confrontations* means.

_____

_____

_____

READING SKILL

Summarize Summarize the impact of Malcolm X on the civil rights movement.

_____

_____

_____

CHAPTER 28 SECTION 1 — Note Taking Study Guide

KENNEDY AND THE COLD WAR

Focus Question: How did Kennedy respond to the continuing challenges of the Cold War?

As you read, list the Cold War crises Kennedy faced and the effects of each event.

Cold War Crisis	Result
Bay of Pigs Invasion	• • •
	• • • •
	• • • • •

CHAPTER 28 SECTION 1

Section Summary
KENNEDY AND THE COLD WAR

The 1960 election featured Democrat **John F. Kennedy** and Republican **Richard M. Nixon.** Both were young, energetic, and intelligent. Kennedy won the election narrowly, in part due to an impressive performance in a televised debate.

As President, Kennedy worked to build up the country's armed forces. He wanted a **"flexible response"** defense policy to prepare the United States to fight any size or any type of conflict. He also wanted to prevent the spread of communism in poor nations around the globe. Like previous leaders, Kennedy believed that democracy combined with prosperity would contain or limit communism's spread. Therefore, he created programs like the **Peace Corps,** which sent American volunteers to help developing countries, to improve the Third World politically and economically.

Kennedy's first major challenge came in Cuba. The revolutionary **Fidel Castro** took over Cuba in 1959 and aligned Cuba with the Soviet Union. Eisenhower had planned an invasion of Cuba to overthrow Castro, and Kennedy executed this plan in 1961. A CIA-led force of Cuban exiles invaded Cuba at the **Bay of Pigs invasion.** The invasion failed and probably ended up strengthening Castro's position in Cuba.

Kennedy's next challenge involved the Soviet premier **Nikita Khrushchev,** who demanded that America remove its troops from West Berlin and recognize the divided city. Kennedy refused. Khrushchev then ordered the construction of a wall between East and West Berlin. The **Berlin Wall** became a symbol of the divide between communism and democracy.

When the Soviets began building nuclear missile sites in Cuba in range of East Coast cities, Kennedy faced his third challenge. During the **Cuban missile crisis,** Kennedy demanded that the Soviets remove the missiles. Nuclear war seemed possible. After several tense days, Khrushchev agreed to remove the missiles. The leaders agreed to install a **"hot line"** telephone system between Moscow and Washington, D.C., to improve communication. A year later, in 1963, the United States, Great Britain, and the Soviet Union signed the first nuclear-weapons agreement.

Review Questions

1. Why did the United States want to overthrow Fidel Castro?

_____

_____

2. Why did U.S. leaders feel threatened by missiles in Cuba?

_____

_____

READING CHECK

Who was the leader of the Soviet Union during the Cuban missile crisis?

_____

_____

_____

VOCABULARY STRATEGY

What does the word *aligned* mean in the underlined sentence? Circle any words or phrases in the paragraph that help you figure out what *aligned* means.

_____

_____

_____

READING SKILL

Understand Effects What effects did the Cuban missile crisis have on the Soviet Union and the United States?

_____

_____

_____

Name _____ Class _____ Date _____

Focus Question: What were the goals of Kennedy's New Frontier?

A. *List the characteristics of John F. Kennedy that appealed to the American people.*

The Kennedy Image
• Youthful
•
•
•
•
•

CHAPTER
28
SECTION 2

Note Taking Study Guide
KENNEDY'S NEW FRONTIER

Focus Question: What were the goals of Kennedy's New Frontier?

B. *As you read, identify details of Kennedy's New Frontier program.*

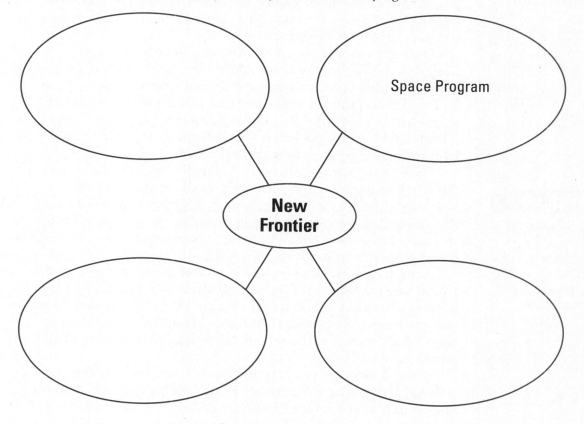

CHAPTER 28 SECTION 2

Section Summary

KENNEDY'S NEW FRONTIER

What was the job of the Warren Commission?

_____

_____

_____

VOCABULARY STRATEGY

What does the word *advocated* mean in the underlined sentence? The word *promoted* is a synonym of *advocated*. Use this synonym to help you figure out the meaning of *advocated*.

_____

_____

_____

READING SKILL

Identify Main Ideas What was deficit spending and why did Kennedy support it?

_____

_____

_____

President Kennedy promised Americans that his administration would blaze a **"New Frontier."** The term described Kennedy's proposals to improve the economy, education, healthcare, and civil rights. He used his charisma and a team of intelligent advisers to win support for his programs.

The high levels of poverty in America troubled Kennedy. Congress was hesitant to make reforms, but Kennedy did achieve an increase in the minimum wage and improvements in the welfare system. He also tried to make sure that women were paid equal wages for "equal work." The **Equal Pay Act** required this. Although it contained various loopholes, the law was an important step on the road to fair and equal employment practices.

The economy was weak when Kennedy took office, and he thought that improving the economy would reduce poverty. Kennedy accepted the "new economics" of John Maynard Keynes that advocated **deficit spending** to stimulate the economy. Deficit spending is the government practice of borrowing money in order to spend more than is received from taxes.

At first, Kennedy moved slowly on civil rights, worried that he would lose the support of the conservatives in his party. By 1963, however, Kennedy realized that African Americans needed the federal government to protect their rights. He introduced a bill that used federal money to aid school desegregation and demanded other reforms.

Perhaps the most visual component of the New Frontier was the active space program. Americans were afraid of falling behind the Soviets in the **"space race."** Kennedy called for a man to be landed on the moon in less than 10 years. The goal was met in 1969.

Kennedy's term as President was ended by his assassination. Lee Harvey Oswald shot Kennedy while he was riding in a car in Dallas, Texas. Although many people questioned whether Oswald acted alone, the **Warren Commission,** which conducted the official investigation of the shooting, declared that Oswald acted alone. The senseless murder deeply saddened Americans across the nation. It seemed as if part of America's innocence had died with Kennedy.

Review Questions

1. Why did Kennedy want a change in the minimum wage?

_____

_____

2. What did Kennedy do to advance the space program?

_____

_____

CHAPTER 28 SECTION 3 — Note Taking Study Guide

JOHNSON'S GREAT SOCIETY

Focus Question: How did Johnson's Great Society programs change life for most Americans?

Identify details about the Great Society programs.

The Great Society			
Education	**Healthcare**	**Immigration**	**Poverty**
•	• Medicare	•	•
•	•		•
			•
			•

CHAPTER 28 SECTION 3

Section Summary

JOHNSON'S GREAT SOCIETY

READING CHECK

What programs did Johnson create to fight poverty?

_____

_____

_____

VOCABULARY STRATEGY

What does the word *outcome* mean in the underlined sentence? Circle any words or phrases in the paragraph that help you figure out what *outcome* means.

_____

_____

_____

READING SKILL

Identify Main Ideas What did the Civil Rights Act accomplish?

_____

_____

_____

Lyndon B. Johnson, who became President after Kennedy's assassination, shared the same goals as his predecessor. Johnson's rise to the top was not easy. He was born in a small town in Texas. After attending a state college, he taught in a poor, segregated school for Mexican Americans. After teaching for several years, he was elected to Congress and began working his way up.

Johnson proved to be an excellent politician. One of his first successes after becoming President was ensuring that Congress passed the **Civil Rights Act,** an important bill introduced by President Kennedy. The outcome of this bill was an end to discrimination in voting, education, and public accommodations.

The **War on Poverty** was a big part of Johnson's plans. He wanted to provide more training, education, and healthcare to those who needed it. The **Economic Opportunity Act** began this process by creating agencies such as Job Corps, VISTA, and Head Start.

After being elected President in 1964, Johnson called his vision for America the **Great Society.** He said the Great Society demanded "an end to poverty and racial injustice." In 1965, Congress began to pass Johnson's Great Society legislation.

One area of reform was in healthcare insurance. Johnson created **Medicare,** a program that provided basic hospital insurance for older Americans. He also created **Medicaid,** which provided basic medical services to poor and disabled Americans.

Education and immigration policy also saw reforms. The 1965 Elementary and Secondary Education Act aided schools in poorer communities. The **Immigration and Nationality Act of 1965** relaxed the nation's immigration policies. Over the next two decades, millions of immigrants poured into the United States.

During the 1960s, the Supreme Court was also interested in reform. The court decided cases on controversial social, religious, and political issues. Led by Chief Justice Earl Warren—and often called the **Warren Court**—this liberal court supported civil rights, civil liberties, voting rights, and personal privacy.

Review Questions

1. What did Johnson say was necessary for America to be the Great Society?

_____

_____

2. What is Medicaid?

_____

_____

Name _____ Class _____ Date _____

Focus Question: Why did the United States become involved in Vietnam?

As you read, describe the Vietnam policies of Presidents Truman, Eisenhower, Kennedy, and Johnson.

U.S. Policy in Vietnam		
Truman/Eisenhower	**Kennedy**	**Johnson**
•	•	•
•	•	•
•		• Gulf of Tonkin Resolution

CHAPTER 29 SECTION 1

Section Summary
ORIGINS OF THE VIETNAM WAR

Who were the Vietcong?

_____

_____

_____

France had controlled Vietnam as a colony since the 1800s. After World War II, however, a strong independence movement took hold. The movement was led by **Ho Chi Minh,** who had been fighting for Vietnamese independence for 30 years. Ho Chi Minh had fled Vietnam in 1912. During his travels around the world, he embraced communism and had formed ties with the Soviet Union.

The United States became involved in Vietnam for several reasons. First, it wanted to keep France as an ally. To ensure French support in the Cold War, President Truman agreed to help France regain control over Vietnam. Second, both Truman and Eisenhower wanted to contain the spread of communism. They believed in the **domino theory.** This idea held that if Vietnam fell to communism, its closest neighbors would follow. Communism would then spread throughout the entire region.

Despite billions of U.S. dollars in support, France lost its hold on Vietnam. In 1954, French troops were trapped at a military base at **Dien Bien Phu.** After 56 days, the French surrendered. At a peace conference in Geneva, Switzerland, France granted independence to Vietnam. The Geneva Accords divided the country into North Vietnam and South Vietnam. Ho Chi Minh's communist forces took power in the north, and an anticommunist government, supported by the United States, ruled in the south.

VOCABULARY STRATEGY

What does the word *ensure* mean in the underlined sentence? Circle any words in the surrounding sentences that could help you learn what *ensure* means.

_____

_____

_____

The United States channeled aid to South Vietnam through the **Southeast Asia Treaty Organization (SEATO).** However, a communist rebel group was determined to undermine the government. Communist guerrilla fighters, called **Vietcong,** were supplied by communists in North Vietnam. They attacked South Vietnamese government officials and destroyed roads and bridges.

In 1961, President Kennedy began sending U.S. troops to South Vietnam. President Johnson increased U.S. involvement after North Vietnam attacked a U.S. destroyer patrolling the Gulf of Tonkin. Congress passed the **Gulf of Tonkin Resolution,** which gave Johnson the authority to use force to defend American troops. This resolution gave the President the power to commit U.S. troops to fight without asking Congress for a formal declaration of war.

READING SKILL

Summarize Why did the United States help France in Vietnam?

_____

_____

_____

Review Questions

1. What was the domino theory?

_____

_____

2. How did the Gulf of Tonkin Resolution expand the powers of the presidency?

_____

_____

Note Taking Study Guide
U.S. INVOLVEMENT GROWS

Focus Question: What were the causes and effects of America's growing involvement in the Vietnam War?

As you read, fill in the outline with details about the escalation of the American war effort.

I. **"Americanizing" the War**

   A. _____

      1. _____

      2. _____

   B. _____

      1. _____

      2. _____

   C. _____

      1. _____

      2. _____

II. _____

   A. _____

      1. _____

      2. _____

   B. _____

      1. _____

      2. _____

   C. _____

      1. _____

      2. _____

III. _____

   A. _____

      1. _____

      2. _____

   B. _____

      1. _____

      2. _____

CHAPTER 29 SECTION 2

Section Summary
U.S. INVOLVEMENT GROWS

READING CHECK

Which group in Congress opposed the war in Vietnam?

_____

_____

_____

VOCABULARY STRATEGY

What does the word *doctrine* mean in the underlined sentence? Circle the words in the surrounding sentences that could help you learn what *doctrine* means.

_____

_____

_____

READING SKILL

Identify Supporting Details Why did President Johnson raise taxes?

_____

_____

_____

In February 1965, President Johnson took the United States deeper into the Vietnam War by ordering a large bombing campaign called Operation Rolling Thunder. Despite massive and sustained airstrikes, communist forces continued to fight. Johnson then ordered more troops to fight them on the ground. This more active strategy came primarily from Secretary of Defense Robert McNamara and General **William Westmoreland,** the American commander in South Vietnam.

In addition to conventional bombs, American pilots dropped napalm and sprayed Agent Orange. **Napalm** is a jellied gasoline that covered large areas in flames. Agent Orange is an herbicide that destroys plant life. It was used to disrupt the enemy's food supply.

When the U.S. troops fought on the ground, it was rarely in large battles. The Vietcong and North Vietnamese Army fought with guerrilla tactics in the jungle, trying to wear the United States down because they knew they could not win a traditional war. They followed Ho Chi Minh's doctrine, which stated that fighting should never be on the opponents' terms. Communist forces used hit-and-run attacks, nighttime ambushes, and booby traps. It was also difficult for the U.S. troops to know which Vietnamese person was a friend or an enemy.

By 1967, the war had become a stalemate. By 1968, more than 30,000 Americans had been killed in Vietnam. Despite the many times Johnson asserted that victory was near, each year yielded little progress. Troop morale began to fall.

The costs of the war had also grown each year, straining government finances. Government spending had lowered the unemployment rate at home, but it had also led to rising prices and inflation. President Johnson was forced to raise taxes, and social programs at home had to be cut.

The war was being questioned in Congress, as well. In 1967, Congress was divided into two camps: hawks and doves. **Hawks** supported the war and believed they were fighting communism. **Doves** questioned the war on moral and strategic grounds. They were not convinced that Vietnam was a vital Cold War battleground.

Review Questions

1. Why did President Johnson commit more troops to fight on the ground in Vietnam?

_____

_____

2. What tactics did the communist forces use against U.S. troops in Vietnam?

_____

_____

Focus Question: How did the American war effort in Vietnam lead to rising protests and social divisions back home?

Note the events leading up to the 1968 election.

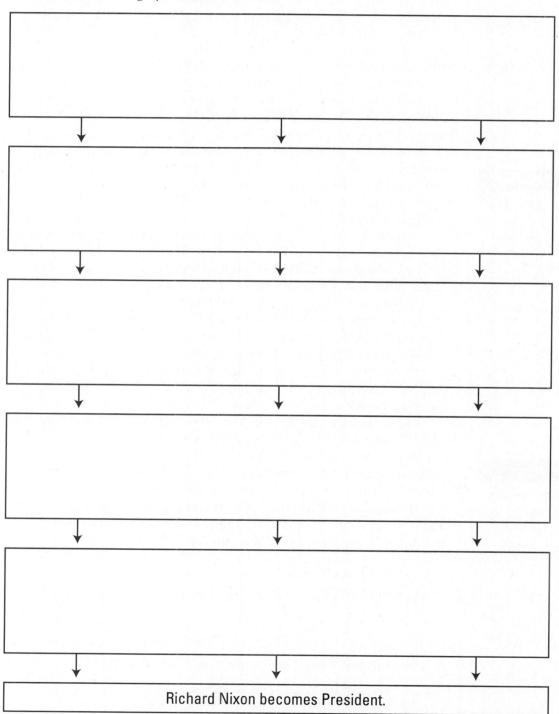

Richard Nixon becomes President.

CHAPTER 29 SECTION 3

Section Summary
THE WAR DIVIDES AMERICA

READING CHECK

READING CHECK

Why did the Tet Offensive shock Americans?

_____

_____

_____

VOCABULARY STRATEGY

What does the word *deferments* mean in the underlined sentence? Circle the words in the surrounding sentences that could help you learn what *deferments* means.

_____

_____

_____

READING SKILL

Recognize Sequence How did the protests at the Democratic National Convention in 1968 help Richard Nixon?

_____

_____

_____

The war in Vietnam divided Americans and opened a deep emotional rift in American society. To provide enough soldiers for the war, the government drafted young men into service. Some of these **draftees,** however, thought that the selection method was unfair. Draft boards were allowed to grant deferments to college students and men who worked in certain occupations. The result was that most of the men who served in Vietnam came from working-class and poor backgrounds. The number of African Americans in Vietnam was also disproportionately high.

College campuses became centers of antiwar sentiment. The **Students for a Democratic Society (SDS),** formed in 1960 to fight racism and poverty, became a leading antiwar group. College students and police clashed during antiwar demonstrations. Nightly television coverage of the war fueled opposition to the conflict. The differences between war accounts given by journalists and the optimistic progress reported by the government created a **"credibility gap."**

Because of the government's reports on the war, the public was greatly surprised by the **Tet Offensive.** This major offensive by the North Vietnamese Army showed that the enemy was still strong. The United States repelled the offensive, but after these attacks, American leaders seemed less confident of a quick end to the war.

Meanwhile, the 1968 presidential campaign began. Senator **Eugene McCarthy,** the antiwar Democratic presidential candidate, made a surprisingly strong showing in an early primary election. Democratic senator **Robert Kennedy** also announced his candidacy for President. Soon thereafter, Johnson announced that he would not run for another term as President.

The spring and summer of 1968 saw violence at home. First, civil rights leader Martin Luther King, Jr., was assassinated. Then, Robert Kennedy was assassinated after winning the California primary. In August, major protests erupted at the Democratic Convention in Chicago. Police clashed with antiwar protesters in the streets outside the convention center. The chaos and civil disorder helped Republican Richard Nixon win the presidency in 1968. Nixon promised to achieve "peace with honor" in Vietnam.

Review Questions
1. Why did some people think that the draft system was unfair?

_____

_____

2. How did television play a role in the Vietnam War?

_____

_____

CHAPTER 29 SECTION 4

Note Taking Study Guide

THE WAR'S END AND IMPACT

Focus Question: How did the Vietnam War end, and what were its lasting effects?

A. *Note the similarities and differences between Nixon's Vietnam policy and that of Lyndon Johnson.*

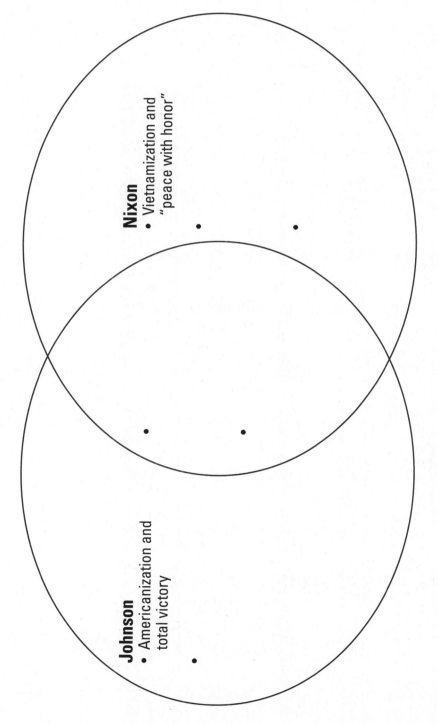

Nixon
• Vietnamization and "peace with honor"

Johnson
• Americanization and total victory

Note Taking Study Guide
THE WAR'S END AND IMPACT

Focus Question: How did the Vietnam War end, and what were its lasting effects?

B. *As you read, use the concept web below to identify the effects of the Vietnam War.*

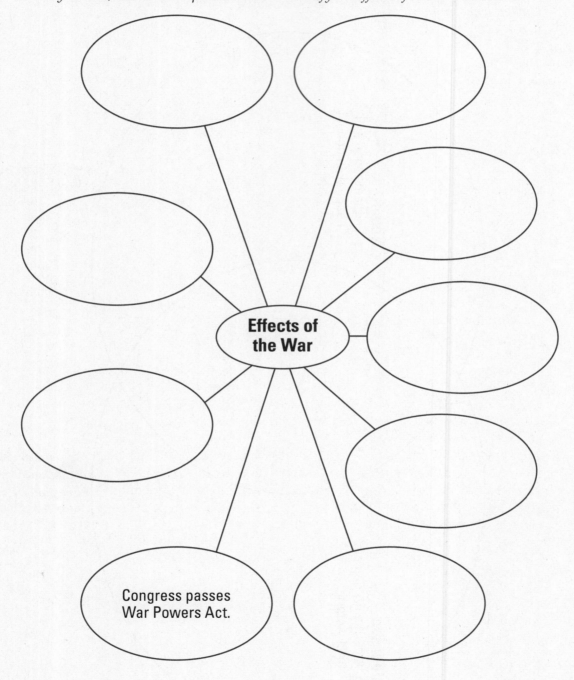

Effects of the War

Congress passes
War Powers Act.

CHAPTER 29 SECTION 4 — Section Summary

THE WAR'S END AND IMPACT

When Nixon became President, he believed that a peace deal could be negotiated with North Vietnam. When these negotiations stalled, however, Nixon gradually began to pull American troops out of Vietnam. He believed that the South Vietnamese Army should fight on its own and called this approach **Vietnamization.** He hoped that American supplies to the South Vietnamese Army would be sufficient for the army to secure and hold South Vietnam.

In 1970, however, Nixon ordered a ground attack on communists in Cambodia, which angered antiwar activists at home who claimed that Nixon was widening the war, not ending it. Protests erupted on many college campuses. At **Kent State University,** members of the National Guard fired into a group of protesters, killing four. This led to demonstrations on other campuses, including Jackson State in Mississippi, where two students were killed.

Other events also outraged the public. American troops killed over four hundred unarmed Vietnamese in the village of **My Lai.** The **Pentagon Papers** showed that the government had been dishonest with the public and with Congress about the Vietnam War.

American bombing finally induced the North Vietnamese to resume negotiations. In January 1973, the United States, South Vietnam, North Vietnam, and the Vietcong signed the **Paris Peace Accords.** American troops would withdraw from South Vietnam, and North Vietnamese troops would remain in South Vietnam. The war was over for the United States, but fighting continued in Vietnam. The Soviet-supplied North Vietnamese Army defeated the South Vietnamese Army, and Vietnam was united under a communist regime.

More than 58,000 American troops and over 2 million Vietnamese had been killed in the Vietnam War. Turmoil troubled Southeast Asia for many years afterward. After the difficult experience in Vietnam, Americans were less willing to intervene in the affairs of other countries. Americans had less trust in their leaders, as well. In 1973, Congress passed the **War Powers Act,** which restricted the President's authority to commit American troops to foreign conflicts. The fear of "another Vietnam" would affect American foreign policy for decades to come.

Review Questions

1. What was Vietnamization?

_____

_____

2. Why did the Pentagon Papers outrage Americans?

_____

_____

READING CHECK

How many American troops were killed in Vietnam?

_____

_____

_____

VOCABULARY STRATEGY

What does the word *induced* mean in the underlined sentence? Circle the words in the underlined sentence that could help you learn what *induced* means.

_____

_____

_____

READING SKILL

Recognize Effects What was one effect of the Vietnam War on American foreign policy?

_____

_____

_____

Note Taking Study Guide

CHAPTER 29 SECTION 5

NIXON AND THE COLD WAR

Focus Question: How did Richard Nixon change Cold War diplomacy during his presidency?

As you read, describe Nixon's Cold War foreign policies in dealing with China and the Soviet Union.

Nixon's Cold War Strategies	
China	**Soviet Union**
• Normalization of relations will drive wedge between China and Soviet Union. • •	• Diplomacy with China will create Soviet fear of isolation. • •

CHAPTER 29 SECTION 5

Section Summary

NIXON AND THE COLD WAR

During his years as President, Richard Nixon fundamentally reshaped the way the United States approached the world. His leading adviser on national security and international affairs, **Henry Kissinger,** helped him.

In foreign affairs, Nixon and Kissinger shared the idea of **realpolitik,** a German word meaning "real politics." According to this idea, a nation's political goals around the world should be defined by what is good for the nation instead of by abstract ideologies. Nixon and Kissinger argued that a flexible, pragmatic foreign policy would benefit the United States in many ways.

Nixon had built his career as a strong opponent of communism. Therefore, his first bold move, to normalize relations with China, came as a surprise. In the 1960s, the United States still did not officially recognize communist China. Nixon understood that communist China could not be ignored. He tried to accomplish several goals by reaching out to China. First, he wanted to drive a wedge between China and the Soviet Union. Second, China could be a good trading partner. Third, perhaps China could pressure North Vietnam to accept a negotiated peace and end the Vietnam War. In 1972, Nixon traveled to China and met with Premier **Zhou Enlai** and Chairman Mao Zedong. The visit was a historic first step toward normalizing relations between the two countries.

Nixon's trip to China was met by an immediate reaction from the Soviet Union. Soviet leader Leonid Brezhnev invited the President to visit Moscow, where they signed the first **Strategic Arms Limitation Treaty.** This agreement froze the deployment of intercontinental ballistic missiles and placed limits on antiballistic missiles. The treaty was a first step toward limiting the arms race.

The United States and Soviet Union now implemented a new policy called **détente** to replace the prior foreign policy, which was based on suspicion and distrust. Détente eased tensions between the two nations.

Nixon's foreign policy changed the nation's stance toward communism. In the short term, the new relationships he forged helped to end the Vietnam War. In the long term, his foreign policy moved the world closer to the end of the Cold War.

Review Questions

1. Why did Nixon want to normalize relations with China?

_____

_____

2. What was the effect of détente?

_____

_____

READING CHECK

What is realpolitik?

_____

_____

_____

VOCABULARY STRATEGY

What does the word *pragmatic* mean in the underlined sentence? Circle the words in the underlined sentence that could help you learn what *pragmatic* means.

_____

_____

_____

READING SKILL

Categorize Circle the statement that most accurately reflects President Nixon's attitudes toward communism.

- If Vietnam fell to communism, its closest neighbors would follow, spreading communism throughout the region.
- A flexible, pragmatic foreign policy would benefit the United States in many ways.
- The United States should support all independence movements, no matter what their political beliefs.

Name _____ Class _____ Date _____

Focus Question: What was the counterculture, and what impact did it have on American society?

As you read, use the concept web below to record main ideas about the counterculture.

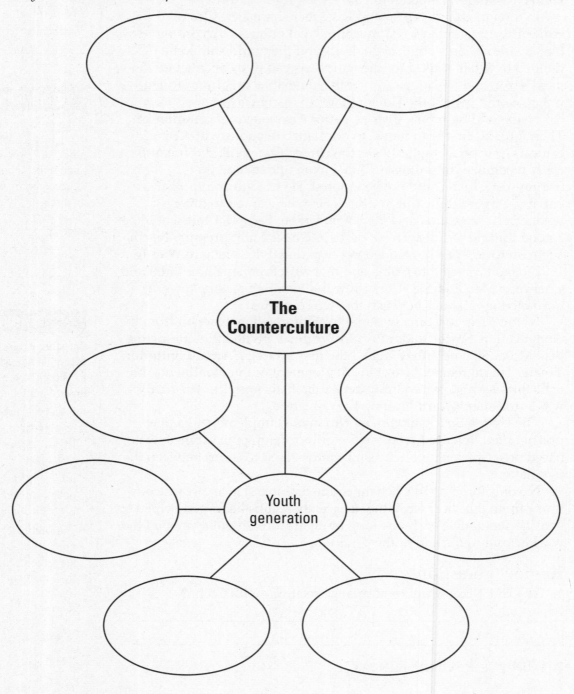

CHAPTER 30 SECTION 1

Section Summary

THE COUNTERCULTURE

The **counterculture** grew out of the Beat movement's emphasis on freedom from materialism and the civil rights movement's questioning of traditional boundaries. The Vietnam antiwar movement's distrust of authority fostered a spirit of rebellion. Members of the counterculture, known as hippies, valued youth, spontaneity, and individuality, and promoted peace, love, and freedom. Their experimentation with drugs, new styles of dress and music, and freer attitudes toward sexual relationships contradicted traditional values and boundaries. This rebellion led to misunderstanding between the older and younger generation, a situation that was called a **generation gap.**

Born after World War II, the younger generation had an enormous influence on American society, driving changes in attitudes and styles in everything from clothes to music and art. Rock-and-roll music by bands such as the **Beatles** came to define the decade. Hippies rejected many traditional restrictions on sexual behavior in what became known as the "sexual revolution." Many also often adopted new living patterns, residing in **communes,** small communities where people shared interests and resources.

The center of the counterculture was the **Haight-Ashbury** district of San Francisco. Here hippies experimented with drugs and listened to rock music and speeches by political radicals such as **Timothy Leary,** who encouraged youths to "tune in," "turn on" to drugs, and "drop out" of mainstream society.

Some hippies sought spirituality outside of the Judeo-Christian tradition, exploring Eastern religions and practices of Native Americans. Some sought to live off the land in harmony with nature. These beliefs impacted the growing environmental movement.

By the late 1960s, several key figures of the counterculture were dead of drug overdoses, and many people had become disillusioned with the movement's excesses. Most hippies eventually rejoined the mainstream, but the seeds of protest sown during the 1960s would influence the growing "rights revolution."

Review Questions

1. How did social and political events help shape the counterculture?

_____

_____

2. In what ways did the counterculture influence American culture?

_____

_____

READING CHECK

What district in San Francisco was at the center of the counterculture?

_____

_____

_____

VOCABULARY STRATEGY

What does the word *contradicted* mean in the underlined sentence? Circle the words in the underlined sentence that could help you learn what *contradicted* means.

_____

_____

_____

READING SKILL

Identify Main Ideas The counterculture's music, art, and style of dress reflected a rejection of what aspect of society?

_____

_____

_____

Name _____ Class _____ Date _____

Note Taking Study Guide
THE WOMEN'S RIGHTS MOVEMENT

Focus Question: What led to the rise of the women's movement, and what impact did it have on American society?

Record the causes, effects, and main figures in the women's movement in the chart below.

The Women's Movement		
Causes	**Proponents/ Opponents**	**Effects**
•	•	•
•	•	•
•	•	•
•		

CHAPTER
30
SECTION 2

Section Summary
THE WOMEN'S RIGHTS MOVEMENT

The first wave of feminism began in the 1840s and culminated in 1920 with women winning the right to vote. **Feminism** is the theory of political, social, and economic equality for men and women. The second wave of feminism was born in the 1960s. Inspired by successes of the civil rights movement, women wanted to change how they were treated as a group and to redefine how they were viewed as individuals.

The role of housewife was seen as the proper one for women, but many women found it deeply unsatisfying. Those women who did work experienced open and routine discrimination, including being paid less than men. **Betty Friedan** described women's dissatisfaction in her 1963 book *The Feminine Mystique*. Friedan later helped establish the **National Organization for Women (NOW),** which sought to win equality for women. The group campaigned for passage of the **Equal Rights Amendment (ERA),** an amendment to the Constitution that would guarantee gender equality under the law. NOW also worked to protect a woman's right to an abortion. Radical feminists went further, conducting protests to expose discrimination against women. One radical feminist was **Gloria Steinem,** who sought to raise consciousness through the media and helped co-found *Ms.* magazine in 1972.

Not all women supported these efforts. **Phyllis Schlafly,** a conservative political activist, denounced women's liberation as "a total assault on the family, on marriage, and on children." The ERA failed to pass partly due to her efforts.

Women did, however, gain new legal rights. Title IX of the Higher Education Act of 1972 banned discrimination in education and the Equal Credit Opportunity Act made it illegal to deny credit to a woman on the basis of gender. The 1973 Supreme Court decision in *Roe* v. *Wade* gave women the right to legal abortions.

Changes in the workplace came slowly. Today, more women work, and more work in fields such as medicine and law that were once limited to them. Despite these gains, the average woman still earns less than the average man, partly because women continue to work in fields that pay less.

Review Questions

1. What was the goal of the Equal Rights Amendment?

_____

_____

2. What causes did the National Organization for Women work toward? Did its efforts succeed or fail?

_____

_____

READING CHECK

Who founded *Ms.* magazine?

_____

_____

_____

VOCABULARY STRATEGY

What does the word *gender* mean in the underlined sentence? Look for context clues in the sentence and surrounding sentences to help you identify what *gender* refers to.

_____

_____

_____

READING SKILL

Identify Causes and Effects
What inspired the second wave of feminism?

_____

_____

_____

Name _____ Class _____ Date _____

Focus Question: How did the rights movements of the 1960s and 1970s expand rights for diverse groups of Americans?

A. *Compare and contrast the Latino and Native American rights movements in the Venn diagram below.*

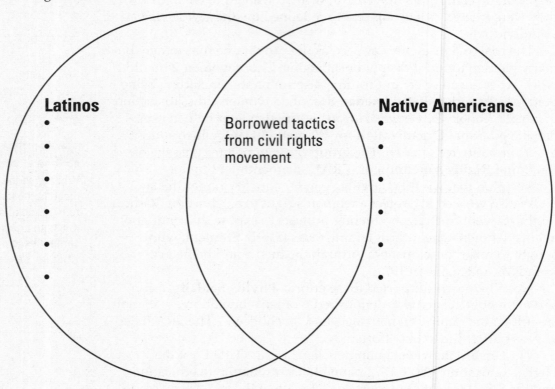

Latinos
-
-
-
-
-
-

Borrowed tactics from civil rights movement

Native Americans
-
-
-
-
-
-

B. *As you read, identify causes of expanding rights for consumers and those with disabilities.*

Consumer Advocacy	Disabled Advocacy
•	•
•	•

Growing Movements Expand Rights

CHAPTER 30 SECTION 3

Section Summary

THE RIGHTS REVOLUTION EXPANDS

Mexican and other Latin American immigrants came to the United States during and after World War II, filling the need for cheap labor. Mexican immigrants came as temporary farmworkers. Other immigrants came from Puerto Rico, Cuba, and the Dominican Republic. The *bracero* program allowed Mexicans to work on American farms. After passage of the Immigration and Nationality Act Amendments in 1965, immigration from Latin America surged.

Following the lead of the civil rights movement, Latinos began fighting for their rights. The most influential Latino activist was **Cesar Chavez,** who formed the **United Farm Workers (UFW).** This union implemented a strike and boycott of grapes that secured safer working conditions for **migrant farmworkers.** These workers were often exploited as they moved from farm to farm to pick fruits and vegetables. A broader movement known as the **Chicano movement** worked to raise consciousness, reduce poverty and discrimination, and attain political power for Latinos.

Native Americans formed their own protest groups. One group took over the island of Alcatraz and claimed it for the Sioux. Another group, the **American Indian Movement (AIM),** was founded in 1968 to ease poverty and help secure legal rights and self-government for Native Americans. In February 1973, AIM took over Wounded Knee, South Dakota, to protest living conditions on reservations. That protest that led to the deaths of two AIM members. Laws helping Native Americans were passed in the 1970s, including the Indian Self-Determination Act of 1975, which granted tribes greater control over resources on reservations.

The consumer rights movement started after **Ralph Nader** published *Unsafe at Any Speed,* a book that investigated the link between flawed car design and deaths in automobile accidents. The book prompted Congress to pass laws to improve automobile safety. Americans with disabilities, due in part to activism by Korean and Vietnam war veterans, also secured additional rights. Several laws were passed in the 1970s guaranteeing equal access to education for those with disabilities.

Review Questions

1. What factors encouraged Latinos to immigrate to the United States during and after World War II?

_____

_____

2. What changes did those fighting for consumer and disabled rights help bring about?

_____

_____

READING CHECK

What organization did Cesar Chavez help organize?

_____

_____

_____

VOCABULARY STRATEGY

What does the word *implemented* mean in the underlined sentence? Look for clues in the surrounding words, phrases, and sentences. Circle the words in the underlined sentence that could help you learn what *implemented* means.

_____

_____

_____

READING SKILL

Compare and Contrast Compare and contrast the results of the UFW's work and Ralph Nader's book.

_____

_____

_____

Focus Question: What forces gave rise to the environmental movement, and what impact did it have?

As you read, record major events in the environmental movement in the flowchart below.

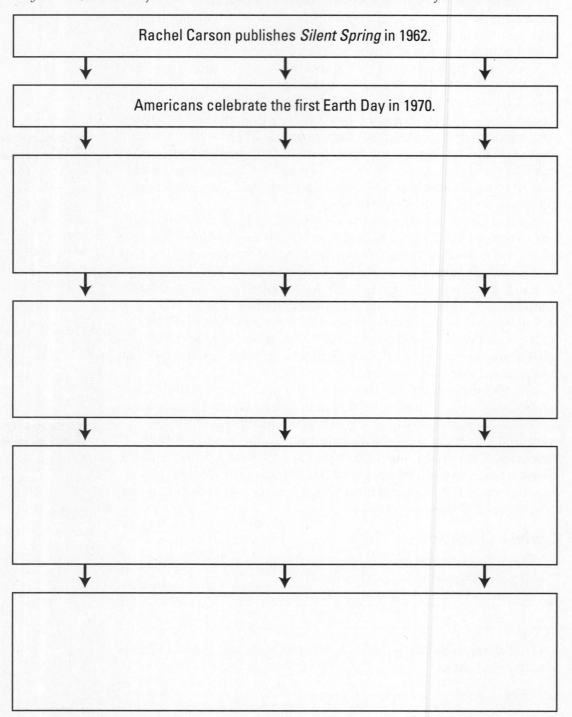

Rachel Carson publishes *Silent Spring* in 1962.

Americans celebrate the first Earth Day in 1970.

CHAPTER 30 SECTION 4

Section Summary
THE ENVIRONMENTAL MOVEMENT

Published in 1962, *Silent Spring*, by **Rachel Carson,** inspired much environmental activism. The book describes the deadly impact that pesticides were having on birds and other animals. Carson argued that humans were drastically altering the environment and had a responsibility to protect it. <u>Protests sparked by the book eventually compelled Congress to restrict use of the pesticide DDT.</u>

Other environmental concerns included **toxic waste** such as coal smog—poisonous byproducts of human activity. One response to environmental concern was **Earth Day.** Close to 20 million Americans took part in the first Earth Day, held on April 22, 1970, and it has since become an annual event.

Public outcry over environmental issues convinced President Nixon to support environmental reforms. Under his leadership, Congress created the **Environmental Protection Agency (EPA)** in 1970 to protect "the entire ecological chain." The EPA worked to clean up and protect the environment and sought to limit or eliminate pollutants that posed a risk to the public's health. Nixon also signed a number of environmental laws. The **Clean Air Act** (1970) combated air pollution by limiting the emissions from factories and automobiles. The **Clean Water Act** (1973) reduced water pollution by industry and agriculture. The **Endangered Species Act** (1973) helped to protect endangered plants and animals.

In the late 1970s, several crises reinforced the public's environmental concern. Toxic waste in the ground was blamed for high rates of birth defects and cancer in Love Canal, New York. Later, a nuclear reactor at Three Mile Island in Pennsylvania malfunctioned and the core began to melt.

While these events solidified some people's support for environmental regulation, other people questioned and opposed the government's actions. Conservatives complained that regulations took away individuals' property rights. Others argued that private property owners rather than the government should protect the environment. Industry leaders worried that too much environmental regulation would harm business.

Review Questions

1. What environmental protection laws were passed during President Nixon's tenure?

_____

_____

2. What arguments did some people make against the U.S. government's role in environmental protection?

_____

_____

READING CHECK

What agency works to limit or eliminate pollution?

_____

_____

_____

VOCABULARY STRATEGY

What does the word *compelled* mean in the underlined sentence? Look for clues in the surrounding words, phrases, and sentences. Circle the word below that is a synonym for *compelled*.

• forced

• voluntary

READING SKILL

Recognize Sequence What people and events influenced President Nixon's environmental reforms?

_____

_____

_____

Note Taking Study Guide

NIXON AND THE WATERGATE SCANDAL

Focus Question: What events led to Richard Nixon's resignation as President in 1974?

A. *Record Nixon's major domestic policies and goals in the chart below.*

Nixon's Domestic Policies and Strategies	
New Federalism	**Southern Strategy**
•	•
•	•
•	•
•	

B. *Use the chart below to record the causes and effects of the Watergate crisis.*

Watergate Crisis

Causes	Effects
• Break-in at Democratic Party headquarters	• Connections revealed between burglars and White House
•	•
•	•
•	•
•	•

CHAPTER 31 SECTION 1
Section Summary
NIXON AND THE WATERGATE SCANDAL

In 1968, Richard Nixon narrowly defeated Democrat Hubert Humphrey to win the presidency. During the campaign, Nixon claimed to represent the **silent majority,** the working men and women who made up Middle America. He believed that they were tired of "big" government. <u>However, he also believed that they wanted the government to address social problems like crime and pollution.</u> He proposed revenue sharing, in which the federal government gave money to the states to run social programs. He also sponsored programs to regulate workplace safety, to administer the federal war on illegal drugs, and to enforce environmental standards. Nixon's presidency was plagued by a combination of recession and inflation that came to be known as **stagflation.** When the **Organization of Petroleum Exporting Countries (OPEC)** placed an oil embargo on Israel's allies, oil prices skyrocketed.

Nixon set out to expand his base of support. His **southern strategy** targeted southern whites, who had traditionally voted for Democrats. He appointed conservative southern judges and criticized the court-ordered busing of school children to achieve desegregation. However, he also supported new **affirmative action** plans in employment and education. Nixon won the 1972 election easily, becoming the first Republican presidential candidate to sweep the entire South.

In June 1972, burglars broke into the Democratic Party headquarters at the Watergate complex in Washington. After their conviction, one of them charged that administration officials had been involved. Nixon denied any wrongdoing in what came to be known as the **Watergate** scandal. In the fall of 1973, Vice President Agnew resigned in the face of an unrelated corruption scandal. Under the **Twenty-fifth Amendment,** Nixon nominated Gerald Ford to become his new Vice President. Nixon refused to turn over secret tapes of Oval Office conversations. He claimed **executive privilege,** which is the principle that the President has the right to keep certain information confidential. However, the Supreme Court ordered Nixon to turn over the tapes. These tapes provided evidence of Nixon's involvement in the coverup. In order to avoid impeachment and conviction, Nixon resigned in August 1974.

Review Questions
1. What was Richard Nixon's attitude toward "big" government?

_____

_____

2. How did Watergate lead to a showdown between the President and the Supreme Court?

_____

_____

READING CHECK
What was Nixon's southern strategy?

_____

_____

_____

VOCABULARY STRATEGY
What does the word *pollution* mean in the underlined sentence? Look for context clues in the surrounding words, phrases, and sentences. Circle the word below that is a synonym for *pollution.*

• contamination

• purification

READING SKILL
Identify Main Ideas In what areas did Nixon expand the federal government's role?

_____

_____

Note Taking Study Guide

THE FORD AND CARTER YEARS

Focus Question: What accounted for the changes in American attitudes during the 1970s?

Use the outline below to record the political, economic, and social problems of the era and their impact on American society.

I. Gerald Ford's Presidency

    A. Major Domestic Issues

        1. _____

        2. _____

        3. _____

        4. _____

II. _____

    A. _____

    B. _____

    C. _____

    D. _____

III. _____

    A. _____

    B. _____

    C. _____

    D. _____

    E. _____

Gerald Ford had a long record of public service. When he became President after Nixon's resignation, he had the support of Democrats as well as Republicans. However, he lost support when he announced that he had **pardoned,** or officially forgiven, Nixon for any crimes he might have committed as President. The pardon was meant to heal the nation's wounds, but Ford's critics accused him of having made a secret deal. The 1974 congressional elections showed the public's disapproval of the pardon and the impact of Watergate. The Republicans lost 48 seats in the House of Representatives.

Former Georgia governor **Jimmy Carter** won the presidency in the 1976 election. He was a born-again Christian who won the support of many **Christian fundamentalists.** He also was a Washington outsider who had no close ties with the Democratic leadership in Congress. Most of the bills he submitted to Congress did not pass without major changes by his own party. A day after his inauguration, he granted **amnesty** to Americans who had evaded the draft, in the hope of moving the nation beyond the Vietnam War. Severe inflation continued, fueled by the ongoing energy crisis. Carter contended with the oil crisis by calling on Americans to conserve energy.

The migration of Americans to the Sunbelt and the growth of the suburbs continued during the 1970s. The Sunbelt's political power also grew. An influx of immigrants from Latin America and Asia also occured. The divorce rate more than doubled between 1965 and 1979, and the number of children born out of wedlock nearly tripled. The 1970s are sometimes called the "me decade" because many Americans appeared to be absorbed with self-improvement. This included an increased interest in fitness and health. Millions began to jog and eat natural foods.

The 1970s also witnessed a resurgence of fundamental Christianity. **Televangelists** such as Jerry Falwell preached to millions on television. Religious conservatives opposed many of the social changes begun in the 1960s that had gone mainstream in the 1970s. They began to form alliances with other conservatives to forge a new political majority.

Review Questions

1. What events cast a shadow over Gerald Ford's presidency?

_____

_____

2. How did Jimmy Carter deal with the energy crisis?

_____

_____

READING CHECK

Why were the 1970s called the "me decade"?

_____

_____

_____

VOCABULARY STRATEGY

What does the word *contended* mean in the underlined sentence? Note that the word is a verb. Ask yourself what kind of action President Carter was taking in relation to the oil crisis. Use this strategy to help you figure out what *contended* means.

_____

_____

_____

READING SKILL

Identify Main Ideas How did being an outsider in Washington hurt Carter's presidency?

_____

_____

_____

CHAPTER 31 SECTION 3

Note Taking Study Guide

FOREIGN POLICY TROUBLES

Focus Question: What were the goals of American foreign policy during the Ford and Carter years, and how successful were Ford's and Carter's policies?

Use the concept web below to record the main ideas and details about the foreign policies of Ford and Carter.

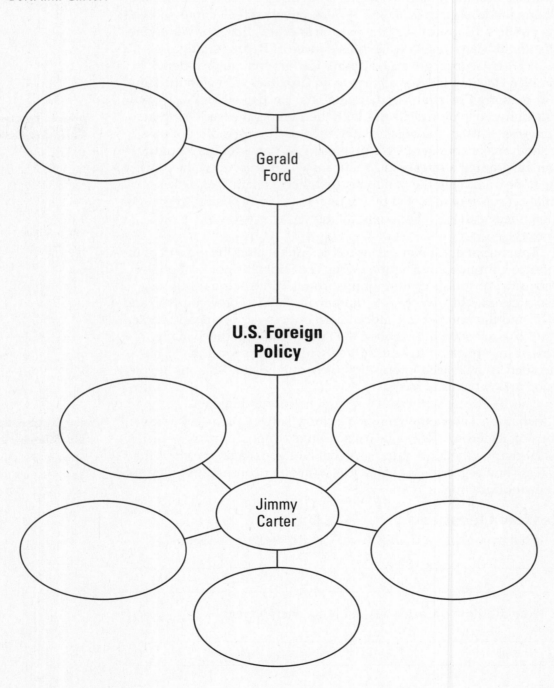

Relations with the Soviet Union were central to U.S. foreign policy during the Ford and Carter administrations. President Gerald Ford and Soviet leader Leonid Brezhnev met twice and endorsed the **Helsinki Accords.** In this document, the nations of Europe expressed their support of **human rights.** However, Ford chose to put arms control ahead of human rights. The United States continued disarmament talks with the Soviets. When South Vietnam fell to the communists, hundreds of thousands of Vietnamese tried to escape in rickety boats. These **boat people** represented the largest mass migration by sea in modern history.

Early in his presidency, Jimmy Carter announced that his foreign policy would be guided by a concern for human rights. He tried to use his foreign policy to end acts of politicial repression, such as torture. Carter also worked to achieve détente, and in 1979, he signed the **SALT II** treaty to limit nuclear arms production. However, relations between the two superpowers took a frosty turn after the Soviet Union invaded Afghanistan in December 1979. Carter responded by imposing **sanctions** on the Soviets, including a boycott of the 1980 Summer Olympic Games in Moscow. Carter also hoped to change the way the United States dealt with the **developing world.** His emphasis on human rights led him to alter the U.S. relationship with a number of dictators.

Carter's greatest foreign policy success and setback were both in the Middle East. Egypt and Israel had been enemies since Israel's founding in 1948. In 1977, Carter invited the leaders of the two nations to the presidential retreat. The result was the **Camp David Accords,** which led to a peace treaty in which Egypt recognized Israel. In January 1979, the U.S.-backed Shah of Iran was forced to flee. Fundamentalist Islamic clerics, led by the **Ayatollah Khomeini,** took power. Iranian radicals invaded the U.S. Embassy and took 66 Americans hostage. The Khomeini government took control of both the embassy and the hostages to defy the United States. The hostage crisis consumed Carter's attention during his last year in office. His failure to win the release of the hostages was viewed as evidence of American weakness.

Review Questions

1. Compare the foreign policies of Gerald Ford and Jimmy Carter.

_____

_____

2. How did the Iran hostage crisis affect the last year of Carter's presidency?

_____

_____

READING CHECK

Why did the United States boycott the 1980 Summer Olympic Games?

_____

_____

_____

VOCABULARY STRATEGY

What does the word *repression* mean in the underlined sentence? Look for context clues in the surrounding sentences to help you figure out the meaning of *repression.*

_____

_____

_____

READING SKILL

Identify Supporting Details List two details that support the following statement: Carter's greatest foreign policy challenges were in the Middle East.

_____

_____

_____

CHAPTER 32 SECTION 1

Note Taking Study Guide
THE CONSERVATIVE MOVEMENT GROWS

Focus Question: What spurred the rise of conservatism in the late 1970s and early 1980s?

As you read, summarize the rise of the conservative movement in the outline below.

I. Two Views: Liberal and Conservative

   A. Liberal ideas and goals

      1. _____

      _____

      2. _____

      _____

      3. _____

      _____

   B. _____

   _____

      1. _____

      _____

      2. _____

      _____

      3. _____

      _____

Section Summary
THE CONSERVATIVE MOVEMENT GROWS

The two major political parties in the late twentieth century were the Democrats, many of whom were "liberals," and the Republicans, often labeled "conservatives." **Liberals** believed that the federal government should play an active role in improving the lives of all Americans. They supported social programs and government regulation of industry, and favored cooperation with international organizations such as the United Nations.

Conservatives believed that the free market, private organizations, and individuals, instead of the government, should care for the needy. They opposed big government, favored tax cuts, and supported a strong military.

Many things contributed to the conservative movement known as the **New Right,** which grew rapidly during the 1960s and 1970s. The Vietnam War and urban riots of the 1960s divided the country. The counterculture had alienated many Americans. Watergate, the oil crises of the 1970s, and the Iran hostage crisis further weakened the public's faith in the federal government. When the economy stagnated, conservative beliefs became more attractive.

Conservatives blamed liberal policies for the economic problems of the late 1970s. They believed that the government taxed too heavily and spent too much money on the wrong programs. They complained about **unfunded mandates,** programs required but not paid for by the federal government.

In 1979, Reverend Jerry Falwell founded the **Moral Majority,** a political organization based on religious beliefs. Supporters worried about the decline of the traditional family. They were also concerned that the new freedoms brought by the counterculture would lead to the degeneration of modern youth.

The conservative movement swept the Republican presidential candidate, former actor and two-term California governor **Ronald Reagan,** to victory over Democratic incumbent Jimmy Carter in the 1980 election. Reagan's conservative beliefs, charm, and optimism convinced Americans that he would usher in a new era of prosperity and patriotism.

Review Questions

1. What events contributed to the rise of conservatism?

_____

_____

2. What did the Moral Majority dislike?

_____

_____

READING CHECK

What is the term for programs that the federal government requires but does not pay for?

_____

_____

_____

VOCABULARY STRATEGY

What does the word *degeneration* mean in the underlined sentence? Circle the word below that is a synonym for *degeneration.*
- advancement
- decline

READING SKILL

Summarize Describe the differences between the liberal and conservative viewpoints of government.

_____

_____

_____

CHAPTER 32 SECTION 2
Note Taking Study Guide
THE REAGAN REVOLUTION

Focus Question: What were the major characteristics of the conservative Reagan Revolution?

Identify the main ideas behind Reagan's policies.

Reagan Era		
Reaganomics	**Conservative Strength**	**Challenging Issues**
•	•	•
•	•	•
•		•
		•
		•
		•
		•
		•

CHAPTER 32 SECTION 2

Section Summary

THE REAGAN REVOLUTION

President Reagan's economic policies, or "Reaganomics," were based on the theory of **supply-side economics,** which assumes that reducing taxes gives people more incentive to work and more money to spend, causing the economy to grow. The government would then collect more tax dollars without raising taxes. Congress passed the Economic Recovery Act of 1981, which reduced taxes by 25 percent over three years.

Reagan called for **deregulation,** or the removal of government control over industries, including airline and telecommunications industries. He also appointed conservative judges to federal courts.

The economy experienced a severe recession from 1980 through 1982 but rebounded in 1983. Inflation fell and the Gross National Product increased. Still, the number of poor increased and the richest grew even richer. Reagan increased defense spending but failed to win cuts in other areas of the budget, leading to a **budget deficit,** a shortfall between money spent and money collected by the government. The **national debt,** the amount of money the government owes to owners of government bonds, also rose. Deficit problems worsened when the government had to bail out depositors of the nearly 1,000 Savings and Loan banks that failed in the **Savings and Loan (S&L) crisis** of 1989.

Reagan faced other problems. American students were scoring lower on standardized tests, prompting conservatives to further lobby for **vouchers,** or government checks that could be used by parents to pay tuition at private schools. The nation also faced a new disease—**Acquired Immunodeficiency Syndrome (AIDS).** By the end of the 1980s, AIDS was the biggest killer of men between the ages of 20 and 40.

Despite these problems, Reagan remained popular and was overwhelmingly reelected in 1984. <u>However, his momentum did not lead to a triumph for conservatives in Congress.</u> Democrats retained control of the House of Representatives.

Review Questions

1. What occurred in the economy during the early 1980s?

_____

_____

2. What was the budget deficit, and what event made it worse?

_____

_____

READING CHECK

What disease became the biggest killer of men between the ages of 20 and 40 by the late 1980s?

_____

_____

_____

VOCABULARY STRATEGY

What does the word *momentum* mean in the underlined sentence? Circle any words or phrases in the paragraph that help you figure out what *momentum* means.

_____

_____

_____

READING SKILL

Identify Main Ideas Describe the central idea of Reagan's economic policies.

_____

_____

_____

Focus Question: What were Reagan's foreign policies, and how did they contribute to the fall of communism in Europe?

A. *As you read this section, use the flowchart below to sequence major events related to the fall of communism in Europe and the Soviet Union.*

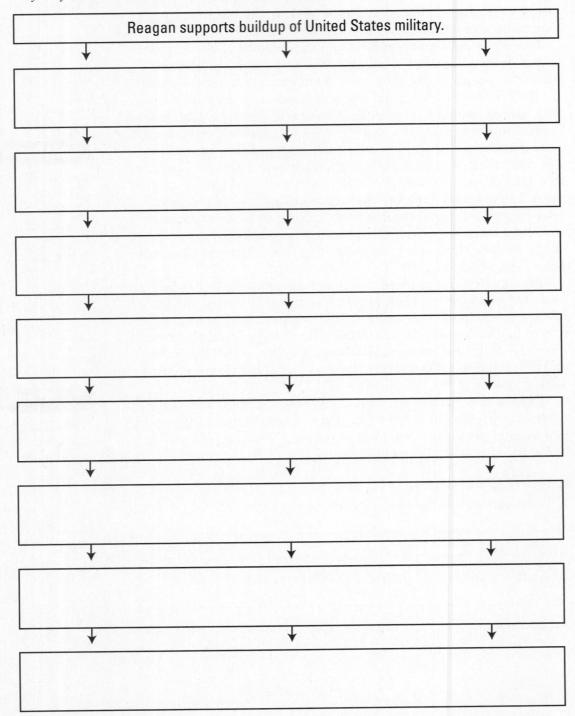

Reagan supports buildup of United States military.

CHAPTER 32 SECTION 3

Note Taking Study Guide

THE END OF THE COLD WAR

Focus Question: What were Reagan's foreign policies, and how did they contribute to the fall of communism in Europe?

B. *Record the main ideas related to events in the Middle East during Reagan's presidency in the concept web below.*

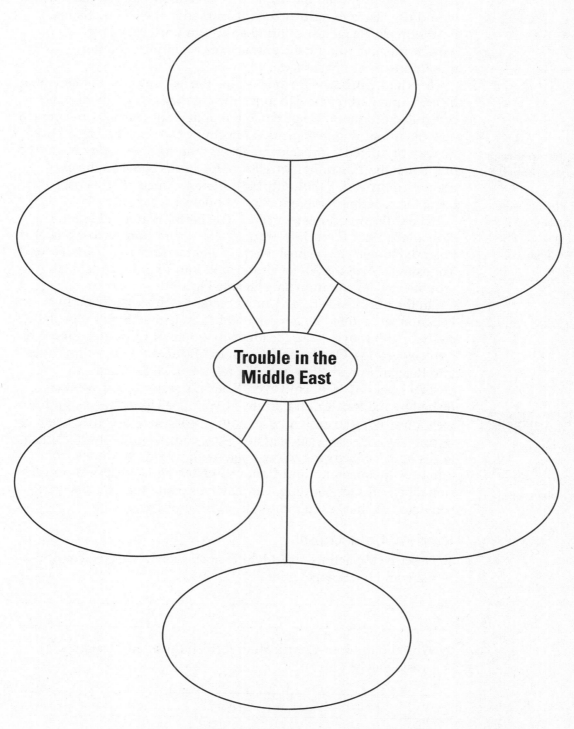

CHAPTER 32 SECTION 3

Section Summary
THE END OF THE COLD WAR

Under President Reagan, the United States worked to weaken communism and the Soviet Union by committing to the largest peacetime military buildup in its history. Reagan believed that the Soviet Union would be unable to match U.S. defense spending. Reagan also proposed the **Strategic Defense Initiative (SDI),** which would use lasers to destroy missiles aimed at the United States. Furthermore, Reagan supported anticommunist rebellions worldwide, including the **Contras,** anticommunist counter-revolutionaries in Nicaragua.

Mikhail Gorbachev, who became the leader of the Soviet Union in 1985, initiated reforms to move the country away from a state-controlled economy. He pursued the policies of *glasnost,* meaning a new openness, and *perestroika,* reforming the Soviet system. As Reagan predicted, Gorbachev realized that the Soviet Union could not match the U.S. military buildup. Relations between the two nations improved. Eventually both signed a nuclear arms pact and began negotiating for a reduction of nuclear weapons.

The Cold War came to an end. The Berlin Wall tumbled in November 1989. From 1989 through 1991, communists lost power in Poland, Hungary, Czechoslovakia, Bulgaria, Romania, Albania, and Yugoslavia. And the Soviet Union split into 15 independent republics when communism collapsed in 1991.

In the Middle East, 241 United States Marines stationed in Lebanon were killed by a truck bomb. The United States repeatedly clashed with Libya, whose leader Muammar al-Qaddafi supported terrorist groups. One breakthrough in Middle East affairs, minutes into Reagan's presidency, was the release of all 52 American hostages held by Iran. However, Reagan's second term was tarnished by the **Iran-Contra affair.** In 1985, the United States sold weapons to Iran in exchange for Iran's promise to pressure Lebanese terrorists to release American hostages, contradicting the administration's policy of refusing to negotiate with terrorists. Money from this sale was then used to fund Contras in Nicaragua, despite a congressional ban on such funding. Ultimately, several top officials were convicted of charges stemming from the scandal.

Review Questions

1. Describe the actions President Reagan took to weaken communism and the Soviet Union.

_____

_____

2. Why did the Iran-Contra affair tarnish President Reagan's presidency?

_____

_____

Name _____ Class _____ Date _____

Focus Question: What actions did the United States take abroad during George H.W. Bush's presidency?

Use the chart below to summarize Bush's major foreign policy decisions.

Post-Cold War Foreign Policy	
America's new role in the world	**Persian Gulf War**
•	•
•	•
•	•
•	
•	
•	

CHAPTER 32 · SECTION 4

Section Summary

FOREIGN POLICY AFTER THE COLD WAR

Under President George H.W. Bush, the United States took a leading role in world affairs. Bush continued the war on drugs, and in December 1989, U.S. troops invaded Panama and arrested its dictator, **Manuel Noriega.** Noriega was convicted of drug trafficking and sentenced to 40 years in an American prison.

In the spring of 1989, Chinese students staged pro-democracy protests in Beijing's **Tiananmen Square.** Americans hoped that communism might fall in China. Instead, China crushed the protest and jailed many of the activists. President Bush condemned these actions and suspended arms sales to China but retained economic and diplomatic ties.

In the early 1990s, the oppressive South African system of segregation called **apartheid** ended, in part because of American economic sanctions. Many American firms **divested,** or withdrew investments, from South Africa. **Nelson Mandela,** the previously imprisoned leader of the antiapartheid movement, was elected leader of South Africa in 1994.

In the former Soviet Union, Yugoslavia was fighting a bloody civil war. Bush chose not to intervene with troops. However, later he did send United States Marines to Somalia on a humanitarian mission called "Operation Restore Hope."

Iraq's invasion of Kuwait in August 1990 was one of Bush's greatest foreign policy challenges. **Saddam Hussein,** Iraq's dictator, sought to control Kuwait's rich oil deposits and increase his power in the region.

President Bush made it clear that he would not tolerate Iraq's aggression against its neighbor. He worked to build an international coalition and backed a United Nations resolution demanding that Iraqi troops withdraw. Hussein did not comply. Under the name **Operation Desert Storm,** American, British, French, Egyptian, and Saudi coalition forces attacked Iraqi troops on January 16, 1991. On February 23, coalition forces stormed Kuwait, and within five days, Iraq agreed to a UN cease-fire. In accordance with the UN resolution, Iraqis left Kuwait, but Saddam Hussein still ruled Iraq. The entire conflict later became known as the Persian Gulf War.

Review Questions

1. Why did President Bush send troops to Panama?

_____

_____

2. Describe non-military actions Bush took to help resolve world conflicts during his presidency.

_____

_____

Name _____ Class _____ Date _____

Focus Question: How have technological changes and globalization transformed the American economy?

As you read, fill in the flowchart below to help you categorize technological changes and their impact.

Technology Revolution		
Computers	**Communications**	**Globalization**
•	•	•
•	•	•
•	•	•
•	•	
•	•	

CHAPTER 33 SECTION 1

Section Summary
THE COMPUTER AND TECHNOLOGY REVOLUTIONS

READING CHECK

What is globalization?

_____

_____

_____

VOCABULARY STRATEGY

What does the word *access* mean in the underlined sentence? Circle any words or phrases in the surrounding sentences that help you figure out what *access* means.

_____

_____

_____

READING SKILL

Categorize Which technological change discussed in this section has had the greatest effect on the American economy? Explain.

_____

_____

_____

The rapid pace of technological change in the twentieth century touched every aspect of modern life. One of the most important innovations was the computer. The first modern computer was developed in 1946 and filled an entire basement. As technology improved, small computers called personal computers were introduced. By the 1980s, **personal computers** were transforming American business and industry. They changed medical science as well and helped create a new field called **biotechnology,** in which technology is used to solve problems affecting living organisms.

The late twentieth century ushered in the "information age." **Satellites** orbiting Earth increased the speed of global communications. Cellular telephones using satellite technology enabled people to communicate away from their homes. <u>By the 1990s, the **Internet** made communication and access to information almost instantaneous, which in turn profoundly altered commerce, education, research, and entertainment.</u>

These technological changes influenced how and where people worked. Fewer Americans worked in factories or on farms. Instead, they provided services. Satellites and computers increased **globalization,** the process by which national economies, politics, cultures, and societies become integrated with those of other nations around the world. A **multinational corporation** might have its financial headquarters in one country and manufacturing plants in several other countries. It might get raw materials from many different places and sell its products to a worldwide market.

Some economists say that the United States now has a **service economy.** Jobs in the service sector vary widely, from some of the highest paying, such as lawyers, to some of the lowest paying, such as fast-food workers. With the rise of the service economy and the decline of industries such as mining and manufacturing, the political power of labor unions has decreased and the average wages of workers have fallen.

Review Questions

1. How have recent developments in communications affected the way people live today?

_____

_____

2. How has the rise of the service sector affected the American economy?

_____

_____

CHAPTER 33 SECTION 2
Note Taking Study Guide
THE CLINTON PRESIDENCY

Focus Question: What were the successes and failures of the Clinton presidency?

Complete the outline below as you read to summarize information about the Clinton presidency.

I. The 1992 Election

    A. Bush's popularity plummets.

    B. Clinton runs as "New Democrat."

    C. Clinton carries the election.

II. Clinton's Domestic Policies

    A. _____

    B. _____

    C. _____

III. _____

    A. _____

    B. _____

    C. _____

    D. _____

IV. _____

    A. _____

    B. _____

    C. _____

    D. _____

CHAPTER 33 SECTION 2

Section Summary
THE CLINTON PRESIDENCY

Twelve years after the Reagan Revolution, Americans were ready for a change in the White House. The Democrats nominated **William Jefferson Clinton,** governor of Arkansas, to run against President Bush in the 1992 election. Texas billionaire **H. Ross Perot** ran as an independent. Clinton carried the election, and Democrats retained control of both houses of Congress.

Early in his presidency, Clinton focused on domestic issues. He signed the **Family Medical Leave Act,** which guaranteed most full-time employees unpaid leave each year for personal or family medical reasons. Clinton also oversaw passage of the **Brady Bill,** which placed a five-day waiting period on sales of handguns. Another important issue for Clinton was healthcare reform. Clinton's wife, Hillary, led a task force to investigate ways to guarantee healthcare for all Americans. The committee's proposal never won congressional support and was ultimately dropped.

VOCABULARY STRATEGY

What does the word *ultimately* mean in the underlined sentence? The term *finally* is a synonym of *ultimately.* Use this synonym to help you figure out what *ultimately* means in this sentence.

_____

_____

_____

In the 1994 midterm elections, Georgia congressman **Newt Gingrich** led the opposition to Clinton. He galvanized Republicans around his **Contract With America,** a plan that attacked big government and emphasized patriotism and traditional values. Winning the votes of Americans who felt the federal government was too big, too wasteful, and too liberal, Republicans captured the House, the Senate, and most state governorships. Once in office, Republicans passed much of Gingrich's program. Two years later, Clinton was reelected by a wide margin, although Congress remained under Republican control.

President Clinton had dodged scandals from his first day in office. One concerned investments the Clintons had made. Special prosecutor **Kenneth Starr** investigated the case for seven years but failed to uncover evidence of the Clintons' guilt. In the process, however, Starr investigated the President's relationship with a White House intern. When Clinton admitted he had lied about the affair under oath, Starr recommended **impeachment** proceedings. The House of Representatives impeached Clinton on the charges of perjury and obstruction of justice. Clinton was tried and acquitted by the Senate in February 1999.

READING SKILL

Summarize What were the most significant events of Clinton's presidency?

_____

_____

_____

Review Questions

1. What bills did President Clinton sign after taking office?

_____

_____

2. What was the Contract With America?

_____

_____

CHAPTER 33

SECTION 3

Note Taking Study Guide

GLOBAL POLITICS AND ECONOMICS

Focus Question: What role did the United States take on in global politics and economics following the Cold War?

Complete the flowchart below to help you identify main ideas about global politics and economics.

U.S. Global Policy		
Free Trade	**Foreign Intervention**	**Middle East**
• NAFTA • •	• • •	• • •

CHAPTER 33 SECTION 3

Section Summary
GLOBAL POLITICS AND ECONOMICS

VOCABULARY STRATEGY

Find the word *intervention* in the underlined sentence. What does *intervention* mean? Circle any words in the surrounding sentences that help you figure out what *intervention* means.

_____

_____

_____

READING SKILL

Identify Main Ideas What role did the United States play in global economics during the 1990s?

_____

_____

_____

In the 1990s, the United States was the world's sole superpower, wielding influence over economic and political events worldwide. Among the issues influenced by the United States was free trade. The **European Union (EU),** which coordinates monetary and economic policies among European nations, is an example of a free trade bloc. When the EU threatened U.S. economic leadership, the United States joined with Canada and Mexico to pass the **North American Free Trade Agreement (NAFTA).** NAFTA created a free trade zone in North America.

Clinton supported NAFTA and other free trade agreements, although many Democrats didn't. In 1994, he signed the revision to the **General Agreement on Tariffs and Trade (GATT)** aimed at reducing tariffs worldwide. In 1995, he signed the accords of the **World Trade Organization (WTO),** which replaced GATT and had greater authority to negotiate agreements and settle disputes.

On the political scene, many Americans opposed military involvement in foreign affairs, but Clinton found it necessary to intervene in conflicts in Somalia and Haiti. When civil war broke out in the former Yugoslav republic of Bosnia, Bosnian Serbs attacked and murdered Muslims and Croats. This state-sanctioned mass murder became known as **ethnic cleansing.** In 1995, Clinton asked NATO to bomb Serbian strongholds. <u>This intervention brought about a cease-fire, but violence flared in another former Yugoslavian republic.</u> NATO troops, including U.S. troops, responded again.

The ongoing conflict between Israelis and Palestinians escalated in the 1990s. Clinton led negotiations that produced a short-lived agreement between Israeli and Palestinian leaders. That involvement in the Middle East made the United States a target of a terrorist group called **al Qaeda.** The group launched several attacks on U.S. targets at home and abroad.

Review Questions

1. What challenge did the European Union pose to the United States?

   _____

   _____

2. Why did Clinton encourage NATO to become involved in the Bosnian conflict?

   _____

   _____

CHAPTER 33 SECTION 4 — Note Taking Study Guide

BUSH AND THE WAR ON TERRORISM

Focus Question: What was the impact of Bush's domestic agenda and his response to the terrorist attack against the United States?

Record the sequence of events in Bush's presidency in the flowchart below.

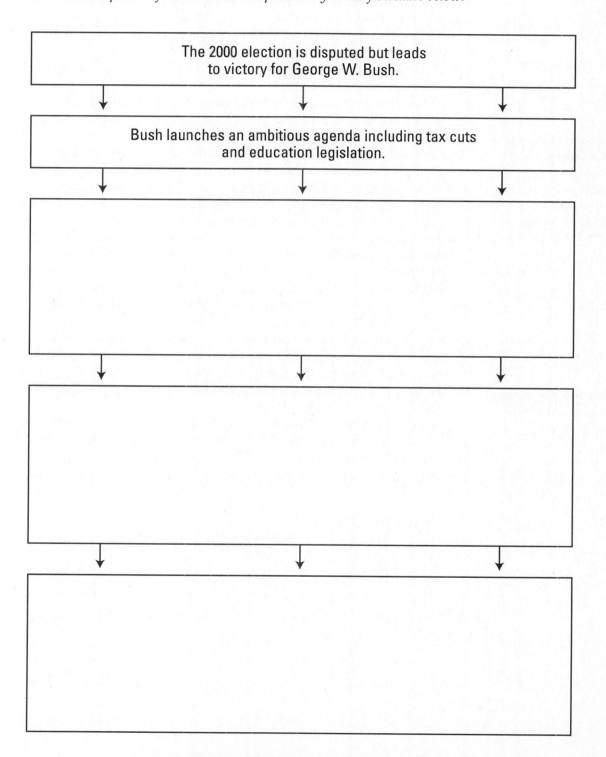

The 2000 election is disputed but leads to victory for George W. Bush.

Bush launches an ambitious agenda including tax cuts and education legislation.

CHAPTER 33 SECTION 4

Section Summary
BUSH AND THE WAR ON TERRORISM

Clinton's Vice President, Al Gore, Jr., was the Democratic candidate for President in 2000. He faced Green Party candidate Ralph Nader and Republican **George W. Bush.** On election day, Gore received more popular votes than Bush, but not enough Electoral College votes to win. Florida's 25 electoral votes would decide the presidency, but the vote there was very close. Democrats demanded a hand recount, which Republicans sued to prevent. The Supreme Court ruled on the issue in *Bush* v. *Gore.* It ended the recounting by a 5-to-4 decision and Bush won.

Less than a year after Bush took office, on September 11, 2001, the United States was attacked by Osama bin Laden's al Qaeda network. When the Islamic fundamentalist **Taliban** government of **Afghanistan** refused to turn over bin Laden to U.S. custody, Bush sent American forces into Afghanistan. The Taliban was overthrown, and several al Qaeda leaders were captured, but bin Laden escaped.

On the home front improving national security became a priority. Congress passed the **Patriot Act** to give law enforcement broader powers to monitor suspected terrorists. A new Cabinet-level **Department of Homeland Security** was created to coordinate domestic security matters.

Bush next turned his attention to Iraq. He asserted that Iraqi dictator Saddam Hussein had **Weapons of Mass Destruction (WMD)** and was a threat to U.S. security. In March 2003, American and British military forces invaded Iraq, and on May 1, Bush announced victory. However, American troops remained and violence erupted between ethnic groups and against American forces. Public support for the Iraq war and Bush's tax cuts waned as the war dragged on and the federal deficit grew larger.

Th 2008 election was historic. Barack Obama became the first African American to be chosen by a major political party as a Prresidential candidate. Obama ran against Republican John McCain. Obama wins and becomes the nation's first African American President.

Review Questions

1. Why was the outcome of the 2000 presidential election unusual?

_____

_____

2. How did the terrorist attacks on the United States affect domestic policies?

_____

_____

Note Taking Study Guide

AMERICANS LOOK TO THE FUTURE

Focus Question: How was American society changing at the beginning of the twenty-first century?

Record supporting details about the changing American society in the table below.

A Changing Society	
Immigration	**Demographics**
• Immigration policies relax. • •	• Family structures change. • •

CHAPTER 33
SECTION 5

Section Summary
AMERICANS LOOK TO THE FUTURE

READING CHECK

What is the purpose of affirmative action?

_____

_____

_____

As the twenty-first century dawned, American society looked very different than it had a hundred years before. The **Immigration Act of 1990** had increased quotas by 40 percent and eased most restrictions. Since then, almost one million immigrants arrived in the United States each year. Most of the new immigrants were Latinos. They have had a profound social, cultural, and political impact. Asians make up the second-largest source of the new immigration.

Some people worry that immigrants take jobs and social services away from native-born Americans. They oppose **bilingual education,** in which students are taught in their native languages as well as in English. Proponents of immigration argue that immigrants contribute to the economy and help the nation maintain its population. Much of the debate concerns illegal immigrants. The **Immigration and Control Act of 1986** aimed to stop the flow of illegal immigrants by penalizing businesses that hired them, but illegal immigrants still regularly cross U.S. borders.

American demographics have changed, with many people moving from the Midwest and Northeast to the Sunbelt. The American family changed as well. Divorces and single-parent households are now more common than just 40 years ago.

Affirmative action was created in the 1960s to help minorities and women overcome past discrimination by giving them preference in school admissions and job applications. Today, such programs are being challenged and in some cases, ended. Even so, women and African Americans continue to make social and political gains. More African Americans now earn middle-class incomes and hold college degrees. Women are protected against unfair treatment in the workplace. The 1994 **Violence Against Women Act** increased federal resources to apprehend and prosecute men guilty of violent acts against women.

As the baby boom generation reaches retirement, falling birthrates mean there may not be enough workers to pay for their Social Security benefits. President Bush proposed **privatizing** Social Security. This change would allow younger workers to invest some of their earnings in individual retirement accounts. Opponents defeated his proposal and the debate continues.

VOCABULARY STRATEGY

What does the word *discrimination* mean in the underlined sentence? Use context clues to help you figure out the meaning of *discrimination*.

_____

_____

_____

READING SKILL

Identify Supporting Details
What law increased resources to prosecute men guilty of violence against women?

_____

_____

_____

Review Questions

1. What led to a dramatic increase in immigration to the United States at the end of the twentieth century?

_____

_____

2. How have American demographics changed in recent decades?

_____

_____

Name _____ Class _____ Date _____

Global Interdependence

 Essential Question: Is global interdependence good for the American economy?

1500s
Columbian Exchange
Exchange of products and
ideas between hemispheres

1944
World Bank
World Bank and
International Money Fund

2000s
**Globalization
Debated**
Benefits and
drawbacks

1500	1820	1860	1900	1940	1980	2020

1812
War of 1812
U.S. goes to war to protect
trade rights

1990s
World Trade Increases
NAFTA and World
Trade Organization

I. WARMUP

As nations have traded with one another over the centuries, they have become interdependent. Today, the United States economy depends on trade with countries around the world. The timeline on this page shows some key events in the development of this interdependence.

Global interdependence affects all Americans. For example, it affects the availability of products, prices of goods, costs of doing business, and the outsourcing of jobs.

1. How does this interdependence affect you? Fill in the concept web to show some of the products on which you depend in your daily life.

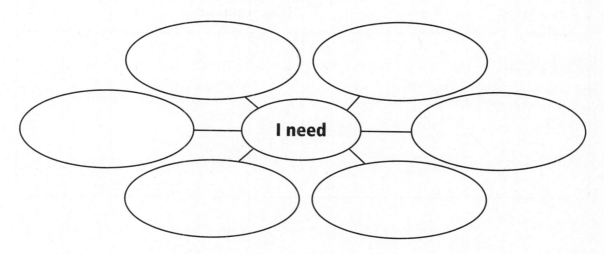

American Issues Journal

2. **a.** Which products on your list were produced in another country?
   b. Which products were produced in the United States?

Foreign Goods	U.S. Goods
_____	_____
_____	_____
_____	_____
_____	_____

3. How might global interdependence affect stores and restaurants in your community?

_____

_____

_____

II. EXPLORATION

Now that you have explored the way global interdependence affects your life, consider the way global interdependence affects the nation.

A. World Trade Increases

In the chapter "Into a New Century" about the twenty-first century, you learned how technology has helped shape globalization.

What are three advantages of globalization? What are three disadvantages?

Advantages	Disadvantages
•	•
•	•
•	•

American Issues Journal

B. Find Out

1. Read the section about NAFTA in the chapter "Into a New Century." What is NAFTA?

_____

_____

2. Why was NAFTA created?

_____

_____

3. What does the term outsourcing mean?

_____

_____

4. Who would most likely support outsourcing?

_____

_____

5. Who would most likely oppose it?

_____

_____

C. What do you think?

Does NAFTA contribute to globalization? Explain.

_____

_____

_____

You may wish to explore this issue further online. Go to:

Internet Research Activity

Transfer Your Knowledge
For: WebQuest **Web Code:** neh-6102

III. ESSAY

Bring together what you have read in your textbook with the information you have gathered online about this American issue. On a separate sheet of paper, answer the essential question: **Is global interdependence good for the American economy?**

Name _____ Class _____ Date _____

American Issues Journal

Expanding and Protecting Civil Rights

 Essential Question: What should the federal government do to expand and protect civil rights?

1791
Bill of Rights
First 10 Constitutional amendments

1964
Civil Rights Act
Bans discrimination in jobs and public places

1990
Americans with Disabilities Act
Bans discrimination for disabilities

| 1820 | 1860 | 1900 | 1940 | 1980 | 2020 |

1868
Fourteenth Amendment
Citizenship for all native-born and naturalized Americans

1920
Nineteenth Amendment
Voting rights for women

I. WARMUP

The scope of civil rights in the United States has grown along with the nation. Over time, the rights stated in the Constitution have been extended and supported by new legislation. The timeline on this page shows important milestones in this history.

Equal rights are guaranteed to all Americans. However, not all Americans enjoy the same privileges. What roles do rights and privileges play in your life?

1. How would you define the term "right"?

_____

_____

2. How would you define the term "privilege"?

_____

_____

What are three rights that matter to you?	What are three privileges that matter to you?
•	•
•	•
•	•

American Issues Journal

3. Why might healthcare or education be considered a right for all people?

_____

_____

_____

_____

II. EXPLORATION

Now that you have explored your civil rights, consider the challenges a nation faces in guaranteeing civil rights for all citizens.

A. Civil Rights Act

You know that the first rights guaranteed to Americans are in the Bill of Rights. However, it has taken more Constitutional amendments and many laws to ensure that these and other rights are extended equally. In some cases, the government has taken additional steps to ensure that some groups have really been able to exercise these rights.

1. Why do you think these groups have had to struggle so much for the rights they have won?

_____

_____

_____

2. What are some ways you enjoy equality? Use the concept map to list four examples.

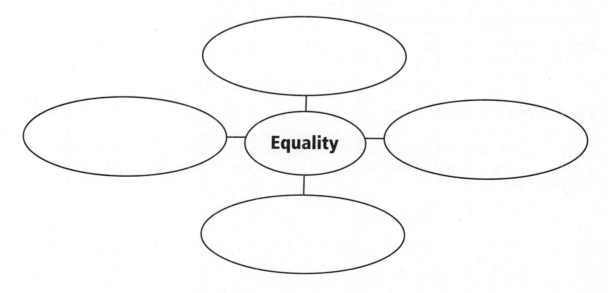

American Issues Journal

B. Find Out

1. Read Section 2 in the chapter "The Civil Rights Movement." How did the Civil Rights Act of 1964 address discrimination?

_____

_____

_____

2. Read Section 3 in the chapter. Why were equal rights for all Americans still not fully enforced after the passage of the Civil Rights Act of 1964? List some of the barriers.

a.

b.

c.

d.

C. What do you think?

Do you think federal protection of civil rights is necessary? Explain.

_____

_____

_____

You may wish to explore this issue further online. Go to:

Internet Research Activity

Transfer Your Knowledge
For: WebQuest Web Code: neh-6502

III. ESSAY

Bring together what you have read in your textbook with the information you have gathered online about this American issue. On a separate sheet of paper, answer the essential question: **What should the federal government do to expand and protect civil rights?**

American Issues Journal

Sectionalism and National Politics

Essential Question: How do regional differences affect national politics?

1812
War of 1812
Westerners and Southerners for war

1861
Civil War
North and South at war

1948
Dixiecrats
Civil rights splits Democrats

| 1820 | 1860 | 1900 | 1940 | 1980 | 2020 |

1787
Three-Fifths Compromise
Slaves counted as three-fifths of a person

1816–1832
Tariffs
North wants tariffs

2004
Presidential Election
Election confirms division between states

I. WARMUP

Throughout U.S. history, different regions or sections of the country have developed conflicting economic, social, political, and cultural interests. These interests have led to differences in views on national matters and have caused regions to respond to events in different ways. The timeline on this page shows the impact of regional conflicts on national politics.

1. Think about the neighborhood in which you live. How does your neighborhood differ from another one in your community?

My Neighborhood:	Other Neighborhood:
•	•
•	•
•	•

2a. How would you define the term "region"?

_____

_____

_____

2b. In what region of the U.S. do you live?

_____

_____

_____

American Issues Journal

3. How might economic factors in your community, such as household income or employment opportunities, affect the way you think about social or political issues?

_____

_____

_____

_____

II. EXPLORATION

Now that you have explored how local differences affect you, consider the ways in which regional differences might affect the nation..

A. Civil War

For more than 70 years, Americans were able to resolve sectional differences through negotiation and compromise. Looming behind many of these differences was the issue of slavery, an issue that had divided the country since its earliest days.

1. How would you define the term "compromise"?

_____

_____

2. What are some benefits of compromise? Some drawbacks?

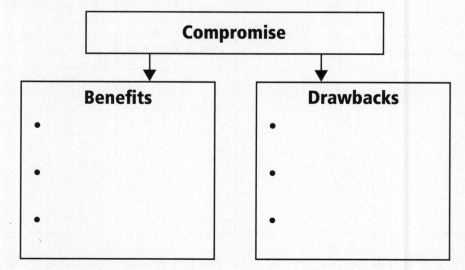

Name _____ Class _____ Date _____

B. Find Out

1. Read the chapter "The Union in Crisis." Why did slavery become a more urgent problem as the nation grew?

_____

_____

2. What were some of the compromises made?

_____

_____

3. Why do you think that the South was willing to make compromises in the early and mid-1800s? Why was the North willing to make compromises? Fill in the speech balloons to show what a Southerner and a Northerner might have said.

North   **South**

C. What do you think?

Why did regional differences matter so much?

_____

_____

_____

You may wish to explore this issue further online. Go to:

Internet Research Activity

Transfer Your Knowledge
For: WebQuest **Web Code:** neh-6702

III. ESSAY

Bring together what you have read in your textbook with the information you have gathered online about this American issue. On a separate sheet of paper, answer the essential question: **How do regional differences affect national politics?**

American Issues Journal

Church and State

 Essential Question: What is the proper relationship between government and religion?

1791 **Bill of Rights** First Amendment	**1840s** **Sabbatarian Controversy** Debate over commerce on Sundays			**1984** **Federal Equal Access Act** Religious clubs at public schools		**2000** **Mitchell v. Helms** Public funds for private schools
1820	**1860**	**1900**	**1940**	**1980**	**2020**	

1947
Everson v. Board of Education
Affirms separation of church and state

I. WARMUP

When Congress approved the Bill of Rights in 1789, it guaranteed freedom of religion to Americans, but it also made clear that Congress could not establish religion. Although the First Amendment set up a separation of church (religion) and state (government), questions have still arisen about the proper relationship between the two. The timeline on this page shows when these issues have come up.

When the government spends money, it is using tax money paid by Americans. The government uses this money to pay for or to support public needs.

1. How would you define the term "public"?

_____

_____

2. How would you define the term "private"?

_____

_____

3a. What are some public places or programs you use that are supported by the government?

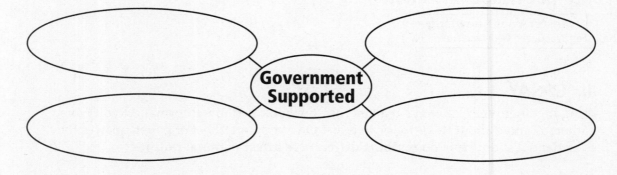

Government Supported

American Issues Journal

3b. What are some private places or programs that you use?

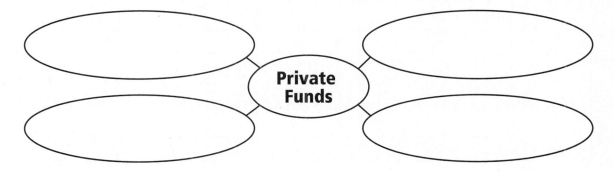

4. Should taxpayer's money be used for a program run by a private organization?

_____

_____

_____

II. EXPLORATION

Now that you have explored the difference between private and public, consider how these differences might affect the role of religion in government.

A. Federal Equal Access Act

You know that not all people have religious freedom. In some nations, government supports or represents a particular religion. Sometimes people are persecuted or prohibited from practicing their religion.

1. As an American, what does religious freedom mean to you?

_____

_____

_____

B. Find Out

1. Read the First Amendment. What does it say the government may not do regarding religion?

_____

_____

_____

American Issues Journal

2. Read the section about the Equal Access Act in the chapter "The Conservative Resurgence." What does the act require?

_____

_____

_____

3. How well do you think the Equal Access Act reflects the First Amendment? Explain.

_____

_____

_____

C. What do you think?

Should there be an Equal Access Act? Why or why not?

_____

_____

_____

You may wish to explore this issue further online. Go to:

Internet Research Activity

Transfer Your Knowledge
For: WebQuest **Web Code:** neh-6802

III. ESSAY

Bring together what you have read in your textbook with the information you have gathered online about this American issue. On a separate sheet of paper, answer the essential question: **What is the proper relationship between government and religion?**

American Issues Journal

Federal Power and States' Rights

Essential Questions: How much power should the federal government have?

1791
Bill of Rights
Tenth Amendment

1831
Nullification Crisis
Calhoun says states can overturn federal laws

1930s
New Deal
Federal government expands power

| 1820 | 1860 | 1900 | 1940 | 1980 | 2020 |

1798
Kentucky and Virginia Resolutions
States claim they can void federal laws

1857
Dred Scott *v.* Sandford
Federal government cannot outlaw slavery in territories

1965
Voting Rights Act
Federal officers register voters

I. WARMUP

The U.S. Constitution provides a federal system of government. One of its basic principles is that power is divided between the central government and the states. Over time, the distribution of power has created controversy. The timeline on this page shows some important events related to this issue.

When the federal government has expanded its power, the power of the states has been affected.

1a. How would you define the term "power"?

_____

_____

1b. What powers do you have?

_____

_____

2. Who are the people, organizations, or governments with power over you?

_____

_____

American Issues Journal

3. Do you think there should be equal power among the branches of government? Explain.

_____

_____

II. EXPLORATION

Now that you have explored how power affects you on a personal level, consider how the power of the federal government might affect your state.

A. The New Deal

You have learned that the New Deal implemented a series of programs to combat problems—unemployment, bank failures, hunger—caused by the Great Depression.

What are some ways that government helps you?

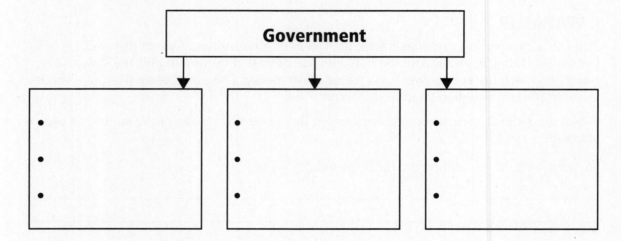

B. Find Out

1. Read the Tenth Amendment to the Constitution. What guarantee does it provide?

_____

_____

_____

_____

_____

American Issues Journal

2. Fill in the thought bubbles below to show different points of view people held about federal power in the 1930s.

President Roosevelt   **States' Rights Advocate**   **Citizen**

C. What do you think?

Is it sometimes necessary for the federal government to broaden its powers? Explain.

_____

_____

_____

You may wish to explore this issue further online. Go to:

Internet Research Activity

> **Transfer Your Knowledge**
> **For:** WebQuest **Web Code:** neh-7002

III. ESSAY

Bring together what you have learned in your textbook with the information you've gathered online about this American issue. On a separate sheet of paper, answer the essential question: **How much power should the federal government have?**

American Issues Journal

Checks and Balances

 Essential Question: Does any branch of the federal government have too much power?

| | | | 1960s
Warren Court
Supreme Court
becomes force
for social reform | 2000s
War on
Terrorism
Congress increases
President's power |

1803
Marbury v. Madison
Right of judicial review

1868
Johnson Impeachment
Congress tries to remove
President

| 1820 | 1860 | 1900 | 1940 | 1980 | 2020 |

1830s
Jackson Presidency
Increase of executive
power

1930s
New Deal
Presidential
power used
to fight the
Depression

1973
War Powers Act
Congress limits
President's power
to wage war

I. WARMUP

When the writers of the Constitution divided the U.S. government into three branches, they created a system of checks and balances. Under this system, each branch has the power to monitor and limit the actions of the other two, thus keeping any one branch from becoming too powerful. However, the balance of power has not always remained equal. The timeline on this page shows times when power has shifted.

Your life is full of checks and balances. For example, you may be able to drive a car, but there are laws that check or limit how you drive it. In this case, the resulting balance of power among drivers ensures safety on the road.

1. Fill in the chart to show other ways checks and balances work in your life.

Power	**Checks**	**Balances**
• to drive a car	• traffic laws	• laws are for all drivers
• _____	• _____	• _____

2. What would happen to the balance if some drivers did not have to obey the laws?

_____

_____

_____

American Issues Journal

3. What are the benefits of checks and balances in your life?

_____

_____

_____

II. EXPLORATION

Now that you have explored how checks and balances work in your own life, consider how they work in the federal government.

A. War on Terrorism

On September 11, 2001, the United States was attacked by terrorists. These attacks changed how Americans viewed terrorism and how the federal government viewed national safety.

How did you feel about the security of the nation before September 11? After it?

Before	After
• • •	• • •

B. Find Out

1. Read Articles I, II, III, and Section 4 of Article IV of the Constitution. How does the Constitution provide checks and balances?

_____

_____

_____

American Issues Journal

2. What powers does the Constitution give the executive branch?

_____

_____

_____

C. What do you think?

Did the War on Terrorism result in too much power for any branch of government?
Explain your answer.

_____

_____

_____

You may wish to explore this issue further online. Go to:

Internet Research Activity

Transfer Your Knowledge
For: WebQuest **Web Code:** neh-7202

III. ESSAY

Bring together what you have read in your textbook with the information you have
gathered online about this American issue. On a separate sheet of paper, answer the
essential question: **Does any branch of the federal government have too much power?**

Name _____ Class _____ Date _____

American Issues Journal

Technology and Society

? **Essential Question:** What are the benefits and costs of technology?

Late 1700s **Factory System** Production increases; worker's conditions worsen		**1930s** **Polymers** Plastics products; pollution increases		**2000s** **Genetic** **Engineering** Benefits; Costs

1780	1800	1820	1840	1860	1880	1900	1920	1940	1960	1980	2000

1859
Oil Refining
Industrial growth;
pollution worsens

1940s
Nuclear Reactor
Nuclear energy; threats
of nuclear waste

I. WARMUP

Technology has played an enormous role in American life and has been responsible for many economic and social benefits. However, technological advances also have drawbacks or costs. The timeline on this page shows some technological advances that have had both benefits and costs.

1a. What does the term "technology" mean to you? How would you define it?

_____

_____

1b. How would you define the term "benefit"?

_____

_____

1c. How would you define the term "cost"?

_____

_____

2. Fill in the chart to show some ways that you use technology for your personal needs at home or at school.

Personal Uses of Technology
•
•
•

American Issues Journal

3. What kinds of costs might there be with the technology that you use for personal purposes?

_____

_____

_____

II. EXPLORATION

Now that you have explored some ways that technology affects your life, consider how it might affect society.

A. Plastics

Plastics are long chains of molecules called polymers. Your home, school, and community are filled with these synthetic products. Plastics are useful materials that can be easily shaped. They often replace other materials such as metal, wood, stone, paper, ceramics, and glass.

1. What are some common plastic products that you use? Use the concept web to list four examples.

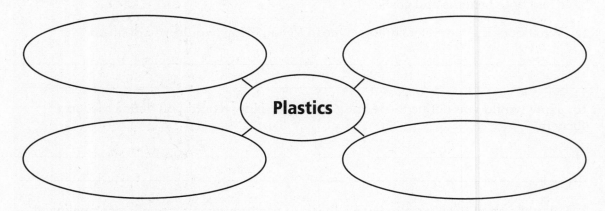

B. Find Out

Many people are concerned about the harmful effects of the disposal of plastic materials on the environment. Read Section Four in the chapter called "An Era of Protest and Change."

1. What is its main point about the impact of the Environmental Movement?

_____

_____

_____

American Issues Journal

2. List four plastic items that you have thrown away or will throw away today.

1.

2.

3.

4.

3. How does your school or community address the problem of plastic items in garbage?

_____

_____

_____

C. What do you think?

Do the costs of using plastics outweigh the benefits?

_____

_____

_____

You may wish to explore this issue further online. Go to:

Internet Research Activity

Transfer Your Knowledge
For: WebQuest **Web Code:** neh-7302

III. ESSAY

Bring together what you have read in your textbook with the information you have gathered online about this American issue. On a separate sheet of paper, answer the essential question: **What are the benefits and costs of technology?**

American Issues Journal

Migration and Urbanization

Essential Question: How does migration affect patterns of settlement in America?

1862
Homestead Act
Free land brings settlers
to Great Plains

1910–1930
Great Migration
Southern blacks
move north

1970s–Present
Sunbelt Growth
Movement to warmer,
southern areas

| 1820 | 1860 | 1900 | 1940 | 1980 | 2020 |

1889–1920
Urban Migration
Movement from
farms to cities

1950s
Suburban Flight
Movement from cities
to suburbs

I. WARMUP

Since the first settlers arrived, Americans have been on the move. The settlement patterns of people have been shaped by several migration trends. The timeline on this page shows times when large migration trends changed settlement patterns.

1. Have you or members of your family ever moved? If so, what were the main reasons for moving?

_____

_____

_____

2a. How would you define the term "migration"?

_____

_____

2b. How would you define the term "patterns of settlement"?

_____

_____

3. How might moving change a person's life?

_____

_____

_____

American Issues Journal

II. EXPLORATION

Now that you have explored moving as it might affect you, consider how migration affected settlement patterns in the United States.

A. Suburban Flight

You have learned that millions of Americans migrated from rural to urban areas between 1890 and 1920. Thirty years later, large groups of people began moving again, this time to the suburbs.

How do suburbs differ from cities? How are the two areas alike? Use the Venn diagram to identify similarities and differences.

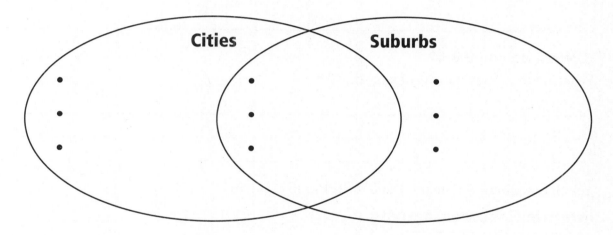

B. Find Out

1. Read Sections 1 and 2 in the chapter "Postwar Confidence and Anxiety." Why did so many people move to the suburbs after World War II?

_____

_____

_____

2. What kinds of buildings and organizations did suburbs need to establish to support their growing populations?

_____

_____

_____

American Issues Journal

3. What were the benefits of living in the suburbs? What were the costs?

Benefits	Costs
•	•
•	•
•	•

C. What do you think?

What are the social benefits of migration?

_____

_____

_____

You may wish to explore this issue further online. Go to:

Internet Research Activity

Transfer Your Knowledge
For: WebQuest **Web Code:** neh-7402

III. ESSAY

Bring together what you have read in your textbook with the information you have gathered online about this American issue. On a separate sheet of paper, answer the essential question: **How does migration affect patterns of settlement in America?**

American Issues Journal

American Indian Policy

Essential Question: How should the federal government deal with Indian nations?

1787
U.S. Constitution
Gives government power to regulate trade with Native Americans

1887
Dawes Act
Reservations divided into individual holdings

1975
Indian Self-Determination Assistance Act
Indians get more control over schools and other services

| 1820 | 1860 | 1900 | 1940 | 1980 | 2020 |

1824
Bureau of Indian Affairs
Agency for handling relations with Native Americans

1934
Indian Reorganization Act
Tribal governments gain more control

I. WARMUP

Relationships between Native Americans and the federal government have often been characterized by confrontation, misunderstanding, and broken promises. Government policy regarding Native Americans has shifted several times since the country's early days. The timeline on this page shows periods when important changes have taken place.

Numerous treaties and agreements defined how the government has dealt with Indian nations. In the past, many of these treaties were broken or disregarded.

1. Why do you think treaties or contracts are important?

_____

_____

_____

2. What happens when a contract is broken? For example, suppose a person signs a contract to buy a used car. What consequences might result if the contract is broken?

_____

_____

_____

American Issues Journal

3. Is breaking a contract ever justified? Explain.

_____

_____

_____

II. EXPLORATION

Now that you have explored how contracts affect your life, consider the challenges of how treaties affected the relations between the federal government and Native Americans.

A. Indian Self-Determination and Educational Assistance Act

You have learned about the struggles for rights of various groups in the United States. Successes in achieving rights by one group encouraged other groups to develop rights movements as well. One goal of the Indian nations was self-determination.

Define the term "self-determination."

_____

_____

B. Find Out

Review the material in Section 2 in "The South and West Transformed" chapter. Then, read Section 3 of the chapter "An Era of Protest and Change."

1. What conditions caused Native Americans to form the activist organization AIM?

American Issues Journal

2. What tactics has AIM used to fight for equality and social justice?

_____

_____

_____

3. What were some results of the protests staged by AIM in the 1970s?

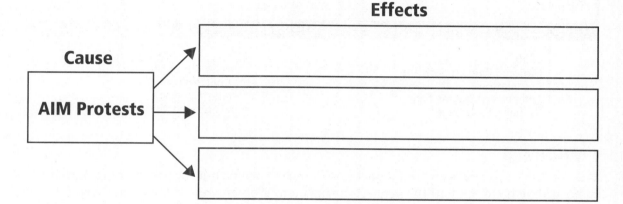

C. What do you think?

Are Native Americans justified in trying to reclaim land they believe still belongs to them? Explain.

_____

_____

_____

You may wish to explore this issue further online. Go to:

Internet Research Activity

Transfer Your Knowledge
For: WebQuest **Web Code:** neh-7502

III. ESSAY

Bring together what you have read in your textbook with the information you have gathered online about this American issue. On a separate sheet of paper, answer the essential question: **How should the federal government deal with Indian nations?**

American Issues Journal

Women in American Society

? Essential Question: Why do Americans disagree over women's rights?

1972
Title IX of the Education Codes
Bans sex discrimination in schools

1848
Seneca Falls Convention
Women meet to support their rights

1920
Nineteenth Amendment
Women gain right to vote

| 1880 | 1900 | 1920 | 1940 | 1960 | 1980 |

1869
National Woman Suffrage Association
Anthony and Stanton fight for women's suffrage

1964
Title VII of the Civil Rights Act
Protection against job discrimination

I. WARMUP

Women have always been a vital part of American society, but for much of the nation's history, they have not had the same rights as men. Women were denied basic legal rights such as voting, owning property, or holding public office. The timeline on this page shows when women finally won some of these rights

1. Who are some of the women you admire in today's society? Make a list of three or four women in different fields. The names you include might be people in your community or nationally known figures.

Name	Field

2. What stereotypes do you think these women had to overcome to succeed?

_____

_____

_____

American Issues Journal

3. How can stereotypes about a group affect its rights?

_____

_____

_____

_____

_____

II. EXPLORATION

Now that you have explored some aspects of rights for women, consider whether full equality for women exists today.

A. Title IX of the Education Codes

Traditional social arrangements do not always accord the same roles or rights to each gender. In the 1960s, a movement for women's rights challenged many of these traditional social arrangements. One piece of legislation that was passed was Title IX of the Higher Education Act. Until that time, most high schools and colleges spent nearly all their athletic funds for male dominated sports. With the passage of Title IX, however, women could demand equal spending for women's sports.

Check a box to show how you stand on spending for high school sports.

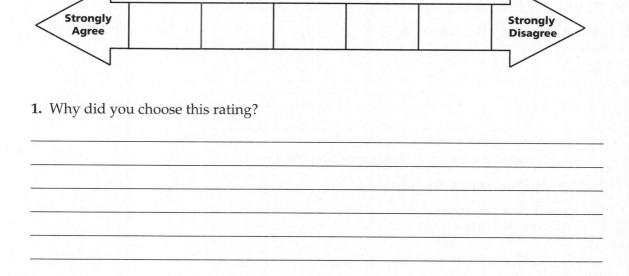

1. Why did you choose this rating?

_____

_____

_____

_____

_____

_____

American Issues Journal

B. Find Out

Read about the legal headway that women made in Section 2 of the chapter "An Era of Protest and Change."

1. Why was banning discrimination in education under Title IX important for women?

_____

_____

_____

2. What are some arguments for and against equal rights for women?

For Equal Rights	Against Equal Rights
•	•
•	•
•	•

C. What do you think?

Should there be a law requiring equal spending for women's and men's sports in public schools? Explain.

_____

_____

_____

You may wish to explore this issue further online. Go to:

Internet Research Activity

Transfer Your Knowledge
For: WebQuest Web Code: neh-7602

III. ESSAY

Bring together what you have read in your textbook with the information you've gathered online about this American issue. On a separate sheet of paper, answer the essential question: **Why do Americans disagree over women's rights?**

American Issues Journal

Social Problems and Reforms

Essential Question: What are the most pressing problems, and how can we solve them?

1990s–2000s
Healthcare Reform
High costs of
healthcare
challenged

1790s–1820s
Second Great Awakening
Christians start reforms

1890–1920
Progressivism
Reformers

1820	1860	1900	1940	1980	2020

1830s–1850s
Abolitionism
Antislavery forces

1950s–1960s
Civil Rights
Racial equality reforms

I. WARMUP

Throughout U.S. history, injustices and pressing needs have produced challenging social problems. In most cases, this has led to reforms. However, not all reforms have been equally welcomed; some have met with fierce opposition. The timeline shows periods in America's history when reform movements have occurred.

1a. How would you define the term "social problem"?

_____

_____

1b. How would you define the term "reform"?

_____

_____

2a. What are the most pressing social problems in your school? Use the chart to list them.

Social Problems in My School
1.
2.
3.
4.

2b. How do you think the social problems in your school might be solved?

_____

_____

_____

American Issues Journal

3. Would these solutions be considered reforms? Explain.

_____

_____

_____

_____

II. EXPLORATION

Now that you have explored social problems and reform at your school, consider how social problems could be resolved by the federal government.

A. Healthcare Reform

Without insurance, few Americans can afford the high costs of healthcare. Two government healthcare programs are in place. One of them is Medicare, a program that supplies basic hospital insurance to people in the Social Security system who are age 65 and older. The other program, called Medicaid, provides basic medical services to poor and disabled Americans. Even so, millions of Americans do not qualify for these programs and have no health insurance.

Do all Americans have the right to health insurance? Show where you stand on this issue by checking one of the boxes below.

Strongly Agree ← | | | | | → Strongly Disagree

1. Why did you choose this rating?

_____

_____

_____

B. Find Out

1. Read the information about healthcare reform in Section 2 of the chapter "Into a New Century." Summarize its main idea.

_____

_____

_____

_____

American Issues Journal

2. What might be some pros and cons about a universal healthcare program or one that would guarantee free insurance coverage for all Americans?

Pros	Cons
•	•
•	•
•	•
•	•

C. What do you think?

Should the U.S. have universal healthcare coverage? Explain.

_____

_____

_____

You may wish to explore this issue further online. Go to:

Internet Research Activity

Transfer Your Knowledge
For: WebQuest **Web Code:** neh-7702

III. ESSAY

Bring together what you have read in your textbook with the information you have gathered online about this American issue. On a separate sheet of paper, answer the essential question: **What are the most pressing problems, and how can we solve them?** Healthcare is one pressing problem. You can choose to discuss any other problem you have read about in your textbook, such as education or immigration.

Name _____ Class _____ Date _____

American Issues Journal

Territorial Expansion of the United States

Essential Question: Should the United States expand its territory?

1803
Louisiana Purchase
Jefferson buys Louisiana without congressional approval

1848
Mexican Cession
U.S. gains Mexican lands after war

1893
Hawaiian Revolt
Americans overthrow queen; pave way to annexation

1820	1860	1900

1845
Texas Annexation
Texas joins Union

1867
Alaska Purchase
U.S. buys Alaska

1898
Spanish-American War
U.S. control over Spanish lands

I. WARMUP

Throughout its history, the U.S. has increased the size of its territory many times and in various ways. While this territorial expansion has broadened the global power of the U.S., it has also caused considerable debate among Americans. The timeline on this page shows how the nation has expanded.

1. How would you define the term "expansion"?

_____

_____

_____

2a. How would you feel if someone moved into your home without your permission? Use the thought bubble to explain your reaction.

Thoughts . . .

American Issues Journal

2b. What actions might you take to reclaim your home?

_____

_____

_____

3. What might be some benefits of one person taking over the property of another? Explain.

_____

_____

_____

II. EXPLORATION

Now that you have explored the concept of territorial expansion on a small scale, consider the national and international effects of territorial expansion by the United States.

A. Mexican Cession

1. Read the chapter "Manifest Destiny." What does the term "Manifest Destiny" mean?

_____

_____

2. How did Manifest Destiny lead to war with Mexico?

_____

_____

B. Find Out

When the U.S. won a war with Mexico in 1848, it acquired a vast area of land known as the Mexican Cession. This territory now comprises the states of Arizona, California, Utah, Nevada, and part of Colorado and New Mexico.

1. There are always many points of view to consider when studying an historical event. Consider the reactions of a Mexican citizen and President Polk after the Mexican War. What might each one have said about the war and the Mexican Cession? Write your thoughts in the chart below.

Mexican Citizen	President Polk

American Issues Journal

2. Ralph Waldo Emerson predicted the United States would win the war against Mexico but said that "Mexico would poison us." How did the Mexican Cession "poison" the United States?

_____

_____

_____

_____

C. What do you think?

Was the U.S. justified in acquiring land from Mexico? Explain.

_____

_____

_____

You may wish to explore this issue further online. Go to:

Internet Research Activity

Transfer Your Knowledge
For: WebQuest **Web Code:** neh-7802

III. ESSAY

Bring together what you have read in your textbook with the information you have gathered online about this American issue. On a separate sheet of paper, answer the essential question: **Should the United States expand its territory?**

American Issues Journal

America Goes to War

Essential Question: When should America go to war?

1917–1918
World War I
Fought after
Germany violated
American
neutrality

1812
War of 1812
Fought to stop Britain from
seizing American ships

1960s–1970s
Vietnam War
Fought to halt spread
of communism

| 1820 | 1860 | 1900 | 1940 | 1980 | 2020 |

1860s
Civil War
Fought over slavery, states'
rights, and saving the Union

1940s
World War II
Fought after Japan attacked
Pearl Harbor

I. WARMUP

The United States came into existence through a revolutionary war and has had many reasons for going to war since then. The timeline on this page shows some of the occasions when the nation went to war.

1. The list below shows some of the reasons America has gone to war. Rank the list from 1 to 6 to show what you think are the most important to the least important reasons. Number 1 is the most important; number 6 is the least important..

___ protect itself

___ protect rights and freedoms

___ expand borders

___ gain economic benefits

___ aid allies

___ increase power and influence

2. Which of the reasons on the list do you think are worth fighting and possibly dying for?

_____

_____

3. Are all wars equally justified? Explain.

_____

_____

American Issues Journal

II. EXPLORATION

Now that you have explored some reasons nations are willing to fight, consider the effects of one war in which the U.S. fought.

A. Vietnam War

Read the chapter "The Vietnam War."

1. Which President introduced the domino theory?

_____

2. Define domino theory.

_____

_____

_____

3. How was this theory used to justify sending troops to Vietnam?

_____

_____

_____

B. Find Out

Opposition to the war lead to a strong anti-war movement. There were two groups—the Hawks and the Doves.

1. How did the Hawks and the Doves differ in their thinking about the war? Fill in the chart with your answers.

Hawks	Doves
• •	• •

American Issues Journal

2. Although not everyone fights in a war, a war affects a nation's citizens in different ways. The war in Vietnam had profound effects on the American people. Use the concept web below to show some of the ways the war impacted the nation.

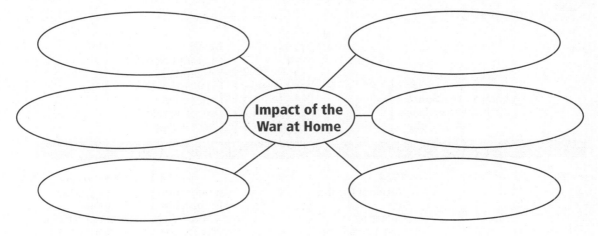

C. What do you think?

Should the U.S. have fought in Vietnam? Explain.

_____

_____

_____

You may wish to explore this issue further online. Go to:

Internet Research Activity

Transfer Your Knowledge
For: WebQuest **Web Code:** neh-7902

III. ESSAY

Bring together what you have read in your textbook with the information you have gathered online about this American issue. On a separate sheet of paper, answer the essential question: **When should America go to war?**

American Issues Journal

U.S. Immigration Policy

 Essential Question: How should the government regulate immigration?

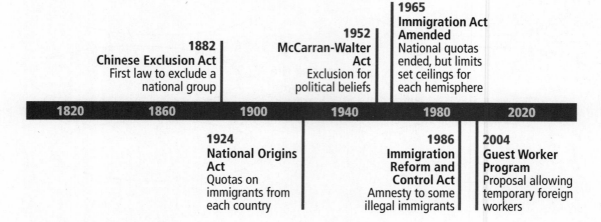

1882
Chinese Exclusion Act
First law to exclude a national group

1952
McCarran-Walter Act
Exclusion for political beliefs

1965
Immigration Act Amended
National quotas ended, but limits set ceilings for each hemisphere

1820   1860   1900   1940   1980   2020

1924
National Origins Act
Quotas on immigrants from each country

1986
Immigration Reform and Control Act
Amnesty to some illegal immigrants

2004
Guest Worker Program
Proposal allowing temporary foreign workers

I. WARMUP

The history of immigration to America is long and complex. It began during the colonial era with both voluntary and involuntary arrivals. The timeline on this page reflects the national policy of immigration after 1850.

1. What are some reasons that immigrants have come voluntarily to the U.S?

_____

_____

_____

2. Why did the U.S. begin to limit immigration?

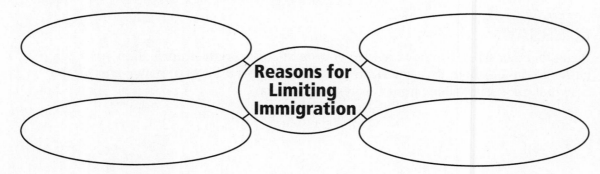

Reasons for Limiting Immigration

American Issues Journal

3. Is the U.S. right to limit immigration? Explain.

_____

_____

_____

II. EXPLORATION

Now that you have started to explore the issue of immigration, consider how immigration continues to affect the nation.

A. Immigration Reform and Control Act

1. Read Section 5 of the chapter "Into a New Century." What was the purpose of the Immigration Reform and Control Act?

_____

_____

2. How did laws restricting immigrants contribute to an increase in illegal immigration?

_____

_____

_____

3. Why do you think immigrants risked entering the U.S. illegally?

_____

_____

_____

B. Find Out

Read the poem by Emma Lazarus in the Documents of Our Nation section at the back of your textbook.

1. How does its message differ from the Immigration Reform and Control Act?

Immigration Reform and Control Act	"The New Colossus" Poem

American Issues Journal

2. Based on what you have read, how do you think each of the following would feel about the Immigration Reform and Control Act?

**Illegal
Immigrant**

**Border Patrol
Worker**

Employer

C. What do you think?

Should there be an Immigration Reform and Control Act? Explain.

_____

_____

_____

You may wish to explore this issue further online. Go to:

Internet Research Activity

Transfer Your Knowledge
For: WebQuest **Web Code:** neh-8002

III. ESSAY

Bring together what you have read in your textbook with the information you have gathered online about this American issue. On a separate sheet of paper, answer the essential question: **How should government regulate immigration?**

American Issues Journal

Government's Role in the Economy

Essential Question: What is the proper balance between free enterprise and government regulation of the economy?

1890
Sherman Antitrust Act
Curbs power of monopolies

1913
Federal Reserve Act
Controls money supply

2001
Tax Cuts
Taxes lowered to promote economic growth

| 1820 | 1860 | 1900 | 1940 | 1980 | 2020 |

1906
Pure Food and Drug Act
Regulates safety of food and medicine

1933
Agricultural Adjustment Act
Payments to farmers create high crop prices and farm profits

I. WARMUP

The U.S. economy operates under a free enterprise system. However, the role of the government has varied in response to different events. For example, during the 1960s and 1970s, demand for government protection of consumers and the environment led to the creation of new government agencies and regulations. The timeline on this page shows other periods in history when the government used regulation to control the economy.

The balance between regulation and free enterprise affects all Americans. How might the balance affect your life? One way is in protecting you as a consumer. For example, the sanitary conditions in which foods are produced are closely regulated.

1a. How do you define the term "free enterprise"?

_____

_____

_____

1b. How do you define the term "regulation"?

_____

_____

_____

2. Research, then list below three products you use that are regulated by consumer protection laws.

_____

_____

_____

Name _____ Class _____ Date _____

American Issues Journal

3. Should the government be allowed to control items that might be dangerous to consumers? Explain.

_____
_____
_____

II. EXPLORATION

You have looked at one way that government regulation can benefit the consumer. Now consider the steps the government takes to regulate the economy.

A. Tax Cuts

In the Constitution, the first power given to Congress is the power "to lay and collect taxes" to pay for debts, defense, and the common welfare.

You have read about the scope of the New Deal and how it increased the role of the federal government. For example, the government began taking taxes directly from the paychecks of workers. What does the government use tax money for? Use the chart to list four things.

TAXES

B. Find Out

Read the section in the Economics Handbook about Tools for Moderating the Business Cycle: Fiscal Policy.

1. What is fiscal policy?

_____
_____
_____

American Issues Journal

2. Read Section 4 in the chapter "Into a New Century." Why did President Bush want a a tax cut in 2001?

_____

_____

_____

3. What were the positive and negative effects of the tax cut?

_____

_____

_____

4. Why do you think taxpayers are usually in favor of tax cuts and against tax increases?

_____

_____

_____

C. What do you think?

Should the government raise and lower taxes to regulate the economy?

_____

_____

_____

You may wish to explore this issue further online. Go to:

Internet Research Activity

Transfer Your Knowledge
For: WebQuest **Web Code:** neh-8202

III. ESSAY

Bring together what you have read in your textbook with the information you have gathered online about this American issue. On a separate sheet of paper, answer the essential question: **What is the proper balance between free enterprise and government regulation of the economy?**

Name _____ Class _____ Date _____

Civil Liberties and National Security

Essential Question: What is the proper balance between national security and civil liberties?

1790s
Undeclared War with France
Alien and Sedition Acts

1940s
World War II
Internment of Japanese Americans

2001
War on Terror
Patriot Act

| 1820 | 1860 | 1900 | 1940 | 1980 | 2020 |

1860s
Civil War
Habeas Corpus suspended

1950s
Cold War
Red Scare

I. WARMUP

Throughout its history, the U.S. government has faced moments when the safety of the nation seemed more important than preserving all the rights and liberties of its citizens. The timeline on this page shows when this issue surfaced in U.S. history.

The balance between national security and civil liberties affects all Americans. But how might the balance between safety and liberty surface in your life?

1. (a) How do you define the term "safe"?

_____

_____

1. (b) How do you define the term "freedom"?

_____

_____

2. Schools are places where students assemble to learn, discuss ideas, and acquire essential skills to become active citizens. Schools are also organizations with rules and regulations to ensure student safety.

A. What are three things that you think make your school safe?	B. What three freedoms do you think students should have in school?
• • •	• • •

American Issues Journal

3. How does the need for safety in schools affect students' freedom?

_____

_____

_____

II. EXPLORATION

Now that you have explored the issues of safety and freedom in your school, consider the challenges of these issues for the nation.

A. Civil Liberties during the Civil War

In the chapter on the Civil War, you read about President Lincoln's response to Americans who sought to undermine the northern war effort. To keep the Union secure, Lincoln suspended the constitutional right of *habeas corpus* and empowered soldiers to arrest people suspected of disloyalty.

1. Civil liberties are freedoms that are or should be protected by the law. As an American, what three freedoms do you value most?

_____

_____

_____

National security is the protection of a nation's citizens and institutions from threats.

2. What do you think makes a nation safe? Use the concept web to list four ways.

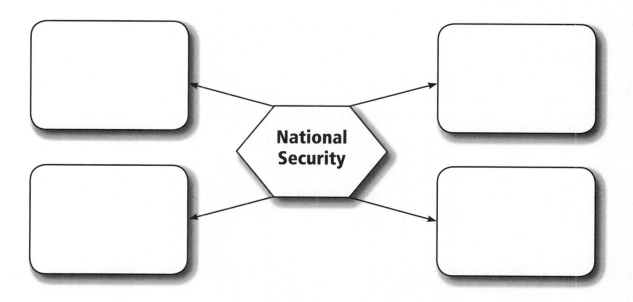

American Issues Journal

B. Find Out

1. Read Article II of the Constitution. What does it say about the powers of the President during time of war?

———————————————————————————————

———————————————————————————————

———————————————————————————————

2. Read Article I, Section 9, Clause 2 of the Constitution. What does it say about habeas corpus?

———————————————————————————————

———————————————————————————————

———————————————————————————————

C. What do you think?

Should Lincoln have suspended habeas corpus? Explain.

———————————————————————————————

———————————————————————————————

———————————————————————————————

You may wish to explore this issue further online. Go to:

Internet Research Activity

Transfer Your Knowledge
For: WebQuest **Web Code:** neh-8502

III. ESSAY

Bring together what you have read in your textbook with the information you have gathered online about this American Issue. On a separate sheet of paper, answer the essential question: **What is the proper balance between national security and civil liberties?**

American Issues Journal

Voting Rights

Essential Question: What should the government do to promote voting rights?

1820s–1830s
Age of Jackson
Move toward
universal white
male suffrage

1920
Nineteenth
Amendment
Vote for women

1971
Twenty-sixth
Amendment
Voting age
lowered to 18

2000
Presidential Election
Polling-place
irregularities lead to
some reforms

1820   1860   1900   1940   1980   2020

1870
Fifteenth Amendment
Vote for African American men

1965
Voting Rights Act
Strengthening of African
American voting rights

I. WARMUP

As you have learned, ensuring voting rights for all American citizens has been a long and sometimes embattled process. Over time, however, more and more Americans have gained suffrage. The timeline on this page shows some key events in the struggle for voting rights.

1. How would you define the term "voting rights"?

_____

_____

2. In a democracy, people vote all the time to make choices about things. Often, these choices are about leaders of a group, actions that a group will take, or rules that a group will follow. As a student, you probably voted for class president. What other school issues did you vote for?

_____

_____

_____

American Issues Journal

3. What are two important responsibilities of a voter?

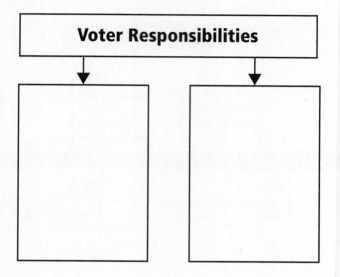

4. Why do groups use voting as a way of deciding things?

_____

_____

_____

II. EXPLORATION

Now that you understand the importance of voting, explore the efforts of different groups of citizens to obtain this right.

A. Twenty-sixth Amendment

The U.S. government has lifted voting restrictions several times throughout its history to broaden the number of citizens who can vote.

Look at the amendments listed on the timeline. Identify any amendments that have helped to make you eligible to vote in the next Presidential election.

_____

_____

_____

B. Find Out

Read Section 3 of the chapter "The Vietnam War Era" and the Twenty-sixth Amendment to the Constitution. The amendment was in part a response to student protests during the Vietnam War.

American Issues Journal

Not everyone thinks that eighteen-year-olds should be allowed to vote. What might be some arguments for and against the Twenty-sixth Amendment?

Arguments for 26th Amendment	Arguments Against 26th Amendment
•	•
•	•
•	•

C. What do you think?

Should the government raise the voting age to 21? Explain.

_____

_____

_____

You may wish to explore this issue further online. Go to:

Internet Research Activity

Transfer Your Knowledge
For: WebQuest Web Code: neh-8702

III. ESSAY

Bring together what you have read in your textbook with the information you have gathered online about this American issue. On a separate sheet of paper, answer the essential question: **What should the government do to promote voting rights?**

American Issues Journal

Poverty and Prosperity

Essential Question: How should Americans deal with the gap between rich and poor?

1800s
Community Aid
Private charities aid poor

1900
Poverty Level
About 40% of Americans living in poverty

1964
War on Poverty
Programs to reduce poverty

1996
Welfare Reform
Limit on welfare programs

| 1820 | 1860 | 1900 | 1940 | 1980 | 2020 |

1933
New Deal
Federal government aids poor

1980s
Reaganomics
Business growth to reduce poverty

I. WARMUP

From the earliest days of the nation, Americans have not been equal in wealth. To balance the extremes between wealth and poverty, some people have supported federal government policies to distribute wealth. Others believe the role of helping needy people should be left to nonprofit charitable organizations. The timeline on this page shows when various efforts to close the gap between rich and poor have occurred.

1. Have you ever worked with a community, religious organization, school, or other local group to help people in need? How did you help? Check the ones that apply.

__ soup kitchen   __ food bank   __ clothing drive
__ recycling toys   __ holiday gifts   __ fuel drive
__ other

2. If you have not joined in these efforts to help the poor, what other ways would you suggest helping those in need in your community?

_____

_____

3. What do you think? How effective are community-level organizations in addressing poverty?

_____

_____

_____

American Issues Journal

II. EXPLORATION

Now that you have started exploring local ways to help those in need, consider these issues on a national level.

A. War on Poverty

1. What are some things that poor people have to struggle for?

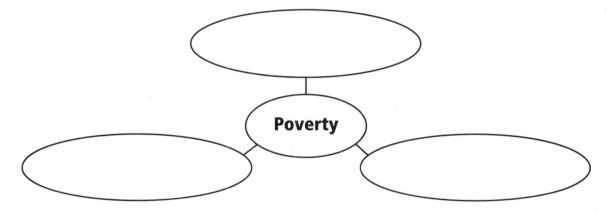

2. Michael Harrington wrote about poverty in the cities, or urban poverty. Do you think urban poverty still exists? Explain.

_____

_____

_____

_____

B. Find Out

1. Read Section 3 of the chapter on "The Kennedy and Johnson Years." What was the goal of the War on Poverty?

_____

_____

2. Why do you think the word "war" was used to name this program?

_____

_____

_____

_____

American Issues Journal

3. What were three important programs set up during the War on Poverty? What issue did each program address?

Program	Purpose

C. What do you think?

Should the government be responsible for creating social programs to help the poor? Explain.

_____

_____

_____

You may wish to explore this issue further online. Go to:

Internet Research Activity

Transfer Your Knowledge
For: WebQuest **Web Code:** neh-8802

III. ESSAY

Bring together what you have read in your textbook with the information you have gathered online about this American issue. On a separate sheet of paper, answer the essential question: **How should Americans deal with the gap between rich and poor?**

American Issues Journal

America and the World

 Essential Question: What is America's role in the world?

I. WARMUP

As he left office in 1796, George Washington warned the nation against foreign alliances. For many years, the U.S. did try to avoid involving itself in the affairs of other nations. However, much has changed since the late 1700s, and the U.S. has played an active role in more and more world affairs as the timeline on this page shows.

Have you ever been in a position where you were the strongest or most able member of a team or group? Because of your status, perhaps you helped the group by using your strength or ability in some way such as scoring a winning point or proposing a plan.

1. Use the graphic below to show what happened.

SITUATION	MY ROLE	WHAT I DID
_____ _____ _____	_____ _____ _____	_____ _____ _____

2. How do you think the other members of the group might feel about your role?

_____

_____

_____

American Issues Journal

3. Should it be your responsibility to help others because of your status?

_____

_____

_____

II. EXPLORATION

Now that you have explored roles you might play as the strongest member in a group, consider the roles the U.S., as a superpower, plays in the world.

A. War on Terrorism

The United States has for many years been one of the most powerful nations in the world. It is also one of the wealthiest. What are some leadership roles you think a nation such as the U.S. should play in the world? For example, should the United States try to settle international disputes?

Show your ideas by filling in the concept web below.

B. Find Out

1. Read the end of Section 3 in the chapter "Into the New Century." What did Americans learn about terrorism?

_____

_____

_____

2. Read the speech on terrorism by President George W. Bush in the section of your textbook entitled Documents of Our Nation. Summarize his main point about the U.S. role in world affairs.

_____

_____

American Issues Journal

3. Read Section 4 in the chapter "Into the New Century. " Why did the U.S. invade Afghanistan and Iraq?

Afghanistan	Iraq

C. What do you think?

Should the U.S. get involved in the affairs of other nations?

_____

_____

_____

You may wish to explore this issue further online. Go to:

Internet Research Activity

Transfer Your Knowledge
For: WebQuest **Web Code:** neh-8902

III. ESSAY

Bring together what you have read in your textbook with the information you have gathered online about this American issue. On a separate sheet of paper, answer the essential question: **What is America's role in the world?**

American Issues Journal

Interaction with the Environment

Essential Question: How can we balance economic development and environmental protection?

1872
Yellowstone
First national park

1962
Silent Spring
Carson's book
exposes pesticide
dangers

1973
**Endangered
Species Act**
Protection for
threatened species

1820	1860	1900	1940	1980	2020

1916
**National Park
Service**
National Park
system created

1970
**Clean Air
Act**
Air quality
standards
established

1997
Kyoto Protocol
U.S. fails to ratify
global treaty on
greenhouse gases

I. WARMUP

Although the government has long worked at conserving public lands and parks, concern about protecting the environment was not an important issue until the 1960s and 1970s. Rachel Carson's book *Silent Spring,* published in 1962, helped make people aware of how human actions were altering the environment in harmful ways. Her book not only inspired the modern environmental movement; it also exposed the connection between economic growth and environmental protection.

1a. How would you define the term "economic development"?

_____
_____
_____

1b. How would you define the term "environmental protection"?

_____
_____
_____

2a. What are some ways that you help to protect the environment? Use the concept web below to list four things you do.

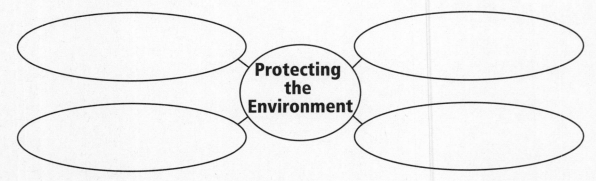

Protecting
the
Environment

American Issues Journal

2b. Why might some industries have unfavorable views of environmental controls?

_____

_____

_____

3. Why should people try to protect the environment?

_____

_____

_____

II. EXPLORATION

You have started exploring the interaction between economic development and the environment. Now consider what role the government should take.

A. Kyoto Protocol

In the chapter "An Era of Protest and Change," you read about the development of the environmental movement. Although many people supported the government's actions, critics felt that it had gone too far in environmental regulation. Some said it hampered U.S. business by diverting funds to clean up projects.

1. List two or three federal or state environmental laws.

_____

_____

_____

2. What impact have these laws had?

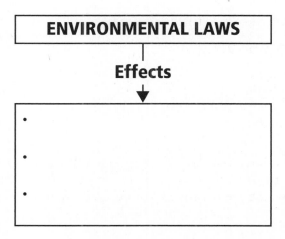

Name _____ Class _____ Date _____

American Issues Journal

Interaction with the Environment (continued)

B. Find Out

In 1997, more than 170 nations met in Kyoto, Japan, to draw up a treaty about global climate change. The resulting Kyoto Protocol addressed the issue of reducing greenhouse gases, a cause of global warming. Although these gases occur naturally, they are also created by human activities such as burning oil and gas. The treaty called for industrial nations that have emitted the most greenhouse gases to take the lead in reducing emissions. Less was expected of developing nations such as China and India.

President Bill Clinton signed the Kyoto treaty, but the U.S. Congress has never ratified it. What might be some of the pros and cons of the Kyoto Protocol for the U.S.? As you complete the chart, think about the effect of the treaty on the U.S. industry as well. Would it hamper or help industry?

Pros	Cons
•	•
•	•
•	•

C. What do you think?

Should the U.S. ratify the Kyoto Protocol? Explain.

_____

_____

_____

You may wish to explore this issue further online. Go to:

Internet Research Activity

Transfer Your Knowledge
For: WebQuest **Web Code:** neh-9002

III. ESSAY

Bring together what you have read in your textbook with the information you have gathered online about this American Issue. On a separate sheet of paper, answer the essential question: **How can we balance economic development and environmental protection?**

Name _____ Class _____ Date _____

Education and the American Society

 Essential Question: What should be the goals of American education?

1600s–1700s
Colonial Education
Emphasis on religious study

1903
Du Bois-Washington Debate
Role of education in lives of
African Americans debated

2001
**No Child Left Behind
Act**
Federal law to raise
student performance
with standardized
testing

| 1600 | 1820 | 1860 | 1900 | 1940 | 1980 | 2020 |

1852
Public Schools
Massachusetts has first
compulsory school
attendance law

1926
Scholastic Aptitude Test
First SAT given

I. WARMUP

Education has long been an important element in American life. While schools in
colonial times had a religious focus, schools in later times have promoted democratic
values. Today, public schools place an emphasis on performance standards. The timeline
on this page shows some key events in American education.

1. What are your goals for your education?

_____

_____

_____

2. How successful do you think you have been so far in achieving these goals? Show
your progress by checking one of the boxes below.

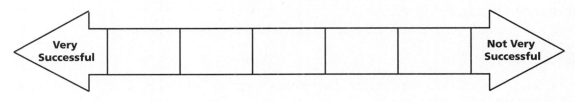

| Very Successful | | | | | Not Very Successful |

3. Explain your choice.

_____

_____

_____

American Issues Journal

4. Why is education important?

_____

_____

_____

II. EXPLORATION

Now that you have explored your own goals in education, consider what goals the government should set for American education.

A. No Child Left Behind Act

As a student, you have no doubt taken many quizzes and tests during your school years. You also know that two teachers of the same subject may give very different tests. A good mark on one test may not be as good on another test.

1. What is the purpose of a test?

_____

_____

_____

2. What other ways are sometimes used to measure what you have learned? List three ways.

_____

_____

_____

3. Does test preparation help you better understand a subject? Explain.

_____

_____

_____

B. Find Out

1. Review the section in the chapter "Into a New Century" on the No Child Left Behind Act. What was the purpose of this?

_____

_____

_____

American Issues Journal

In the U.S. each state has its own school system paid for by state and local taxes. The states also receive federal funds to help support their educational systems. Traditionally, the quality of education has varied significantly from state to state.

1. Do you think federal programs would improve the quality of education? Explain.

_____

_____

_____

2. How does standardized testing affect what is taught? List a possible positive and negative result on the chart.

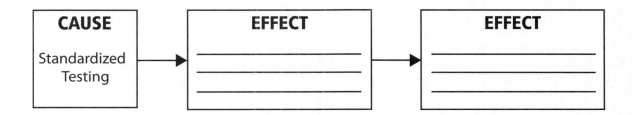

C. What do you think?

Do the advantages of the No Child Left Behind Act outweigh the disadvantages? Explain.

_____

_____

_____

You may wish to explore this issue further online. Go to:

Internet Research Activity

Transfer Your Knowledge
For: WebQuest **Web Code:** neh-9302

III. ESSAY

Bring together what you have read in your textbook with the information you've gathered online about this American issue. On a separate sheet of paper, answer the essential question: **What should be the goals of American education?**